Out of Order

Out of Order

A haphazard journey through
one woman's year

Jane Lapotaire

KYLE CATHIE LIMITED

First published in Great Britain in 1999 by
Kyle Cathie Limited
20 Vauxhall Bridge Road
London SW1V 2SA

ISBN 1 85626 316 9

A Cataloguing in Publication record for this title is available
from the British Library.

Typeset by SX Composing DTP, Rayleigh, Essex
Printed in Great Britain by
WBC Book Manufacturers Limited, Bridgend

contents

This book is dedicated to Jackie McGlone

with special thanks to those who also maintain the Auld Alliance:
David McLellan
Cameron Duncan
and not least of all, Kyle Cathie.

Thanks too to Stephanie Cabot, literary agent at William Morris UK, for support and maintenance during crises of writer's confidence; Caroline Taggart, editor at Kyle Cathie; and Di from 'Pacemakers' Leamington Spa for maintenance of laptop and writer's sanity.

To David McLellan, Maurice Denham, Lis Barat and my son, whose friendship I tested to the full by asking them to read the entire manuscript, which they uncomplainingly and caringly did – my gratitude and love.

JANE LAPOTAIRE, LONDON, JUNE 1998

Some of the material in this book has already been published, in slightly different form by the *Glasgow Herald*. 'Seeds of Faith' was written to accompany six programmes devised for BBC Radio, January 1996; 'Everything Lovely Is in the Garden' accompanied a reading from *The Virago Book of Gardeners' Verse*, March 1996. 'Stratford Upon Haven' was written for a book on Stratford published by Susan Hill and Stanley Wells; and 'The Role is Greater than the Sum of the Part' is abridged from an essay about Katherine of Aragon published by the Cambridge University Press in 1998.

The quotation from Hilaire Belloc's poem 'His Own Country' (p. 56) is reproduced from his *Complete Verse*, published by Random House UK Ltd, by permission of Peters Fraser & Dunlop; the lines from Patricia Beer's 'Middle Age' (p. 158) are taken from *Driving West* © 1975, published by Victor Gollancz Ltd; Gwendolyn Brooks' 'A Sunset of the City' (p. 158) is taken from *The World of Gwendolyn Brooks* © 1960, published by Harper & Row Inc; Sharon Olds' 'Ecstasy' (p. 191) is from *The Dead and the Living* © 1983 by Sharon Olds, reprinted by permission of Alfred A Knopf Inc; Philp Larkin's 'They Fuck You Up, Your Mum and Dad' (p. 191) is reprinted by permission of Faber & Faber; Wendy Cope's 'English Weather' (p. 192) is from *Serious Concerns*, reprinted by permission of Faber & Faber; the quotation from *Monty Python's Flying Circus* (p. 249) is used by permission of Python (Monty) Pictures Ltd.

The photograph on p. 49 is by Maureen Moore; p. 227 by Robert Day; p. 253 by Cherry Morris; p. 268 by Richard Kalina (Elizabeth I costume designed by Paul Farnsworth); p. 270 by Erika Neumann. All other photographs from the author's collection.

Toutes choses sont dites déjà, mais comme personne écoute, il faut toujours recommencer.

ANDRÉ GIDE, 1869–1951

Let me take your hand for love and sing you a song, said the other traveller. The journey is a hard journey, but if we hold together in the morning and the evening what matter if in the hours between there is sorrow.

LAO TZU, C. 6TH CENTURY BC

This would appear to be the beginning of the book, but in fact it's the end. I'm writing the beginning of this book at the end. I mean I've just finished the last bit. And now I'm writing the first. Because when I got to the end, the beginning I had was no longer apt. Time plays these tricks. Just when you've lived through something and have come out the other side, irredeemably wiser of course, when you look back on the journey you've been through, you no longer see it with the same eyes.

This started out as a sort of diary. I say sort of, advisedly, because I wouldn't dare show anyone the genuine article. I take great pains to hide it in preposterous places, though none of my friends who visit have ever expressed the slightest interest in braving the junk-infested heap that is my study, in which it is housed. I guess the hiding is an indication of the level to which I will stoop to keep my very private jottings just that, very private. So I thought this would be the acceptable 'private face in the public place', which, if Mr Auden is correct, is 'wiser and nicer than the public face in the private place'. Though now I suspect some seepage from one to the other has occurred. I pander to the prurient...

But as I progressed through the days and weeks that brought these experiences into my life, or as they progressed through me, I just couldn't make the time fit the events, or the events fit the time. I've always been able to stretch time, or fill the time available with more than would fit in and make it fit. But time stubbornly refused to bend or yield to my plan.

I thought I was writing a diary and I wasn't – it isn't. It's turned out to be a travel book. A journey through a year. Like all travel you can never be sure of what time you leave or what time you arrive. Journeying is such a haphazard business.

Beginnings and Endings

Every day is a new beginning
Listen my heart to the glad refrain,
And spite of old sorrows
And older sinning
Troubles forecasted
And possible pain
Take heart with the day and begin again.

SUSAN COOLIDGE, 1835–1905

I used to hate the New Year when I was younger. Age has a lot to do with it. My birthday falls on 26 December, so the most festive two days of the year are over for me in one fell forty-eight-hour swoop. Apart from being the recipient of post-Yuletide economy – the birthday present and card doubling as Christmas gift and greeting (something that most of us who share birthdays with JC suffer) – my birthday is often characterised by a search for the Alka Seltzer. Or if I'm lucky enough to be working, a matinee performance to greet the bleary day, with an evening show hot on its heels, and falling out of the theatre at 11p.m. to find that I'm another year older with only an hour left to celebrate or mourn it in.

Trying to have a birthday party on Boxing Day itself is near to nigh impossible. I've only done it once. Inevitably friends are away or ensconced with family, and my small house would be hard pushed to encompass an Auntie Rosaleen with her five nephews, and Uncle Didi with his son, brother and father, and that's only the appendages to one of my friends. So I've let sleeping dogs lie and given celebrating my birthday the by-pass. Then no one has to brave the ravages of driving family-filled pantechnicons to Putney without the solace of a mug of my Dr Johnson's punch to kick-start them on the homeward journey, the drink-driving laws being what they are and my version of this punch being what it is.

I did manage a birthday party once in the village hall, complete with Poll and Pip the caterers and their excellent post-Christmas choice: fish or shepherds pie, apple crumble or cherry tart, washed down with gallons of the aforementioned brew by some forty guests – most of whom I'd never seen before, being families of friends who stood around unsure as to what or whom we were feting, to the accompaniment of the Doctors of Jazz à la Acker Bilk from Bromsgrove. But then most people came from the village so they just had to stagger down the hill home, or in our case up the hill, which was harder carrying black plastic bags of rubbish, brooms, tin platters and deflated balloons, footsore from hours of jigging about on the not very smooth floorboards of the village hall circa 1933 rented for the princessly sum of £17 for the purpose of celebrating JL circa 1944.

It was fun. But my abiding memory is of feeding the insatiable electricity meter with fifty-pence pieces from the witching hour of three in the afternoon, to activate the few spindly overhead fires, hands numb with cold from setting up collapsible chairs and green baize-covered whist tables that, true to their nature, collapsed on my feet like rebellious deckchairs, or pinched my unfeeling fingers. The triumph of having it all sorted, balloons blown and last year's pantomime scenery half hidden away behind the stage curtains before Poll and Pip arrived pink cheeked and cheery faced with their car full of food, was somewhat tainted by the sight of their shivering frames and blanched features after less than half an hour in the vast tiled kitchen. Their quick-frozen beings became a template for those of the first intrepid guests who stood around with their coats firmly on and their hands dug deep in their pockets until 8.30 when the punch finally loosened their limbs and 'Stranger on the Shore' had them swaying with nostalgia, and a surfeit of rum.

No, the prospect of the New Year stretching ahead with its brain-clogging grey dampness, and the spiteful sneaky teeth of its biting winds has always had me clinging fast to my Latin roots. Can't do without the sun. SAD nothing. I get Seriously Awfully Depressed without that warm feeling spreading across my back from the SUN. Not that the winter weather is any more clement in the Languedoc, or that my bank balance has ever been in a state that could support the idyll of wintering in the French West Indies. But France is frequently bright when it's cold. And there can be surprising days of warm sunlight when the intrepid can sit out and eat their lunch, much to the astonishment of the locals. It's that surprise that counts. Something happens to the clouds as they cross the channel in this direction. They become predictably constant, and seeped in spirit-clogging greyness. It's then that I yearn for cobbles dappled with yellow sunlight, to be startled by pockets of warmth in the sheltered corners of medieval castle walls and have my spirits lifted by the sight of window boxes perched high in Mediterranean alleys full of brave geraniums that don't have to be taken indoors. So I take comfort in the fact that as far as I and my sun-starved constitution are concerned, British January and February really should be cancelled. Or they should be proclaimed official hibernating time. No one out of their burrows until March. Eat, drink, sit by the fire and read. Heaven.

But my attitude to the first months of the year has changed radically since I met Henry. A tall, aquiline-featured man, surprisingly diffident for an American, quietly spoken with an unassuming intelligence and a vast amount of knowledge, modestly shared.We met over a trestle table of quiche and sandwiches, not the most auspicious introduction, at one of the innumerable fund-raising events at Shakespeare's Globe some six months ago, when the theatre itself was still an incomplete wooden 'O' with only two of its bays thatched and a permanent puddle in the centre where the stage would eventually be once we'd raised yet more money – hence the expensive quiche and sandwiches. The room was full of Globe Friends from every corner of the world cajoled and bullied into supporting us by the wily and indomitable Sam Wanamaker.

'I saw you in *Love's Labour's Lost*,' said Henry, as we loaded our unstable paper plates side by side. Not an auspicious beginning that, either. It could have been the end of a friendship. I hadn't particularly enjoyed working on *LLL* apart from being directed by the inspirational John Barton. Rosaline may well have been modelled on the Dark Lady of the Sonnets, but she's a lousy part. Lady-in-waiting to the Princess of France, she has very few lines. All pertness, cleverness and scheming. The princess has the lion's part. But brunettes get the soubrette. So I got racy Rosaline.

I've learned that it's churlish to colour someone's enjoyment of a play by showing them the bolts and shackles of a role, to force them to accompany you as you retrace your turgid steps through the mud and mire of rehearsals, and have, I hope, trained myself to smile graciously and accept the undeserved compliment. Risking the bathos of a similar Noel Coward remark, as a palliative I ventured, 'The set was good, though.' All trees and leaves and dappled green light. Illuminated by the unfailing humour of a constantly benevolent Richard Griffiths as the slim-line King of Navarre, and the acerbic wit of the much loved Ian Charleson, who was quite probably the most reluctant and the worst Longaville in the history of the play, followed closely by the embarrassed Boyet of Alan Rickman who would mutter laconically at every opportunity his mantra of 'Miscast, miscast'. They made it largely a jolly time. In spite of my paucity of bons mots.

Henry and I chatted Shakespeare, Globe and RSC – the last two subjects not encouraged as conversation topics within the confines of the latter establishment at that particular moment, but now that the finished Globe is an inescapable feature of the London skyline and the work there well on a level to challenge any of the RSC's best, those of us who move between the two have done a little, it is fervently to be wished, in pouring oil on previously competitive waters.

Henry's knowledge of the plays and his vast experience of many productions was daunting and pushed the well-worn buttons of my feelings of inadequacy. Most classical actors if they're lucky can probably, in a normal working lifetime, expect to be in some fifteen or so of Shakespeare's thirty-seven plays. But addicts like Henry, inspired by a genuine love of the work and not simply an academic obligation, have a deep working knowledge and personal experience of most of the canon. It's difficult for an actor confined within an eighteen-month contract at the RSC to leap down the M40, should the inclination so move her, and view all the other bits of the Bard on offer across the board.

The conversation ended in an invitation. I thought, to be honest, the invitation would turn out to be one of those grand gestures made in an unguarded moment, *grace à* the third plastic beaker full of dry white, and would not come to fruition or look quite so rosy in retrospect, when Washington University in St Louis would be approached to finance his wild suggestion that I visit Wash U!

Equally, my third cup of Australian red would have paled considerably had I realised that the previous sporadic bouts of teaching Shakespeare *à la* John Barton that I had done at The Actor's Centre, The Oxford School of Drama, The Bristol Old

Vic Theatre School, Wadham College and the British American Drama Academy were about to crystallise themselves into three jam-packed, very demanding three-hour classes containing terrifyingly bright and inquisitive Ph.D. and MA students as well as impressionable undergraduates, on a campus so large it took me some half an hour to cross it.

So St Louis it was, and is every January now, if I'm not otherwise gainfully employed. Of course, the wind-chill factor in Missouri can rip your face off, and I've never been there to see leaves on the trees, but there have been many days of startling sunshine which assume a kind of Beckettian weirdness against the bare branches. Henry and his wife Patty have become much loved friends, and the warmth of their home and their welcome do much to obliterate the cold which is frequently accompanied by cheeringly bright skies. Also, I get to leave England for a month. So January is to a large extent now cancelled.

St Louis Blues

In the United States there is more space where nobody is
than where anybody is. That is what makes America what it is.

GERTRUDE STEIN, 1874–1946

I've just come back from St Louis, and wish I hadn't. Now don't
get me wrong. I love this country. Bits of it. The snowdrops are
forcing their way bravely through the frozen grey of January.
The Cotswold hills where I love to walk are spiked with the green
spears of the first daffodils and treacherous with hidden acres of
slimy mud, that clings to your boots so that you end up stag-
gering on built-up soles. There's the first quarter's VAT to do,
and the seasonal gas, electricity and phone bills waiting to
welcome the spring. But somehow none of these joys gladden
my heart as much as they used to, before I went AWOL to the
USA. It's become a yearly occurrence now, my teaching
Shakespeare to the very eager, enthusiastic students of Wash U.
(That's Washington University to the uninitiated, and yes,
there's a Washington University in St Louis, Missouri. Don't ask
me why, there just is.)

There's nothing like teaching: where the energy put out, is
matched with the energy received, and there perhaps is the
crux of the problem. I have to say it. What's wrong with this
country? Now I know we know we're in decline. Well, we are,
aren't we? Unemployment; Beef; urban decay; inner city
isolation; Beef; the last days of the Empire; Britannia put to bed;

the diminishing Commonwealth; Beef; the EEC; single currency; Beef and Beef. See what I mean? But where's our energy gone? The great British Tolerance, you know, that live-and-let-live, that not minding about eccentrics because we're supposed to be a nation of them, I think it's all a myth. Or at least, if it used to be true, it isn't any longer. For tolerance, in my book, read Apathy.

I had to go to Sussex University to give a seminar, a few days after my return from where the Missouri meets the Mississippi, and the comparison was horrifying. The train to Brighton was late. No one complained. Perhaps, used to the vagaries of the Southern Railway (one can hardly call it a System, it seems to be so arbitrary) they were worn down by the alarming regularity of its lateness and its propensity for stopping at leaves on the line... There were sweet wrappers and empty drink cans all over the floor of the carriage. Again, no one complained. They sat there in the rubbish. Most of the students looked tired and worn out too; not surprising, as most of them have to hold down a job, if not two, in order to pay for their tuition and board. And as my seminar is an evening class, it's hard to pay attention at 7 p.m. when you've been up since 7 a.m. writing essays before going in to some café or pub to wash up or serve, or both.

Of course it's not fair to compare Sussex University with Wash U – the latter is just below the Ivy League, its fees are $9,634. a semester and there are two a year (that's £15,000 to you) for four years. That's before the little dears lay their weary heads in a dormitory or apartment anywhere (whack on another £8,000), and if after that you're still standing, you can buy them the necessary books, at $500 a year... so we're talking very comfortably off middle-class kids and their deep-pocketed fee-paying parents. And for that money you get two theatres within the university campus that are better equipped and staffed than most provincial theatres in this country.

While I was there I saw the Tyrone Guthrie theatre from Minneapolis do an adaptation of Kafka's *Metamorphosis*; there was a one-man show devised by Robert le Page from Montreal, called *Needles and Opium* – a collage of events from the lives of Miles Davies, Jean Cocteau and a fictitious Canadian visiting Paris... and the dance students did their own evening of in-house work that included ballet and some very modern dance. Costumes, choreography and some of the music was in-house too. When I left, the drama bit of the Performing Arts Department – to which I was attached – had just started rehearsing a full-scale Elizabethan production, complete with sword fights and tights of *Romeo and Juliet*... and that's just one month in one small section of the university syllabus.

Most of these PAD students were in my class. I rarely had to ask for volunteers. Arms shot up whenever a new piece of the Bard was to be tried, illustrating heightened prose or naturalistic verse or, God help us all, rhyme. I rarely had to resort to the cajoling that I normally have to use in England – 'Now who's going to go next?' Silence from the armless ones. 'OK, who's got a birthday nearest to today's date?' These American kids were keen.

Now I know that some of you cynics for keen will read pushy. 'Not backwards in coming forwards, the Americans,' I can hear. 'Probably all those vitamins that they were throwing down their throats just after the war when we were still living on acorn coffee and strawberry jam made out of swede, and no one had seen an egg or a banana since goodness knows when. No wonder they're big.'

Yes they are. Big and keen. They'd hook me into conversations after class and accost me as I was crossing campus – quite difficult, that. It was mostly below freezing while I was there. In fact it was so cold that one day, when I was probably the only person to venture out on foot, my dear hosts happened to be out too, in one of their three cars, so my intention to walk wasn't met with the usual, incredulous 'You're gonna *walk*? You sure are crazy. It's fifteen below and the wind-chill factor is forty-five!' Well this particular day, I don't know what primeval urge it was, but deciding to activate the winter version of 'Mad dogs and Englishmen go out in the midday sun', out I went, armed with my best Marks and Sparks long-sleeved thermal vest and sundry layers of winter woollies. I saw a guy peering into the open bonnet of his car wearing a face mask. Now I knew, unusual as this sight was to me, greenhorn that I am from the quiet backwaters of Putney, that he wasn't a bank robber with carburettor trouble, because the mask he was sporting was knitted. Yessir! A home-made face mask. Not a lot of them about. Not even in the 'Show Me' State.

So you can see that it's not the weather that's the magnet of the mid-west. It's the keenness. And it wasn't just on the campus that I met it. It was the same in church. Packed to the rafters it was. Every Sunday. People looked happy to be there. No wonder. It was *warm.* None of the puritan 'You're not here to be comfortable, or, Lordy me, enjoy yourselves'. They sang hymns – I was going to say songs — with gusto and obvious enjoyment. Some of them were rather bordering on the happy-clappy for my taste, and others wouldn't have seemed out of place in the hit parade. Everyone suddenly burst out singing. Every time. And the family from across the street that I went with (my dear hosts were of the Jewish persuasion) made me feel so warmly welcome to their family worship that their little boy of eleven didn't hesitate for a second at the beginning of the Lord's Prayer, when it was their custom to hold hands in a circle, to grab mine and include me too.

Everywhere I went I met with the same enthusiasm, warmth and openness. Now I know the English accent has a lot to do with it. When I was playing on Broadway, some fifteen years ago now, if I hailed a cab and said, 'Thirteenth, please, between sixth and seventh.' I was often met with an 'Aw, say it again' from the front seat, which of course I would, becoming even more BBC in my second delivery. It might have been the 'please' that did it. New York and New Yorkers are not renowned for their politeness. Sharp elbows and a whiplash tongue are needed to survive in that Metropolis and that's just for survival on the sidewalk.

But provincial America is different. The pace of life is slower. People have time to talk, time to be, even if their geography is somewhat hazy. The bellboy at the Holiday Inn in St Louis, on hearing me speak, said, 'Say, what part of France do you come from?' He could have done his homework on my surname, of course, and been thrown right off the scent. 'London? London? Now where's *that*?' This same hotel, where I had to stay on my first visit before the delights of my host's house were opened up to me, came back with an immortal rejoinder to a friend's request to room service, 'Could I have a cappuccino please?' 'Ma'am, this is the Holiday Inn.' That's one of the great hotel non-sequiturs of the world.

Perhaps part of my malaise at being back in not-so-great Britain is that my host's house was a mansion. The street that this detached three-floored quasi palace was in, had wrought iron gates at either end, one set of which was closed at the main road end on weekends. All its neighbouring houses, mostly mock TudorBethan, but each one unique in its design, stood in their own grounds too, both back and front. The garden at the back of ours – you see how quickly I became proprietorial – was so large that I spent several days marvelling at how quietly the neighbours shared it. I never saw them. It was a while before the dime dropped and I realised that the three-car garage at the bottom, the vast expanse of land and the hot tub – a sort of garden jacuzzi – was all ours, sorry, theirs.

The room I had as my sitting room on the top floor, which was bigger than my entire Putney house from the front door to the back of the kitchen wall, was overlooked by the most exquisite Art Deco skyscraper of some seventy-plus floors, in a pale biscuit-coloured stone. Over each window was a unique bas relief, perhaps haut relief would be more appropriate, of various fruits or flowers and animals. To the left of it, only some fifty yards away, also visible from my window, were two enormous satellite dishes for a local television station. That's 'merica for you.

There was a beautiful coat of arms with cherubs, a shield and several fleurs-de-lys over the main door of our house, and an exquisite triptych of stained glass windows on the stair landing which, when the sun shone diffused a warm pink and yellow glow over all the carved panelling above and beneath it.

Every room was lined with rich dark wood and every room had its own set of finely finished built-in cupboards in the same warm rich American oak, all lovingly finished by an antique hand with a caring eye for detail and craftsmanship. Now I know that our country, and Scotland especially, abounds in marvels of Burne Jones and Rennie Mackintosh stained glass and Jacobean carved doors, but to find these and many other gems of architectural wonders in Middle America was a double delight, and one that most Americans are unaware of too – say that you're in St Louis and most other Americans will laugh, or ask 'Why?'

Arriving so soon after the festive season, I found many of the houses still hung with garlands of pine and fir, entwined with reams of bright red ribbon and alight with little white tree lights (none of that Twelfth Night better take it down or it's bad luck nonsense here). I felt as if I were in a movie. Not in the same sense that you feel that in LA – that if you walk in through a doorway you'll see that it's a one-dimensional facade propped up by stage weights. In fact I have a theory, not original I'm sure, that the whole of LA is one great set. No, I was in a Middle America movie, where the post boy threw the day's newspapers on to the front lawn as he passed, whatever the weather. Mud-encrusted *Post* and *Dispatch*? Yessir. And when it snowed I sang under my breath 'I'm dreaming of a white Christmas,' even though it was January, because the street *was* the movie. Pat Boone could have stepped out on to any of the frost tinged lawns. Front doors were decorated with balloons on birthdays, or in our case on the birth of six (on the second count, seven) kittens.

Pershing Place, where I was so lavishly lodged, had originally been called Berlin Place when it was inhabited by Germans and Russians during the World's Fair in 1904, and its local shops with their Greenwich Village-type artists' cafés and bookshops felt very European – except in their service. Nothing was too much trouble. Ask for hot sliced home-made potato chips in Dressel's, the Welsh pub (a *Welsh* pub!?) on Euclid... and quicker than you could say 'Only $1.75 to the

pound?' they were there, and that was at ten o'clock at night. None of that 'Sorry but the chef doesn't work after 8.30' that we are so familiar with.

Food plays a large part in my memory bank. There were six types of coffee to choose from: hazelnut, amaretto, vanilla, french, mocha and espresso; as many types of bagel: sesame, onion, blueberry, raisin, rye and just plain old sourdough – and that was in the campus café. Lunch at the St Louis Bread Company was a carbohydrate dream, with its glass display cases full of every kind of bread, bagel, roll, cake and biscuit that a foodie like me could ever require, and all made freshly on the premises. Straub's, the local supermarket, had tumbling iced piles of fresh jumbo shrimp, potted mountains of home made fat-free fruit dip, – a delicious pale pink almondy concoction for dipping strawberries into, which I did almost daily. Fat-free is big in the land of the free right now. You can have fat-free chocolate chip cookies, fat-free cup cakes, even fat-free spray-on 'I can't believe it's not butter'. I still can't believe the spray-on bit.

I was taken to Country Kitchen on the Interstate Highway, a gathering place of the not quite middle-class Middle America, sporting their check shirts and baseball caps (worn the right way round) and ploughing their way through the Sunday papers' sporting pages. The menu was a cliché of American food at its best: pancakes and maple syrup, waffles and bacon, home-made hash browns, onion rings, biscuits and gravy, the biscuits being more like scones; I thought it wisest not to ask about the gravy that Came With it, in the same way that Jack Nicholson's hamburger Came With french fries in *Five Easy Pieces.*

In fact all my vegetarian reluctance went well by the board at a later date at Steak and Shake, whose motto, 'If it's in sight it must be right', was blazoned on the paper hats we wore while eating. I had a hand-made vanilla milk shake that I could have taken a knife and fork to, so unctuous and creamy it was (I can always wax poetic about food) and it wasn't the Steak that made me Shake, it was the hamburger that Came With it. I forgot, or tried to, all my misgivings about meat – we're talking non-mad cow meat here – closed my eyes and thought of England, in a manner of eating.

That did it, of course. Several queasy hours, not to say days, later, I remembered the warning of a waggish friend, a Scot from the Borders as it happens, who on seeing me eat snails with my glance averted (this was before my vegetarian days, although I was obviously heading in that direction) retorted, 'You should never eat anything that you can't look in the eye.' Well I've obviously lost the knack of finding the eye of a hamburger.

Food is everywhere in the States. At every intermission at the ice hockey game I was taken to at the vast new stadium – the only time I've ever suffered vertigo from a seat in the stalls – the packed auditorium would, as one, get up and get a hot dog, a bucket of popcorn, a coke or a beer, and there are a lot of intermissions in a game of ice hockey. Now it could well have been comfort food. The St Louis Blues were massacred by The Oilers from Edmonton, a shaming forty-nine to about twelve, I think, much to my host's chagrin. The normally mild-mannered, quietly spoken Henry turned into whatever the male version of a virago is at every Canadian turn of the puck.

I apologise for not being able to remember the score. It was almost half-time before I could work out which way 'our' team was headed. Ice hockey is the opposite of cricket. Things happen so fast you haven't a clue what's going on. Or at least I hadn't. In spite of my host explaining it all with great care and precision, at shouting level in order to be heard above the screams and roars of disbelief and despair. In much the same way, apart from the decibels, the entire staff of the Performing Arts Department, gathered round the television at his house a week or so later, tried to explain to me the intricacies of the Superbowl. I didn't even really begin with that one. I spent the whole match slowly realising it wasn't basketball or baseball, but football with war paint, motorbike helmets and epaulettes.

Now I know you can watch American football on the TV in dear old Blighty, and eat all the fast food I've mentioned, but it's different eating and watching in situ. Like wine from Tuscany never tastes the same in SW15.

They threw me a surprise party the night before I left. My students had just said goodbye at the end of the afternoon's class, and I had to sniff back a whisker of disappointment that this lot, unlike the bunch the previous year, hadn't even signed a farewell card or a Wash U PAD T-shirt. Even the paperback copy of the first folio ordered from a student who worked in the shopping mall bookshop (for shopping mall read mini-city) wasn't forthcoming. I pressed $40 into his hand and made him promise to send it on. When I returned 'home' Patty pleaded a headache and absented herself from the final dinner we had arranged for Henry, myself, her and their two daughters at a local restaurant.

So, disappointed on two counts, off I went with mine host, the two girls and a male friend. The kids jumped up and down all through a rather despondent dinner on my part, to check by phone whether Mom was feeling well enough yet to join us. The answer being consistently negative, it looked like my last evening was going to finish in a flurry of nothing, round about 8.15. So I suggested to the friend that we continue our evening further along with coffee cake and ice cream – I was planning to top up on American food before my departure – but my suggestion was politely declined. 'Wow, I've really scored a hit here,' I thought.

Walking back through the dark streets, my mood even darker, I said on raising my eyes from pavement level, 'There seems to be a lot of people further up the street.' No one answered. As we approached the house I said, 'Henry, there's a lot of people outside your house.'

'I think the neighbours have on some kind of a do,' he answered.

It wasn't until one of the girls sniggered that I realised something was up. My hearing isn't all it might be, but a few steps further and I could detect the tune of an Elizabethan round I had taught them to sing.

Rose, Rose, Rose, Rose,
Will I ever see thee wed?
Ay, marry that thou wilt,
If thou but stay.

There they were, all my students who had so hurriedly and unceremoniously said goodbye that afternoon, lining the path up to the house, holding candles and singing. And there was I, my mouth open in disbelief (there are photos to prove it) and my eyes full of tears. As we walked up the path, my male friend and I, I had to stifle a thought about how like a wedding arch it was, but I didn't stifle the prayer that he wouldn't listen too closely to the words of the song.

Inside, the house was awash with every colour of helium balloon, shiny sparkles were scattered all over the floor, and every member of the PAD was there holding a glass of champagne and sporting huge smiles. Even the drama critic from the local cable station was there, for whom I had done an interview on Shakespeare, and who had then turned up to two of my Saturday morning classes held at the crack of 9.30 a.m. Now there's keen for you. There was an iced cake the size of a small table with 'We love you Jane' on it, and a supermarket trolley-sized basket full of all the tackiest American inventions that I love: Ziplock plastic food bags, fat-free Coffee Mate – vanilla flavour, chocolate chip cookies, fat-free too. Someone had been doing a good bit of pre-party canvassing about my taste, or lack of it, and yes, there amongst the presents was my paperback copy of the first folio that they had all clubbed together to buy and had inscribed with the most heart-wrenching goodbyes and thanks. On almost every window and door were photographs of almost every play, film or TV production I've ever been in. (The memory of some of them could well have spoiled an evening had I been on less of an attention and affection high.)

It was one of the greatest evenings of my life.

'I've never had a party like that – I've never had a surprise party come to think of it,' I mumbled some hours later as we, the family, sat round the kitchen table.

'Well, you should have had' was Patty's simple retort, she of the brilliantly acted headache. It must have taken her weeks to organise that party. Almost as long as it took me the next morning to sweep up the hundreds of sparkles that stuck to the beautiful wooden floor. It wasn't a totally altruistic gesture. I wanted to bring some of the sparkles home with me. Apart from the ones embedded in my memory.

America is still the land where dreams can come true. Is that where our energy has gone, gone with our ability and willingness to dream?

The Soul

While I was in the States I received a request via the wonders of modern science – Henry's fax machine – to write an article to accompany six radio programmes I'd devised that were about to be transmitted. The request had come from a bright-eyed, warm-spirited Scots lady I'd met some months before in the Dirty Duck pub in Stratford – the Life Support System for actors in the RSC in need of liquid refreshment as a reward for having made it relatively safe and sound through yet another performance. The benefits of the alcohol are frequently enhanced by the lively support and encouragement of one Pam, Mine Hostess, who *is* the Dirty Duck pub and without whose acknowledgement no actor can ever seriously regard themselves as a bona fide member of the company.

I'd received the most exquisite bunch of deep purply blue anemones one night after a performance of Mrs Alving in Ibsen's *Ghosts* at The Other Place in Stratford. It wasn't just the comfort of my favourite flowers from an unknown donor that had me intrigued, but that they had probably been sent with a knowledge of the gruelling rigours of the role. Mrs Alving is the emotional Himalayas – the female equivalent of Lear. She starts off lonely, tortured and isolated by the secret of her debauched dead husband's philandering which has caused her many years before to send her son safely away from his father's bad influence and neighbour's gossiping tongues, to find, after his much hoped for return, that she is faced with the dilemma of releasing him from his terminal disease to death, or keeping him alive. This allows her to fulfil the mothering that her sacrifice made her forego, but is contrary to his wishes and the soul-searing promise that he tries to elicit from her at the end of the play. So, post-performance, several large glasses at the Dirty Duck are the order of the day.

'Did you like the flowers?' came gently tinged with a Scottish burr from a small bespectacled woman with dark shiny hair who had edged her way towards me amongst the loudly talking crowd.

'My favourites,' I said thankfully, expecting her to then come out with some post-performance gratitudes which are always welcome, but which often hide a string of further questions which are sometimes tiring. 'It's a killer of a role,' I said, by way of an excuse for my inability to talk coherently, the untouched glass of red still in my hand. I needn't have worried. She knew the play well and talked about it in a refreshing and passionate way. It's always such a relief that a post-performance conversation with a member of the audience isn't a thinly veiled need for a performance after a perfor-mance; to be met with a genuine love of theatre and an astute awareness of the intricacies of the work, not just the impression that the work leaves.

I thought no more about this meeting other than it being an audience highlight in a very debilitating season. I had also been playing Gertrude to Kenneth Branagh's Hamlet, and she's no bundle of laughs either.

I knew no more about this little lady until the red-letter fax day. She, the fax informed me, was the Features Editor of the *Glasgow Herald*. She had seen the advertisement for the radio programmes in the *Radio Times*. With the help of Henry's electric typewriter and bolstered by her generous assumption that I would be able to write an accompanying article for the programmes, ensconced in my palatial top-floor flat under the requisite blue Missouri skies, spiked by the creamy coloured skyscraper that was my nearest neighbour, I wrote. And so began my working relationship and burgeoning friendship with Jackie McGlone.

Looking back now, the aptness of having to write first about my faith and my journey to it (although of course there is no 'it' to travel to, faith being a constantly challenged, ever-broadening understanding, changing state of awareness) is pleasing. My life would be meaningless without a belief in the potential for a transcendent generosity of spirit in us all – to cobble Thomas Carlyle and Matthew Arnold 'for that which in us and around us which is not ourselves,' a conviction of the necessity within the human psyche for what Carl Jung called the Numinous. Looking up the word in the dictionary I find ironically that it is absent and in its place is 'numismatic' – the study of coins, a study which the consumerist world we live in seems amply to have taken to where its heart should be.

But 'what is a man if his chief good and market of his time be but to sleep and feed? A beast, no more'. Perhaps the days of institutionalised religion are over (why should the church be exempt from the deconstruction that has affected every other established organisation?). The organised church seems sadly unwilling and unable to answer questions that doubt and challenge the simplistic grounds on which it was built, that are no longer relevant to this disparate and complex world in which we live. But in the debris of the hard and fast rules that were the tracks laid down for our predecessors lives to run on and within, and in the shambles of new age thinking, 'Modern man's tragedy is not that he believes in nothing but that he believes in anything' – no one is exempt from having to answer to themselves at least, for what they do or don't believe. 'We can believe what we choose, but we are answerable for what we believe.' Life with its inevitable potholes and troughs ensures that confrontation occurs at several points along the road if one has eyes to see.

Faith is a gift – it cannot be commanded or demanded. It cannot be described or proscribed. But the ground can be prepared by an openness of heart, a willingness to learn and a humility to remember from whence we came. 'Trailing clouds of glory' is a hard image to take on board nowadays, and the ego runs rampant under the greedy seduction of Mammon and basks smugly in its brassy omnipotence. Determinism is out of fashion. And institutionalised religions by their nature do not encourage the individual spiritual path. There may be only one God but there are many ways to the Divine.

Seeds of Faith

A faith that sets bounds in itself, that will believe so much and
no more that will trust thus far and no further, is none.

J C AND S W HARE *GUESSES AT TRUTH,* 1827

Know then thyself; presume not God to scan
The proper study of mankind is man.

ALEXANDER POPE *ESSAYS ON MAN,* 1733–4

Like a lot of teenagers I drifted away from churchgoing when
the attraction of its youth club paled in the lights and lure of
the coffee bar. Its frothy cappuccino and Elvis Presley songs on
the juke box became the repository for my collection money, not
the offertory plate at Alan Road Methodist Church in Ipswich,
where, thanks to my foster mother's devout faith, I had been in
regular attendance three times a Sunday since I was old enough
to walk there and sing 'Jesus wants me for a sunbeam'. Probably
unlike a lot of seventeen-year-olds, though, I lied to my foster
mother about the sermon I hadn't heard the Reverend John
Blamey preach, thereby encouraging the development of my
imagination, conversely also assuring my place amongst the well
and truly damned. So religion and things spiritual (and I do
define them differently) were put on hold until many years later.

Faced some ten years ago simultaneously with a dear friend dying of cancer, and the interpretation of the role of Saint Joan – the necessity of helping a loved one relinquish a hold on life, and needing to find empathy with a passionate young woman's hot-line to God – I was forced to take stock of what I actually believed, if anything, about matters of the soul. (I did not then, and have not since, ever doubted the existence of such a thing – and I suspect that anyone who has ever had anything to do with the interpretation of music, great poetry, edifying and life-enhancing thought and language, would whole-heartedly agree with me.)

But between the coffee and the stake came the women's movement of the sixties. I am a feminist. That is to say I am concerned and involved in the fair representation of the feminine in all walks of life. So what place could there be for me in such a patriarchal institution as the Church? Given that at least in some of the most 'advanced' branches of conventional Christianity (and sadly, I am being ironic) we do at least have women priests, but there were women in those positions in the early Christian Church before St Paul and the Roman Christians sanitised blood and fertility out of the act.

However, something sticks in my craw over God the Father, God the Son and God the Holy Ghost. All right, the last-named could be interpreted as asexual. Nevertheless, the odds are mightily stacked against the distaff side, not least in the icon of the Virgin Mary – a level of sanctity that no mere woman could attain, the double role of virgin and mother being well beyond most of our abilities. Could this be one of the reasons why most of our churches stand empty on Sundays? Women, as we know from anthropological studies are nearly always the guardians of the spirit life of the tribe.

Where did this need for a God arise? Is it part of our psyches? Ever since humankind staggered upright on its two back feet, it has exhibited a need for the worship of something grander than itself.

So is our God of our own making? Or is our search for something that we once knew but have lost, 'not in entire forgetfulness'? So is God beyond us? How has our perception of God changed? For many years after St Joan, questions like this buzzed around in my head, leading me into a vociferous reading of psychology, theology and anthropology.

According to one of my guests in these programmes, Swedenborg said as early as the end of the last century that the need for churches was dead. Given that the current inexorable grip of materialism is hard to ignore, in what form does intelligent thought, or better still, informed and articulate faith about God survive? That was one of the spurs that led me to interview three academics in the programmes on 4, 11 and 18 February. And thankfully as the pendulum swings away from the non-satisfaction of acquisitiveness, enter Stage Left the non-attachment to things and states and people – a central role which is now being occupied in a spiritual sense by Eastern religions, their advent tolling the demise of Christianity for the 'modern' thinker. Their many-layered message says the same things as Christianity, but it's too much bother to re-interpret that – to try to see the meanings behind the well-worn phrases and well-known parables – 'novelty is only in request'?

So to Buddhism, which is where I restarted my spiritual journey. After all the reading and the thinking, I realised there was nothing for it but to get down on my butt and *do* it, every day, not just when I felt like it. So meditating became part of my life, for better or mostly worse (and it is like a marriage, there's a nagging if you haven't paid attention to it) about eight years ago. I thought, foolishly, that it was easier than praying. Or perhaps more accurately, I was dissatisfied with what I knew of praying – simply asking for what you wanted, then being fed up when it didn't occur.

Realising the inherent dangers of mapping my own path without recourse or redress to others, I found myself in the congregation of the Russian Orthodox church, where in contrast to the starkness of the Methodist worship of my youth, I found enjoyment in the smells and the bells, the uplift of the glorious music, and the singing in a language I couldn't understand, but that I could use simply as a channel for my worship.

The ease with which we were all free to wander and ponder an icon or light a candle, appealed to my sense of liberty, and the company and modesty of fellow worshippers, kneeling with their foreheads to the ground, kept my rampant ego in its proper place.

So, these six radio programmes were really the charting of my journey from the Gondolier coffee bar, to finding myself once more at the altar rail taking communion (albeit still unable and unwilling to recite the Nicene Creed, because I can't, and won't, say things I don't mean, or things that I think the church isn't honest about). The Nicene Creed was after all a manifesto drawn up under a Roman Emperor in order to reconcile all the different factions and sects of Christianity that had sprung up around the Mediterranean some 400 years AD. Inevitably I find myself wanting to mutter, 'And God the Mother?'

It was a privilege and a pleasure to talk to the six people who comprised these programmes, most of whom I am lucky to have as personal friends. They include a woman priest, the Reverend Elisabeth Arnold, a girl I went to school with, who has no problem with 'God the Father', as I do; David McLellan, the world authority on Marx and a professor in the politics department of Kent University in Canterbury, who is also a devout Roman Catholic and erstwhile Jesuit novice; a poet friend, Peter Abbs, who is Reader in Education at Sussex University, and a Blakean (God as Imagination); medieval biblical historian Dr Lesley Smith of Manchester Theological College, Oxford, who patiently cleared up my fuzzy notions about where ideas of women as second-rate citizens in the Bible come from (surprisingly not, as I thought, from Judaism, but from the Roman attitude to the female fertility and sex); while my hunger for the spiritual in psychology led me to talk to Jungian psychotherapist Eliana Essery, who is also a painter. Together we touched on the resonance of archetypes and symbols throughout all cultures and ages.

The sixth programme – anything but the end of my journey, rather more the starting place for all the questions that the other interviews have raised – was with Shaun de Warren who describes himself as a Life Coach, and who has indeed thrown some very basic assumptions that we all hold dear, well and truly up into the air, and reassembled them with insights gained from Eastern religions, a reinterpretation of Western ones, minus the guilt, delivered with the common sense and positiveness of neuro-linguistic programming.

I wanted these six programmes to show that God, the Divine, Energy, Eternal Love, Light – call it what you will, can be approached in many ways. That the vanguard of Christian thinking is still alive and healthy, battling for survival among acute minds and caring hearts. That by plugging into this Force; by some personal inner connection, to Being, and not Doing, we can then return to our outer lives refreshed, renewed and strengthened in the knowledge that we all come from one and the same Source. That we can then enrich and enhance the lives of those we meet. I hope that my friends in these programmes and their many ways of 'oneing' with the Divine, will have refreshed and renewed the lives of those who tuned in to what the media call 'The God Slot'; marginalised to the unseasonable hour of 11.45 p.m., which says a lot about our priority for the spiritual.

The Garden

I discovered I was happy writing.

I'd wanted to be a writer from a very early age. English was the only subject at which I was evenly remotely adequate in at school. Maths was and still is an unfathomable nightmare. I dwindle into a kind of catatonic trance when faced with a sheet of numbers. They mean nothing. My initial reaction to numbers is often sheer panic. I could lay the responsibility for that persistent terror fair and square at the door of Miss Howell. Miss Howell, presiding dragon over Class 7, under whose steely gaze and strident demand for the right answer I could provoke an asthma attack at will by way of diversion, until, impatient with my speechless wheezing, she would reluctantly relinquish her vice-like attention on my shaking frame and I would be allowed, shamed but nonetheless off the hook, to retreat to my desk. Years later, the memory still smarting, I would reason with and excuse my younger self – how could I possibly have come up with any answer at all, having never understood the question?

Words were different. They were my friends. They provided me, as they do for a lot of 'only' children, with an escape into the imaginary world of books. Books collected from the library in piles and devoured in great feasts of reading at night in my cold bedroom, away from the watchful eyes of my foster mother, for whom my sitting absorbed in a book was a sure sign that I was sickening for some life-threatening disease.

Now in my middle years, when the roles for women in the
classical theatre are thin on the ground, the terror of the blank
page that faces me as a writer and the responsibility for what
goes down on it being solely mine, is a small price to pay for
the necessarily corporate effort that is the production and
performance of a play. Co-operation is sometimes sadly lacking
in the rehearsal room, given all the varying needs, aspirations
and abilities of director, actors and designers. And acting is
such a passive job. Waiting for the phone to ring, waiting for
some director to have your name drop into his mind as ideal
for the role he is pondering. Then being at the mercy of the
chemistry between you and him. (It's nearly always a he, even
in this post-feminist age. In thirty years I've only ever worked
with four women directors and they're not necessarily more
approachable or amenable – the power game of Director as
God is played by the distaff side as well.) You hope too that an
easy working relationship may develop between you and your
opposite number in the play, who may feel he is miscast, hard
done by, inadequate, or may be just sheer bloody-minded.

All these imponderables are well in the future when the
actor agrees to do a play and signs the resultant contract. It irks
me that I am not in the driving seat, or that given my age, my
vehicle has been reduced to that of the leading character's
mother, or worse, maid. Drama is still largely written by men
who, in this country at least, don't see mature women as
protagonists. Younger actors' mothers that's my life......or
somebody's wife. After forty-five, apart from Shaw, a few
Chekhovs and the Greeks, you can say goodbye to holding
the reins and being the motor of the play if you have two X
chromosomes.

All these niggles had been festering away in the stewpot of
my subconscious for some time. When I did find a voice for
them either through lack of self-restraint or sheer despair, my
friends would look at me in unspoken sympathy tinged with,
I suspect, a belief that I was fishing for confirmation of the

continuation of my work as an actor. I wasn't. I wanted encouragement to go back to my first love. Writing.

Again the Scots were trumps. From north of the border came a further request from Jackie McGlone to write an article to go with another radio programme in which I'd recorded some excerpts from *The Virago Book of Women Gardeners*. Somewhere between Scotland and Broadcasting House was a plot to bring what was stewing in my subconscious to the surface. I was grateful, relieved and not a touch terrified to face the inconsistencies of my own electric typewriter. A self-awarded promotion from the old manual that I'd written *Grace and Favour* on, it was a dubious step up as it displayed inexplicable tendencies to devour whole lines of text in a completely unprovoked and volatile manner. I wondered how much it would allow me to write before it would decide to unwrite it and shatter the fragile burgeoning of my writer's confidence.

Everything Lovely
Is in the Garden

Perennials are the ones that grow like weeds,
biennials are the ones that die this year instead of next, and
hardy annuals are the ones that never come up at all.

KATHARINE WHITEHORN, *OBSERVATIONS*, 1970

The phone rang. It was the PR woman from the Press Office of
the BBC.

'We wondered if you'd like to give us a quote for the *Virago
Book of Women Gardeners* programme that you recorded.'

I was not in the best of moods about gardens. The old dear
next door was still feeding the hoards of dratted pigeons that
flocked to her roof three times a day and my garden resembled
some indescribable graveyard-cum-sewage tip of matted feathers
and guano, in spite of my increasingly less and less polite
requests for her to stop. And on the other side... well it's
probably libellous, but suffice to say that the decibel curve of
noise increases in direct proportion to the consumption of
alcohol, and from recent evidence it seemed apparent that we
were on an up. My nerves were not at their best or, as I saw
recently, a more witty way of putting it – 'I have one nerve left,
and you're on it.'

'Isn't it strange,' I said – my biting sarcasm always takes a
while to warm up – 'how you PR people always assume we actors

know something about the subject of a programme we've recorded?' There was the expected pause at the other end. 'That's put her in her place,' I thought nastily.

'Well, the producer said you'd told her you were a keen gardener.' There I was, firmly put in mine.

I wondered in a total panic if she were going to suggest a visit from a photographer. Before she could answer I gave her her quote. 'This programme will make you feel so guilty that you'll don your wellies, grab your trowel and head for the weeds.'

I could feel her beaming at the other end of the line, off which she then got, placated and pleased. I just stood there feeling bad. Bad – and guilty. Bad because of my rudeness to her, and guilty on two counts. I haven't donned or grabbed, and if I did anything as reckless as heading for my garden, I'd end up with concussion,because of the proximity of my neighbour's bottom wall. Yes, it's a plot. My garden, that is. I think in Estate Agent-speak it's a patio, but it's really an L-shaped yard up the other way, or a T with the left-hand bit missing. It used to be a rectangle. The missing bit is where the outside loo used to be, which is now where my kitchen table is, if you see what I mean. You have to use your imagination. I've certainly had to use mine. The plot is about fifteen feet across the T bar bit, and four feet deep. The long bit's about the same. To date, and I've just been to check, I have: fifteen large pots, eleven tubs and twelve window boxes in it. So you see I do deserve the appellation 'keen'. It's just the word 'garden' that's a bit questionable.

'You could build a twenty-two storey block out here,' said one of my builders some eight years ago now, when I was having The Extension done. I remember it as if it were yesterday. Preposterous idea. Whoever heard of a twenty two storey block in space fifteen foot by four, which is, as I say, about the size of it. The depth of the hole, where The Extension was to be built, was something else – in the American sense of the expression.

'You've been down there for days,' I said, peering into the ever increasing murk. Were they working for the gas board, using my garden for yet another of their subterranean

destructions? Or were they secretly drilling for hidden oil? Builders outstaying their welcome have this weird effect on one's thinking.

'It's the junk, yer see.' I didn't. I couldn't. The hole was too deep to see anything. 'Just chucked everything down 'ere, didn't he, the bloke who had this house before you. Rusty tins, plastic cement bags, we've even found the old water tank from the loft.' I wanted to offer some biting witticism about my garden being a veritable treasure trove, or that I was beginning, just beginning, to feel fed up with it looking as much of a rubbish tip *outside* the hole as it evidently did inside. 'Yeah, he just covered it all with a few inches of soil and left it.'

'Eureka,' I thought, 'the junk – that's it!' The occupant of the beds of lost causes was 'Junk'. I wished even more fervently they'd leave, so I could get to the flower-beds. No, I've been guilty of a misdescription – they weren't flower-beds then, they were plant graveyards. Along the left-hand wall, the long bit of the T, was my local garden centre's main profits; they must have thought I owned a mansion with extensive grounds at the rate I wheeled out trolleys and trolleys of bedding plants but they were in fact for the graveyard i.e. patch of ground on which absolutely nothing would grow, or if it did, it was spindly and pale and unstable. And I had tried. Petunias, Geraniums, Narcissi, Daffodils, Asters, Marguerites, Those Brightly Coloured Things That Look Like Daisies But Aren't (you name it, I obviously can't).

My builder's words ringing in my ears, as only builders' words can, I dug up the flower-bed's worth of rusty tins and plastic cement bags – I drew a blank at a water tank, so to speak. I did find the bones of a dead cat. Or at least I hoped that's what they were. Over the freshly dug junk-free earth, I envisioned carpets of brilliant blooms. Is that what I have there now? Sadly no. A carpet of not-so-brilliant variegated ivies. I forgot to say that my back yard is edged on three sides by cascades of wall-covering honeysuckle, jasmine and climbing iceberg roses. At least it was, till the neighbour at the bottom decided to oust his buddleia from our mutual wall, and in the so doing, ran his electric hedge trimmer along the top. What is it with neighbours in Putney? You might well ask. Me too. I no longer had a little green bower, a secret walled garden of delights, a little paradise of green and white, Like-What-I-Saw-in-a-Magazine. I had fifteen black rubbish bags of garden refuse that I had to take to the local tip (sorry, the civic amenities site), and that ten days before Christmas and me with five guests to feed, around a table now facing a half-bare bottom wall. Well you see, this magazine had suggested that All White was a good idea for London gardens, as most Londoners only saw their gardens at night as they got home late – and working in the theatre, I got home later than most. So all white it is. But a paradise? No. At least, not for me. For the snails and slugs that delight in the damp mouldy blanket of leaves that fall from my honeysuckle, jasmine, and roses through every season of the year, yes, it is a paradise – and a permanent picnic.

All sorts of ridiculous slug 'n' snail remedies were suggested by well-meaning friends – heard the one about the mug full of beer to entice them to drown? I'm afraid I'm not that patient, or that generous with alcohol. So, yes, they go by the way of slug pellets – the bright blue grains do rather spoil that swept up look, and yes, my main gardening tool is a broom. Or they go by air, on a curved arc, overarm mostly, towards my neighbours garden. Which one? That would be telling. And I'm not. So in various stages of munched I have: white pansies, a white camellia, white potentilla, white hydrangea, white geraniums, and a thing that looks like a variegated privet but isn't, that shoots stems of white star-shaped flowers in the middle of spring (if ever we get one), and a dark green five-fingered leafy thing that does the same (you knew I wouldn't be able to keep those names going for long, didn't you?), and a large magnolia tree in a tub behind my white wrought-iron table and chair that sit resplendent on the top of a little brick dais, which has never flowered – the magnolia, that is. They say magnolias are like marriages, the first seven years are the worst. Well, we've ridden the storms of the first eleven years, my magnolia and I, and it's never blessed me with one single bloom. But then I wasn't very green-fingered at marriage either.

An abundant magnolia some few terraced gardens down mocks me with its luscious flowers whenever I sit out in the garden. Whenever it's out. The sun, that is. You see it doesn't appear from behind the bottom wall of them with the buddleia until 11.30, and it disappears behind the chimneys of him with the large alcohol consumption by 3.15, and that's on a good day. A good day of sun. And oh, how very good that glass of wine tastes then. The bottle perched on my white wrought-iron table, and me perched on my white wrought-iron seat, my knuckles white from all that sweeping. Good wine and a large smile in my leaf-free, slug-free idyll. What pleasure, what satisfaction.

Similar to the joy I get from seeing the light of the candles burning on my kitchen table, reflected amongst the leaves of many shades of green in the glass of the French windows with which The Extension was finished off. A student friend of mine, Claudia, half way through gratefully slurping her dinner, lifted her head long enough to remark, 'It looks great. But it's such a small space, not many people would have bothered.' Not bothered? A small space? But it's my *garden.*

Maybe I'm just a sucker for a challenge.

Machines

Flush with success – not of the horticultural kind evidently, but of seeing my words in print (why is it that one's words on the page of a newspaper look so much more important, so much more substantial than they ever possibly could on a page sticking out of a typewriter? Well, perhaps given the nasty nature of my electric typewriter, that isn't so surprising) – I made a life-changing and completely uncharacteristic, given my non-relations with machines, decision. I threw caution to the winds and the typewriter into the hands of a very deserving but unsuspecting teenage neighbour and dragged myself into the twentieth century. I decided to buy a laptop. I thought I'd better do it while I was still working – work has a mysterious way of petering out in the face of a major financial decision. By some uncanny sense, unemployment is lured like a magnet to bills over £500. Working, the overdraft had at least a weekly chance of minimal reduction if only in thought, not in deed. The flimsy courage to make this decision was bolstered by the fact that my son was still living at home, if not in deed in theory, and would therefore be comfortingly and theoretically available – on the rare occasions he turned up for food, baths and whatever money I could throw his way – to listen to my inexorable and inevitable cries for help.

Oh, but it wasn't as easy as that. It never is. Not as far as machines and I are concerned. Hoops of fire had to be gone through. I had to survive the junior slopes of technology first. I had to cut my teeth on a fax and a mobile phone.

Yes We Have No Technology

To err is human, but to really foul things up requires a computer.
FARMER'S ALMANAC, 1978

The thing with high tech is that you always
end up using scissors.
DAVID HOCKNEY. THE OBSERVER, 1994

I am frightened of machines. And I have good cause. They make
me feel inadequate, incompetent and downright stupid at best. At
worst I am reduced to being a footstamping, furious five year old,
red faced and tearful, ready to hurl the unsuspecting item which is
the cause of my crashing self-esteem through the nearest window.
I'd better declare at the outset, that the problem is two-way.

Machines seem to know, in my case, rather like horses do
when you get on them and you're nervous, that they are dealing
with total terror. Fear has a smell, and most of the machines that
I've had to deal with lately, have very finely tuned noses. And yes,
I am incompetent. They're right.

I am machine illiterate. I mean you're talking to a woman here
who had to have her son accompany her to the shop to choose a
mobile phone; the situation was so fraught with horror I couldn't
face going it alone. I had to get one you see, whatever my initial
reluctance, because being self-employed, it's rather essential for
the people who can find me work, to be able to get in touch with

me instantly, or down the drain goes all the potential dosh, and these people know, bless 'em, that I rarely listen to my answerphone because I've lost the bleeper that enables me to listen to the calls when I'm not at home. Well actually I didn't lose it. I threw it away by mistake, with the packaging.

I didn't know what it was you see. It looked just like a spare piece of plastic. So out it went. It was only weeks later when something went wrong with the answerphone, that I got out the instruction book and read it. I think that's a pre-requisite of being machine illiterate. Never read the instructions, until it's too late. Paradoxical isn't it? You'd think us technological twerps would need all the help we can get. But instruction manuals these days are like novels. As large. Only not so entertaining. I mean you need to have a degree in Nuclear Physics to understand most of them. I've had a video machine for about four years now that I can only use when I'm there to press the button, and it's playing the channel I want to record, because I've never managed to wade through, let alone understand, the pages and pages of instructions. I have a sneaking feeling that I haven't even managed to tune it to the right wavelengths yet. I'm waiting till I feel strong enough.

So back I went to the mobile phone shop some two days later. 'Could I have another battery please?' I said in my best polite-customer voice. It does help to be an actor in these circumstances. I did a good job of hiding my nervousness.

'But I sold you a battery with the phone only a few days ago,' said the helpful shop assistant. He wasn't fooled by my apparent control of the situation.

'Yes I know, but it's dead now,' I said, rather condescendingly, as if every idiot should know that a mobile phone battery only lasts a short time.

Now it was my turn to be patronised. 'So what have you done with it?' I think shop assistants see me coming. Or maybe the word has gone round the retailers in Putney High Street. I've lived here long enough for my ineptitude to have spread like some infectious disease all over SW15.

'I've thrown it in the bin,' I said, the veneer of calm beginning to crack.

'You've *what?*' he said. Actually he didn't say it. It was more of a chortle. And the grin on his face was still very vivid in my mind when some time later found me, plus rubber gloves, going through the contents of my last weeks' household waste. Old coffee grounds, old tins of catfood, and those unspeakably awful mushy bits that dustbins always seem to attract. Reminds me of that wonderfully stomach-churning Billy Connolly sketch, where he asks why it is everything you vomit always comes up looking like diced carrot? Why is it the everything that lurks in the corner of dustbins resembles furry trifle? Anyway, my son said some days later that I wasn't completely at fault over the battery incident. The man had forgotten to sell me a re-charger. How was *I* to know?

It was the same with the fax machine. Well not quite the same. Again, I need it for my work. Were it not for my work I'd still be in the flat iron stage.

So I said to the man in the fax machine shop, after he'd totally confused me with articles of all shapes sizes and colours, 'I'd like the cream one please, because it goes with my sitting room,' and bravely, 'Don't bother to tell me how to install it, because I'll read the instructions.' I got the smile of approval I was seeking. 'But could you please tell me how to write the message?'

'Well,' he said, rather incredulously, 'you just write the message.'

'Yes,' I said, pointing to the face of the fax, wishing to push home my point. But which *buttons* do I press to write the message?'

'Madam, you take a pen and a piece of paper...'

I left the shop with my cream fax machine and a burning face.

Well honestly. So much for modern technology – you take a pen and a piece of paper. Knowing my predilection for total panic, I planned to put aside the whole of a quiet afternoon with the fax and its instruction book and a cup of tea. Well it was anything but quiet. Oh, I managed to wire it all up, connect it to the answer-phone and even plumb in (I'm sure that's not the correct fax-speak word – that's the trouble with these modern machines, they all have their own very specific vocabulary) the date and the time of day, and several friends' phone numbers. But when I tried to check whether it was working, by ringing my own home number from the sainted mobile phone, all I got was a high-pitched whine.

But that wasn't all the bloke in the shop got when I had to trundle all the way back to the Tottenham Court Road with the fax machine in its box and an even redder face.

'Well, it's obviously not compatible with your answerphone is is?' said the very bothered bloke in the shop, trying to quell the rising decibel level of my very angry voice, and allay the increasingly curious stares of other potential customers. I was also parked on a double yellow line outside which never does much for one's peace of mind in central London.

'You sold me a fax that wasn't compatible with my answerphone when I'd even told you what kind of answerphone I had!'

'But Madam, how am *I* to know?'

Well, if not you, who? And if not now, when?

So I am now the proud possessor of a fax that is compatible with my answerphone. But it's grey.

I wrote *Grace and Favour* some nine years ago on a manual typewriter. 'Now that's what I call *real* skill,' said a friend whose advice I was seeking yesterday about why I had lost an icon from the window of my hard disk. (I think I can hear you shudder at the prospect of what could have gone wrong between me and a computer. With reason. But I was hoping you'd be impressed with my use of the vocab.)

'Oh no,' I said to the friend, not wishing to take credit where credit was definitely not due, 'I had to pay a secretary to type out my typing. It was indecipherable. She cost me almost half what they paid me for the book.'

I did promote myself, as I said, to an electric typewriter some time afterwards, as a celebration of publication, and when I gave it away about a month ago, because I'd bought this laptop, I still hadn't worked out why sometimes the erase button ate up a whole line of typing, and sometimes only a word...

To cut a long laptop disaster story short – much shorter than the time it takes a so-called Helpline to help; which at my present count is about an average of twenty minutes. (Are these people in league with British telecom or what? And that's twenty minutes of Erik Satie piano music meant to calm the nerves – it did little for mine).

It turned out that I had a faulty trackpad button. Never to be wished on one's worst enemy that. So yes, back went the laptop to a shop just off the Tottenham Court Road – the gods were with me.

I found a parking meter, and home came the new laptop. All was just hunky dory until I got a battery-going-flat warning light. Now this was odd because I was plugged into the mains and I had an article to type out for Jackie McGlone and the *Herald* pronto. Several more bill- and blood pressure-raising calls later, the shop agreed to courier me a new mains-to-laptop lead. That was at 12.20. At 4.15 and several more calls to a very helpful Melanie in Dispatch later, we ascertained that the *car* containing my precious piece of electric wire was on Putney Bridge. Now no one in their right minds would send a car to the west of London on a Friday afternoon. A motor bike yes. There are probably, at a conservative guess, about six trillion cars in the west of London on a Friday afternoon. All trying to get out. Mind you, after I'd finished with the bloke in the shop about having sold me a faulty laptop *and* a faulty lead he probably had no mind left. I certainly hadn't. I did however, manage to stop shaking for long enough to finish the article with the power supply coming from the mains through my beautiful new piece of grey plastic lead. I finished at 7.15 and trotted, mission accomplished, downstairs to put it in the fax machine. The fax machine jammed. I grabbed an envelope. I threw on my mac, dashed up the street, and threw it in the post box. Oh, the wonders of modern science.

My mobile phone bill for the month came yesterday. It's normally about £60. It was £235. Blood pressure nothing. This was cardiac arrest time. It transpires that someone has been tapping into my mobile phone number. You can apparently. If you have the necessary equipment, said the mobile phone Helpline very sanguinely. (They only kept me waiting three minutes, and played Mozart.) This bright new dawn of technology holds daily terrors for us all. So there is now a bar on my mobile phone. Which means that whoever has been using it, now can't. Neither can I. Know where I'm going for Easter? To a place I know, where I have to bring in the wood and strike a match to light a fire. And I'm going to take with me a pen and a piece of paper.

Time Off

I was just kidding about the pen. I took my brand new, supposedly idiotproof, laptop and like a proper writer with a country retreat went down to my rented cottage in Warwickshire. Although there were a couple of days when the pen was more mobile than the trackpad. I had the usual beginner's dose of frozen programmes, inexplicable questions that flashed up on to the screen that I had no answer to, as I had never asked the questions in the first place, and the duck quack that I'd plumbed in as my warning sound in case of a wrong move, was in danger of going down with laryngitis. As indeed was the whole machine. Out through my cottage window and down into the street.

I'm very partial to ducks. I know they're not renowned for their intelligence. Perhaps that's why subconsciously I chose the quack as my error indicator. Like pigs, mother ducks walk all over their babies. Perhaps with some babies, though, that's a sensible move.

'From the troubles of the world I turn to ducks, quaint comical things...' Too many ducks, though, and I was very far from being amused. So I withdrew from the twentieth century and, in need of relief for my taut nerves and shattered patience, turned to the hills. My cottage, also known as my bolt hole and sanctuary, is at the foot of one. It's where I go for comfort and solace: my Temenos. I've also been known to call it my lover. Only it doesn't snore, fart or drop its socks.

Hillwalking

Solvitur ambulando – it is solved by walking
St Augustine, 354–430 AD

It is a fine thing to be out on the hills alone. A person can
hardly be a beast or a fool alone on a great mountain.
Francis Kilvert, *Diary*, 1871

If anyone had said to me years ago, you're going to don a
woolly hat and red socks and ramble, I would have replied,
'Get real' or whatever the slang equivalent was, way back then
when I was young. But this is now what I do whenever I can,
and whatever the weather. I haven't had to pay vast fees to join
some exclusive club. I haven't in a manner of speaking had any
expensive training, apart from some costly experiences on my
leg muscles, and the only equipment I've had to lash out on
and lace up was a pair of stout walking boots. In my young days
wild horses wouldn't have dragged me into such unbecoming
footwear, 'slip-ons' being all the rage, the dreaded lace-ups
spurned and to be avoided at all fashion costs. But now my
thick ridged soled boots with their metal tags to catch the laces
as you hook them round and across, are the envy of any mini-
skirted teenager cruising the Kings Road. That's not why I wear
them of course. You can't skimp on footwear if you're going to
be a serious walker. You need boots with ankle support, to

protect your feet from stony and uneven ground, and those edges give you grip in the mud and rain. Mostly.

I really do walk whatever the weather, sometimes in spite of it. I guess it's part of my Capricorn stubbornness, to defy wind and sleet – if I've made my mind up to walk, I'll walk. I have a low in-built tolerance level of city living, which if I exceed, gives me tree and field and space withdrawal. This clock ticks away inside me whenever I'm trapped in town and can't get out to the wide open spaces of the country. Anything over the three-week period and I can turn very nasty. Deprived of my drug, my food for the soul, the balm against tired mind, drained emotions and all the wearing, debilitating occupational hazards of my job, I become short-tempered, irascible and often just plain horrid.

I was introduced to what was to become my fix, or more respectably, my passion, on a visit to the Lake District some fifteen years ago, by a well-meaning friend who had no idea what an addiction it was to become. My son was then about nine, so consequently, whenever he was with us, our walking was really limited to slithering about in the foothills, interspersed with half-hearted games of hide and seek, or rolling down grassy meadows at crazy angles hoping against hope that our trajectory, over which we had no control, of course, would be guided by unseen hands, and steer us clear of the treacherous cowpats that lurked behind every dandelion clump.

But the day came when all this fooling about on the junior slopes ended, and, with my son left in the company of friends with children his own age, we were free to spend the day walking. A whole day. I would have shuddered at that prospect in my teens. In fact I only just managed to get my Walkers' Badge as a member of the Girl's Life Brigade at Alan Road Methodist Church in Ipswich, by sustaining myself against the excruciating boredom of the seemingly never-ending vistas of fields, with bars of chocolate, licorice strips, gobstoppers, aniseed balls, sherbet lemons, and anything else the paucity of my foster mother's purse could run to, by munching something sweet every fifty yards or so. I spent more time peering into crumpled paper bags for the one last one lodged in a corner, than ever I did sweeping the vast expanse of Suffolk sky above me, or noticing the busyness in the hedgerows beside me. That was before I met The Hill, of course.

There aren't a lot of hills in Suffolk. Very flat Suffolk too. Well, my first proper walk was to be a baptism by fire. We met the granpappy of all hills – Red Pike. And we met all the season's weather in one day too. Innocence, of course, is bliss – in my case it was just pig ignorance. I had no idea, when we started out all blithe and gay of a midsummer's morning (being in Wordsworth land has this effect on one's language), armed with rucksacks loaded with home made goodies from the B and B of the lovely pub that nestles in the crook of Lake Buttermere, and footed with my brand new walking boots, what lay in store.

After the post-breakfast wander through leafy shaded lanes, wind rippled lowlands and lush pasture dotted with the black and white specks of peacefully grazing cattle BMC (Before Mad Cow) later in the day found me (after a hastily eaten lunch, taken in what little shelter a dry stone wall could give us against a wind that plucked at our sandwich wrappings, and hurled itself at us through the winding gulleys of the peaks that towered somewhere in the mist above us) flat on all fours. My face screwed up, wind-lashed and rain-stung, gasping for breath at an astonishing 2,479 feet, I prayed for survival, but mostly for the strength to continue. 'Returning were as tedious as go o'er' – not so much tedious as terrifying, I thought as I clung on to treacherous slivers of slate – scree, as I learned later they were called. At the time, as they dislodged themselves under my trembling fingers, stiff and swollen in their rain-soaked gloves, I called them everything under the non-existent sun. This wasn't so much hill walking, more slope crawling.

'Do you want to turn back?' shouted my friend, some dizzying, steeply sloping feet above me. At least I think that's what he said. By then the wind, which in its infancy had lulled the leaves in the lowlands into a gentle dance had, by now, revealed its true gale-force nature, frozen my ears till they ached, and was threatening to shred the hood of my walking jacket as it howled around outside it, and picked at it with icy sneaking

fingers inside it, and then crashing it against my eardrums in a spiteful whine of triumph, as I cowered and ducked and tried hard not to look down or up, but just along.

Of course when we thought we'd finally made it to The Top, we found this was an experience that was to be repeated several times: the lift of the heart that accompanied arrival on a reasonably level slope, lurched and dropped several times too, as yet another slope revealed itself behind the swirling cloud and mist, ahead and above us. But when, at The Top of all the Tops, we eventually could manage to stand upright – a feat not accomplished without clutching each other – there was of course nothing to see as we peered down through the damp grey swirls, except more damp grey swirling. My eyes stung with looking, and my cheeks felt frozen into a grimace of determination and endurance. But oh, the triumph! The incredible sense of achievement and satisfaction! If I had been able to move my face at all, I would have smiled as wide as the ancient peak on which we stood, and as high as the soaring heavens above us. 'Say not the struggle nought availeth.' My heart felt lighter than it had for years, and my head spun with the raw, abrasive mountain air. I breathed out, a breath that seemed to clean and renew every cell in my aching tingling body, and something, somewhere deep inside me shifted into its proper place. A locking into, a connecting with, the universe around me, and an unshake-able conviction growing, that I had at last, come home.

Don't ever believe anyone who says climbing *up* is the hardest part of hill walking. *Going down is torture.* Tired legs begin to shake and tremble uncontrollably, and fighting against the force of gravity, as your natural momentum tricks you into descending faster than is either sensible or safe, is an exhausting business. Rocks that could be tested on the way up with hands and eyes at the same level, before planting feet on them, on the way down look safe and secure enough from above, and then deceitfully give way under the weight of your entire body. I slipped and slithered and covered a large part of the descent, not on my feet, but on my butt. At times I felt like Bambi. Not the velvet-nosed cutie, all eyelashes and coyness, but the jelly legs in every direction. My legs alternated between feeling like water, and then rubber. They were totally beyond my control. I felt like running and jumping for joy, when those dear and familiar pastures and lowlands, now tinted by an evening sun, came into our tired, grateful view. But I couldn't. My legs had their own agenda, which had little to do with me or my intentions. They seemed to describe semi-circles as I lifted them off the ground, and placed them down again. I felt like John Cleese doing his Ministry of Silly Walks. Only not so tall.

A hot bath and several drinks later, as I sat glowing inside and out by the pub fire, I cast a glance outside through the window, into the darkening night. 'Somewhere out there,' I thought, picking an eyeline that was level with the pelmet of the curtain, 'is a hill I've climbed.' I knew how the first men who walked on the moon had felt. And I couldn't wait to get back.

I yelped when I tried to get out of bed the next morning. But the triumph exceeded the pain. It still does. Since those first fine careless raptures I've lifted up mine eyes to the hills whenever they are there to look up to. I feel in some small way, an understanding with Chris Bonington, who, when asked why he climbed Everest, plagiarising Mallory replied simply, 'Because it's there.'

My achievements since have been considerably more modest, but oh, so rewarding and renewing. I've walked with Wainwright (the maps, sadly not the delightful, knowledgeable man) most of the paths and a large extent of the Roman Road round Ullswater. I've tramped across the hills of Cumbria near Alston, to Garrigill, across Cross Fell to High Force, where the torrent cascades down with such a roar that it literally takes your breath away by the sheer energy of it. I've walked with the Roman legions in my head across these majestic, awesome, unforgiving fells. How must they have felt, those men from the sun-drenched, vine-clad slopes of Tuscany and Umbria, here amongst the boulder-strewn, heather-coloured wildness of such a relentless landscape, where no trees grow, where only the long-haired sheep, their matted locks tossed by capricious gusts, cling to the clumps of grass that grow between the grey rocks and fast-flowing rock bed streams of icy clear, brown-scummed water?

'God's last outpost,' said Bob, the Alston taxi driver, in his sing-song Geordie, as he gave the hills that rose steeply behind him a nodding acquaintance, and me a cursory look of such non-under-standing, as he appraised my walking boots, red socks and waterproofs – and this a frosty morning in November. 'Gang walkin', are ye?' He shook his head, clicked his tongue in disapproval, and made off towards the warmth of his Ford Escort to commune with

Radio 2 and a Senior Service, untipped, and I turned in the opposite direction to lift up mine eyes and my feet to the hills.

I've walked the hills round Selkirk in the blistering summer sun, and peered into the depths of the Yarrow, where, as on Skye, the midges have unfailing aim and finely honed teeth. I've hiked in Hawick, till the sweat ran like the butter in our sandwiches.

I've wondered at the unravelling vistas of the blue remembered hills of Shropshire. I pondered all one walk about what the gradations of grey ridges and disappearing hills were called – 'Chiaroscuro?' 'No, no,' said my knowledgeable undergraduate son, till a more knowledgeable friend came to the rescue – 'S'fumato'. So 'S'fumato,' I think, as distance lends enchantment to the view. It doesn't make me enjoy the hills more, but I now spend the time scanning the horizon, and breathing in the mind-renewing space, not searching for a word. Walking isn't for that kind of thinking. It's best to let the mind float free and wander like the feet.

I've climbed Caer Caradoc that overlooks Church Stretton, and picnicked amongst the Stuyper stones on the Long Mynd. Shropshire Blue tastes better at over 500 feet. (There are those who say it tastes of 500 feet...) I've tramped round Matlock in mists, and done the Derbyshire Dales in downpours. There's something about us serious walkers that bad weather acts on like a magnet. 'Huh,' I think, '*summer* walkers!' as I spot clumps of happily chatting rucksacked, Niked or Adidas-ed innocents, 'doing' the Fosseway in my beloved Cotswolds, bordered by fields of scarlet poppies and heavy-eared corn. 'They should be up here when it's snowing, then it's *really* beautiful.'

Actually I don't think they should be up there at all. That's another thing about us walkers-in-all-weathers. We feel that those hills are ours by right, and by dint of having faced them in inclement times. Having struggled, bent double, in a biting March wind against hail or sleet, we feel we have a right to own that hill when we get to the top. When *I* get to the top that is. I walk mostly on my own. There are few who understand what I mean by a walk.

'Where have you been?' asked my horrified stepsister on the first day of my holiday with the family in France last year. Her house faces the peach-treed slopes of the breathtaking Canigou hill just outside Perpignan. My eyes had fastened on its peak within seconds of arriving at 'Villa le Petit Puits' through the fruit-laden orchards of Golden Delicious that were tumbling into the ridges of sunbaked red earth, amongst rust coloured hillocks spiked with clumps of strong-smelling wild thyme and heady lavender. It took me just one morning to be polite and pay my house-guestly duties, and then, in an untimely shower, late that same afternoon, when everyone was sleeping off lunch, I was off, taking Harry the dog with me as a gesture towards family togetherness.

'I've just been for a walk,' I replied calmly.

'A walk!' she repeated. The French have a way of repeating what you say in all innocence, and making it sound like a convictable offence. 'But you've been gone for over two hours!'

'Well, that's only about seven miles,' I said.

'Seven miles!' she repeated. She gave me what we in England would call an old-fashioned look that turned into a withering glance as Harry, sun-burned and parched, lapped up his entire bowl of water and then slunk exhausted along the cool marble tiles, and came to a dazed rest under the kitchen table.

They all walked with me on other occasions, but it wasn't a walk. It's what I would call a stroll. Anything under five miles doesn't count. And anything lower than 200 feet doesn't count either. I've climbed up Montsegur and Peyrepertuse, those astonishing Cathar fortresses hewn directly from the rock in the wild terrain of the Languedoc. Mad dogs and Englishmen... I know, I know. But I never wear shorts – I wouldn't want to frighten the wildlife (or get the backs of my legs cooked in that blazing sun) and I always wear a hat. I have accumulated a large collection over the years during which my addiction has taken hold. I have hats for sun, floppy cotton jobs with large brims to protect the back of my neck; hats for wind, with no brims at all, berets mostly that I pull down right over my ears (the prat-ometer level rising dangerously near its optimum mark); and hats for rain – these are the most well-worn. I have my upper-class hats too. Those lovat green jobs that you see Sloane Rangers toting in the winter, to face the vagaries of shopping in the General Trading Stores and to weather the wilds of Draycott Avenue. I bought it in Woodstock (nowhere more landed gentry than *that*) and wore it with my much-patched green husky when I rented the Georgian stables flat at Admington Hall and used to wander around its hundred-acre estate, complete with trout lake and tennis court, as if I owned it. My best role: class impostor. The dear American owner of this estate, one Joe, used to warn my visiting friends, 'If she asks you to go for a walk, say *no*. She's crazy. She walks in all weathers. She'll freeze your bones!'

Indeed, a very thin friend of mine came back from a walk with me with neuralgia and frozen nerves in her face. I had to hold on to her on the top of Larkstoke hill, to prevent the winds of the four counties that meet there in a swirling dance, from blowing her away. Well, she wouldn't wear a hat you see. Frightened that we might meet some eligible swain and she'd look silly. We met no one. It was minus two.

My love for the Cotswolds, born of many seasons at The Royal Shakespeare Company in Stratford upon Avon (they are the nearest, albeit modest hills to London), has led me into penury. I have an ongoing struggle to find the rent for my small cottage in the village, just a few miles from Shipston on Stour. It is a village of such exquisiteness that I'm loth to name it, its centre being a network of leafy lanes that the car never has, and joyfully never will, penetrate. Its Elizabethan cottages are mostly thatched and beamed, their gardens an abundance of riotous colours, and tended with much love. A stream trickles through these shady walks, and I know now where the first brave snowdrops will pierce the hardened earth and, on the hill where the cottage is, I know which spots of sun will harbour the first primroses, and on which banks the even rarer cowslips will appear. Later in April the first violets unravel their quietly brilliant purple, but you have to know where to look for them. I walk from Mickleton to Chipping Campden and back, a mere eight miles or so, and fortified with a cream tea, I make a detour through Baker's Wood that in late spring is ablaze – if such a cool colour as royal blue can blaze – with bluebells.

It's not all get up and go. I have a favourite spot where four trees join, their roots forming a nook, which overlooks the village, where I just sit and stare. Or just sit and be, using what Wordsworth would call 'the inward eye of solitude'. I like being alone in the country.

It heals the ravages of the town, the demands of a profession where we are continually on show and being torn this way and that by well-meaning people just doing their jobs; make-up here, wardrobe there, publicity somewhere else, and then filming what you've been made up and costumed for, in a completely different location. Being under scrutiny from many eyes.

I like walking alone, because I can't cope with the 'Are we there yet?' syndrome. There's often not a 'there' to get to. I just walk until I feel like turning back. The challenge of the slope ahead, the struggle of legs and the focusing of energy and mind to attain it, the increased heartbeat, and the growing awareness of body and its rising warmth, and the almost indescribable exhilaration and triumph as I look down on the world below, the world that I have left behind, as I stand, a little nearer to the angels, is a modest experience that not everyone can relish or share. I walk alone, but in the company of the spirits of all those who walked there before me. I never liked being alone until I learned to like myself, and I like being alone in the country because it puts the ego into its proper place. How can you feel overwhelmed with trivial matters and worries, faced with hills that have been there for thousands of years before you, and will continue to be there, long after your little life has been rounded by a sleep? I walk not for my body, although the physical exertion brings relief and a welcoming warming tiredness. I walk for my soul. I often sing as I walk, hymns mostly. The sheep don't seem to mind. Cows recently do seem to have a marked sadness about their woebegone faces, but I suspect it's not my tuneless singing, I think they have worries of their own. I must have been a wandering monk in another life, as my feet often guide me to sitting quietly in whatever church or abbey ruins I come across. Bits of poems often nudge out the hymns and float through my mind as I walk:

I shall go without companions
And with nothing in my hand
I shall pass through many places
That I cannot understand
Until I come to my own country
Which is a pleasant land.

The trees that grow in my own country
Are the beech tree and the yew,
Many stand together and some stand few,
But in the month of May in my own country,
All the woods are new.

When I get to my own country
I shall lie down and sleep
I shall watch in the valleys the long flocks of sheep
And I shall dream for ever and all
A good dream and deep.

But I will have climbed a hill first, of course.

More Time Off – Unemployment

All that talk of triumph and boasting about challenges welcomed and embraced, I should have known I was in for it. You see however maverick and eclectic my spiritual beliefs, when life deals a right upper cut, out comes my foster mother's Methodism – the 'Give me a child for the first seven years of its life' syndrome. Whenever the going gets tough out comes the thought of the dreaded, but somehow expected, bucket of shit as a panacea for cocksureness. Or even if it doesn't actually manifest itself, the fact that the 'you've-really-done-it-now' thought has surfaced and will badger me relentlessly is sometimes chastisement enough. This punishment for imagined hubris is a turn of mind I've fought all my life and am still fighting. I've read about neuro-linguistic programming, done Transactional Analysis, become a passionate Jungian – and I've even been to workshops on positive thinking, not something I care to admit to often, but the bottom line when I'm rock bottom is the ineradicable thought that I've somehow brought it on myself. A potent mixture of I deserve it, but why does it always happen to me? An unhappy marriage of Jewish guilt brought about by Christian sin. Given the powerful magnet of having spent more on a laptop than my overdraft could comfortably allow, just around the corner in the pre-requisite bucket lurked unemployment.

Not Resting But Seething

To do nothing is very good, but to have nothing to do
is very bad.

GONVILLE FFRENCH-BEYTAGH,
A GLIMPSE OF GLORY, 1987

I hear the tubes begin to trundle in to Putney East about 4.30 in
the morning, getting ready to take the workforce to their work.
I watch them some hours later, those smart office girls in their
high heels, regulation black stockings and mandatory briefcase,
hurrying up my street, as if lured by some unheard chant
towards the mosque-like building that houses our beloved
District Line. I'm usually awake between these two events. It's my
worrying time. I mean it's the time that my brain seems to set
aside with alarming regularity for Worry. Worry about Money
mostly. Money is something that those of us who are not in the
workforce can get very preoccupied with. Not the 'Oh dear, the
second-hand dishwasher that I bought for £99 six years ago
seems to be rotting into the floor and I haven't got the £500 to
fork out for a new one' type worry, but the 'I'd better wait till
after 6 p.m. before I call you because it's cheaper then', as a
hard-pushed friend said to me last week, and I knew exactly the
area of constraint that she was coming from. Money for phone
bill worry. Money for modest mortgage worry. No work. Big
worry. But actors are supposed to be used to being out of work.
Yes, well.

Of course the recession, which has taken great chunks out of our National Health system and has taken great swipes at our education system, has had a crumbling effect on the entertainment industry too. General cut-backs in the number of film and TV productions, the general gutting of the BBC, provincial theatres (the training ground of young writers, directors and actors, the new blood of the profession) all fighting for their very lives, some sadly having lost the battle and the bricks and mortar. Short-term cuts – long-time cultural losses.

Oh why can't the English be more like the French? They fight like mad to protect their culture. Seems we're hell-bent on destroying ours; and that's the only thing we make a good job of in the Arts. Apart from winning Oscars in an industry most governments don't deem worthy of financial support. Artists of any kind are regarded by the English as not quite *nice*. Not for us the middle-class respectability of the doctor or lawyer accorded to Scandinavian and even Russian thespians. No state dashas for us. The only par we're on with the medics is in car insurance premiums. Top of the bill are actors and doctors. It's the mad pace we live our lives at, see? And actors aren't driving hell-bent to save someone else's. It was only some 180 years ago that actors were allowed the privilege of being buried within the confines of the city wall. Rogues and vagabonds. Actors are all right really when they're winning prizes (except if they make those awful left-wing speeches – biting the hand that feeds them, tut) an actor with a political opinion, tut tut. Oh and by the way, I wouldn't let my daughter marry one.

But actors are used to being out of work. Used to it, yes, but it never gets easier. Loss of earnings equals loss of self-esteem. We know all about that don't we, those of us who make up the faceless statistics of the unemployed. 'Two and a half million without a job' I hear on a news bulletin as I'm driving along in my car. 'Two and a half million plus *one*,' I add dourly but meaningfully to no one in particular. And that's what we are, no one in particular. The quiet prejudice even on seemingly innocuous forms. 'Daytime telephone number'. I don't have a different one because home is where I'm at all day long if I'm not working or teaching or forcing myself to go out to an exhibition or an art gallery just to get out and mix with the world – well, with the retirees who have all the time in the world to look at pictures and not feel guilty about there being something that they ought to be doing to bring in the odd penny or two.

Rising unemployment equals rising hopelessness plus violence. Could the two be linked? That's a rhetorical question. I'm busy dodging feeling hopeless, and if anyone says to me, 'Resting?' with that sympathetic upward inflection reserved for the very sick or the terminally insane I may get violent. 'No,' I say, 'I'm *unemployed*.'

Resting was a term used in the jolly old days of Noel Coward when every self-respecting Actor belonged to the Garrick Club, went to rehearsals with the *Daily Telegraph* open at the crossword page, did what the director told him, and then went home. If he hadn't knocked over the furniture he thought he'd done a good day's work. The female version of this Actor Laddie, now in these PC days also called an *Actor* please – 'actresses' grace the pages usually numbered three, and the projection they are famed for, has little to do with the area occupied by the vocal chords.

The erstwhile Leading Lady had a Treasure who lived in the East Wing who dealt with all the fan mail (then undoubtedly called correspondence) and doubled as a Dresser in the theatre, ironing cocktail dresses for those quiet little moments at The Ivy before the show, and serving champagne to adoring young men in coats with astrakhan collars after it, who came, gardenias in hand, to pay their very circumspect compliments to the well-crimped, primped and be-furred Leading Lady, who was all ready to be taken out to dine. Not for these hothouse plants, with the perfect diction and the Marcel wave, a quick dash round Sainsbury's between the shows, hair still pinned up under a stocking top, ready for the wig to go back on in the evening. They really did rest between jobs. They could afford to.

My diary at the moment stretches ahead in page after page of alarming whiteness. 'Of course something might turn up,' I tell myself. 'That's the wonderful thing about this business, you never know what's round the corner,' actors tell each other. Or 'Things will start to pick up soon,' my agent tells all her clients in the same predicament. 'It's a bit quiet at this time of the year.' (Because it's Christmas, or just before it, or worse, just after it, ditto Easter, and the summer holidays, then the weather's bad, or it's the bombs or the weather's bad again and then we're back to the not-so-festive season for those without work. So there it is, my diary. A blank, my Lord.

Apart from the charity do's. But those are another story.

Whenever I teach these days, which is in direct proportion to the time I'm not acting, though the two do blur, I always paint a very black picture for the would-be thesps. It's a bit like the theory behind employing an au pair. Tell it like it is, only worse and then some, and it still won't be as bad as it can get. Rejection, heartbreak, disappointment, flavour-of-the-month and flash-in-the-pan-itis – a disease prone to those picked up and dropped by fickle casting directors who believe the hype they read in silly showbiz mags, about who's 'in' and who's not 'in' – and that's *before* you get the job.

And that longed-for job? Could be touring round twelve cities on an itinerary devised by committee and a mad one at that – Warwick, Worthing, Blackpool, Oxford, and somewhere round about Norwich prior to Harrogate. Eventually you give up – all the pedestrian shopping precincts look the same in a British winter. All this and heaven too for £350 a week, plus, or rather minus ten per cent to your agent and a place to pay for in London while you're gone. It's a staunch constitution that can play eight St Joans a week as I did in 1986 to sixty-five people a night in the end of the pier Pavilion Theatre, Eastbourne – the end of a lot more than straight drama, Eastbourne. Then you go 'home' to a supper of curry or fish and chips (they're the only places that stay open in such wild night-life towns after 9 o'clock) over a one-bar fire that works on 10ps – yes, they still exist in what used to be known as theatre digs. Would that theatre digs proper still existed. Presided over by those wonderful landladies of both sexes who were prepared to wait up and cook you bacon and eggs at 11.30 at night, all in return for a little bit of theatre gossip. Gone, they are, the way the music halls went.

On top of that, to do the work itself, you have to have – to quote a much-loved drama teacher, Rudi Shelley of the Bristol Old Vic Theatre School – 'the hide of an elephant and the sensitivity of a butterfly'. If, after all that blackwash, would-be actors, the little dears, bless 'em, still want to go ahead and Do It, then there's nothing for it but to send them on their way topped up with determination, fired with encouragement and hefty support, and pray that their doting parents have the means to bale them out when they're broke or disenchanted. Not enough then, for the 'It must be in his blood – no one else in the family ever took to the stage.' They might have to find out the hard way whether the stage takes to them. Prayers too must be said that they themselves have the resilience to ride out the bad bits, or the qualifications for an alternative career 'tween times. The 'tween times could end up being most of the time.

There are 65,000 actors registered with Equity (surprisingly not our frame of mind, but the name of our union) and according to them, only 25 per cent work for more than four months of the year. And when those of us who usually do, don't, we do galas. But that's another story, as I said.

Of course, if *they* see you on TV, *they* think you're millionaires. *They* don't know about the three months out of work before you got the job, the months of editing before you graced the tiny screen, and the months after it before you were employed again... And of course some actors *are* millionaires, or as near as dammit. Dammit. Not those of us who work in the subsidised theatre, of course. Best thing Peter Hall ever said was, 'It's the actors who subsidise the subsidised theatre.' You don't read about *them* in newspapers night-clubbing in exclusive places in Mayfair and Chelsea till the early hours and having their houses photographed for *Hello* magazine at various times of the day and night. You'd have to be a millionaire to have a different outfit for all of those rooms. Most jobbing actors are too damn knackered after eight shows a week to do anything apart from crawl to the nearest pub if it's still open, or to a friend's nearby flat with a six-pack if it's not.

We moan about the work when we have it, and we moan about it even more when we don't. Being out of work for anyone creative (I hate the word artist, or its even worse playmate, artist*e*) is doubly hard. The fact that you are not wanted is a rejection of your very self. We are our Stradivarius. If that sounds too high-fallutin' – remember that we can't blame our level of performance on the boss's out-of-date computer. If we don't get the job, it's our voice, our face, our ability to interpret, our understanding of life, the way we move and think and have our being, that's on the line, or worse the reject file. The result? Crisis of confidence, which leads to crisis in pocket. Creative energy is a very volatile master. Don't use it, and it will turn in on itself and start to devour you.

That's why, when I teach, one bit of extra-curricular advice that I give, old-fashioned as it may sound, is, get a Hobby. As long as there's something you can be absorbed in that makes the hours whizz by, chances are you can stop that steam of frustration coming out of your ears, and more importantly, you'll stand a bat's chance in hell of saving whatever relationship you're in. And if that Hobby can earn you a few extra pennies so much the better. I've never drawn the dole. Well, that's not quite true. I did until my son was nine months old. He's now twenty-five. No, I wasn't overcome by a rash of social altruism – 'there are people worse off than me who could well put my National Insurance contributions to better use!' It was all the fault of The Woman who looked after the letter L way back in those dark ages when I used to sign on at Chadwick Street labour exchange. What a misnomer. The only thing that was being exchanged was condescension – hers to me, but I refused it, and the whatever it was then that went with it – £18 a week or thereabouts.

'Sign on at eight thirty,' trilled The Woman behind the grille.

'But I can't,' I said aghast, clutching my dribbling, crying baby – from an early age he's shared my dislike of civil service bureaucracy.

'Eight thirty,' she repeated.

'Have you any idea what time I'd have to get up, to get the baby fed, washed and dressed to be here by eight thirty in the rush hour?' My voice was becoming shrill. People were beginning to turn round and stare.

'Eight thirty,' came the reply to my increasingly frazzled self. I'd noticed by this time that she hadn't been employed for her conversational tactics, but as I just stood there feeling helpless, about to be overcome by waves of delayed post-natal depression, she ventured, 'So how do you manage when you work?' in a very patronising tone. I wanted to say, 'Don't talk to me like that. I'm only unemployed, I'm not mentally deficient.

'Well, when I work, I can just about afford someone to take care of him,' I said swallowing hard, not wanting to add to the popularly held belief that actors are such emotional creatures, and anyway, I thought, what business is it of yours? You're behaving as if the £18 is coming out of *your* pocket.

Conversationalist she wasn't, but she must have been psychic. 'Eight-thirty,' she reiterated.

It was at this point that I had wild ideas about changing my name to Smith, the man who looked after the S–W had a kindly face, but I thought better of it – someone had got there before me. I gave The Woman what I hoped was a withering stare that I wished would stay with her and haunt her days, pulled my baby closer to my thumping chest, mustered what little dignity I had left, and left. I've never been back. I may have given the many managers who have passed through my bank over the years sleepless nights worrying about my rising overdraft (that makes two of us), but I've never had to undergo that dreadful talking down to.

Of course now that attitude of 'When are you going to get a proper job?' has been taken up by successive governments, if one can describe such disparate entities as an entity. No dole for actors is the latest hue and cry. And 'Retrain for another job after the allotted span of time out of work.' 'What do you mean you've been trained to use your voice, to recognise an iambic pentameter at twenty paces, and you're a mean mime? We've got this great job here for you as a filing clerk.' No play, no pay now takes on a different meaning altogether. 'When *are* you going to get a proper job?' Holding the mirror up to Nature isn't one, you see. The little grey men in suits with their little grey minds don't want to look. They might, of course, see something they don't like. Something that doesn't fit in with their spreadsheet mentality.

'What do you mean if you put award-winning director with top scriptwriter and a cast of very famous actors you can't *guarantee* that the piece will be a box-office hit?' No, sir. The Arts don't work like that. You can't quantify them. It's not like over-seeing a production line. Isn't that annoying? That old Human Nature factor. So unpredictable. So unspreadsheetworthy. Mediocrity rules and it's not OK. Anything large or colourful, flamboyant or out of the ordinary has no place. And what is the theatre if it is none of those things? Politics, too, come to think of it. Oh where are the politicians of yesteryear? The orators like Aneurin Bevin and Disraeli?

'Where there is no vision the people perish.' No vision but a preponderance of suits. 'Thank God it's Friday,' said the receptionist at my agent's just now on the phone, bringing me back to things more mundane. 'Two days off.' I bit back my instant rejoinder, 'It's difficult to have days off when *all* your days are days off,' and just said, 'Have a good weekend.' That's what those secretaries are going to have, returning home now, offloading from the full to bursting Tube, clutching their bulging Marks and Sparks bags full of weekend treats. And me? I've got this silly song going through my head. I think George Formby used to sing it. I'm thinking of joining in:

If I were not upon the stage, someone else I'd like to be,
If I were not upon the stage, a window cleaner me,

You'd hear me all day long, a-singing out this song
Cleaning windows, cleaning windows, running up steps
      all day......

Yes, I'm going to clean my filthy windows. I'm on a retraining
programme. Well, it'll please the government.

Motherhood

One of the joys of unemployment is the freedom to go and do and be wherever you want. Providing it doesn't cost any money of course. So that rather narrows the field. Before Warwickshire exerted its irresistible pull on my heart and bank balance my only means of escape to the hills was from a dear friend's Georgian home with its compound of little Victorian cottages in Alston, Cumbria. It's the highest market town in England, often cut off by snow during the winter months, but the starkness of its awesome terrain, which lifts the spirits and cuts the breath, makes up for the inclemency in the weather. For those of us who don't live there all the time of course. The winter months are long and can stretch from September to May in a bad year, but in the summer the brightness and clarity of the air can rival the uplift of the Pyrenees. Returning from one such escape during a particularly warm blessing, I arrived back in London earlier than expected.

As a young parent the area of protection of one's child is largely confined to the elastoplast on the knee, support and encouragement against the trials of the playground and classroom, the vagaries of passing friendships, help with difficult homework and, in the home, constant warmth, food, comfort and affection. Of course children don't realise that the parent continually struggles to keep up with the various stages of their growth, each stage bringing new lessons and new awareness for both. I remember thinking, 'I've only just mastered adding an egg to his bottle feed and now the clinic says I have to start him on solids!' Something as trivial as that can seem like a mountain to a new mum, overtired, alone and taking each new step in the dark. But nothing prepares one for the strength of will needed to keep one's mouth shut when the heir to the family fortune turns up with a completely unsuitable girlfriend. Not just unsuitable in my eyes, but as it turned out in everyone else's too. Everyone's except his, of course.

Standing back and letting children make their own mistakes with a knowledge of the possible resulting emotional pain is the hardest thing of all. I found it very hard to hide my feelings, being a what-you-see-is-what-you-get person. But I've learned. My introduction to the keeping-my-mouth-shut course was a tough one.

Only the names have been changed to protect the guilty.

Meeting Rita

Alas, regardless of their doom
The little victims play
No sense have they of ills to come
No care beyond today.

THOMAS GRAY, 1716–61

The young have aspirations that never come to pass;
the old have reminiscences that never happened.

SAKI, 1870–1916

As meetings go it wasn't of the best. The young friend, Stefanie, I was with said, 'Do you think you ought to ring and tell him? We *are* two hours early.' I brushed away the suggestion. I'd been driving for nearly six hours, apart from a stop at the horrendous motorway cafe – where the salads, which had that kind of crusty look of vegetables that hadn't been moved for a considerable time, were doing a passable imitation of those moulded plaster foods we used to play with as kids, and the hot grey liquid sold as coffee had never had even a passing acquaintance with a bean. Consequently I didn't want to stop again. I couldn't face the tortuous tracks up the slip roads and through the bewildering no man's land of petrol pumps and forecourts, to the village of glaring, congested shops, to find a phone which wouldn't work or if it did would need a card, which I didn't have.

So on we ploughed, having left the bleak and majestic hills of Cumbria far behind us, through the desolate terrain of suburban London, with little to uplift the soul, apart from the imminence of a proper cup of tea in my own kitchen and a chance to stretch my legs further than the accelerator pedal or the brake, and the even greater relief of being able to get out of earshot of my friend's increasingly fractious five-year-old on the back seat.

I should have know something was up. I rang the doorbell twice. No answer. Against the full-blown sound of blaring rock music the tinny doorbell didn't stand a chance. I rang again. Surely he couldn't have gone out and left this din, which threatened to rattle the foundations of my somewhat rickety house, and the unstable equanimity of the neighbours. I have been known to leave the radio on when going away for a few days – Radio 4 of course. No, I'm not paranoid about burglars, it's company for the cat. And no doubt educative too. All those programmes, and advice about gardening and growth of the soul. I also leave the central heating on for him. It's a sort of unspoken deal. If I leave him with warmth, he won't sick fur balls all over the not-quite-so-new-now Axminster. It's a deal I don't think my feline friend has ever quite come to grips with, unlike the corners of my armchairs, which he has. The consumer programmes are obviously way above his head and tastes, as he sticks rigidly to the same diet of tuna fish and sliced turkey morning and evening, and any attempt by me to introduce variety into his predictable eating habits over the years, has been met with a quick glance at his questionable dish, followed by a sniff of disgust and a whirl of his very furry tail, which then follows him very rapidly out of the cat door. He's obviously taken the gardening programmes to heart, though. Especially the bits about digging. Sole he's never cared for.

Anyway, there was no need for the central heating to be left on during this brief exit from my beloved place of abode, as Mother Nature herself was doing a passable imitation of a global grill. It was ninety degrees plus in the shade, where we weren't – my front door faces due west, and it was now about four in the afternoon. It felt like Tuscany, without the wine and holiday humour. The hot weather, which had shown no signs of breaking for four unbelievable weeks, was causing havoc with everybody's nerves, and deteriorating the already rapidly declining standard of driving in central London, until the traffic resembled a low-grade dodgem ride. But the screams weren't screams of joy and delight. Cut and thrust was the order of the day, with vocal abuse high on the list. I was glad to be out of it.

I put down the heavy bags I was carrying, and rang the doorbell again, irritably and for some considerable time. Wiping the sweat off my forehead, I noticed the usual greasy gritty flecks that came with it, a sure and depressing harbinger of being back in city living. I heard the five-year-old ask querulously, 'Can I have a drink?'

'Not here in the front garden you can't, dummy,' I wanted to bite back, but then realised that actually if I could muster my already sapped energy, and rummage in one of the many bags that were now threatening to topple over and spill out into a parched flower bed, I might manage to find my front-door key. As I wearily bent down to start the search, I saw the bottom of the front door open. Relieved, I stood up and came face to face with my son, wearing nothing but a pair of boxer shorts and a very anxious expression. The smile of welcome and feeling of pleasure at seeing him again that began to break over me was short lived.

'Oh God,' he said. 'Oh God. Oh no.'

Now my son has been complimented, since a very early age, on his grasp of the English language. Talking not walking was big on his agenda. In fact he showed no interest in walking at all. He would sit on his bottom and string whole sentences together at about eighteen months. In fact the pair of Kickers that my mother, embarrassed by his lack of interest in mobility, had bought him as an enticement to stagger upright, remained pristinely clean on the soles and heels, the only sign of wear being where he had scuffed them on the backs as he shuffled about the place on his bottom. 'It's not normal,' she said.

That was rich coming from her, whose entire life has been manifestly lacking in such a quality. 'For goodness sake!' I retorted. 'No one's going to know when he's thirty-seven and a chartered accountant, that he didn't walk till he was two!' At this precise moment, though, he was an obviously overwhelmed undergraduate, and thoughts of a lifetime of Inland Revenue returns were far from his mind.

'Oh God,' he repeated again, not moving, but staring at me in disbelief. At least I *think* that's what he said. My hearing isn't all it might be, and over the cacophony of heavy metal (it certainly resembled saucepan bashing) it could have been, for someone less able to lip-read, quite difficult to decipher.

'Oh God, it couldn't be worse.' Things were looking up. We must have been standing at the front door for about four minutes by now, and he was, at last, using more than three words. The word 'worse' could have triggered a negative reaction in me, given the heat, the noise, the third-degree burns from the sun on my back (Tuscany? More like Delhi) and the five-year-old now falling into his mother's skirts with exhaustion and repeating, like a stuck record, 'Can I have a drink?' But somewhere deep in the subconscious minds of all mothers is an innate knowledge that whatever your offspring think is a dramatic problem usually isn't, and inevitably and more frequently of course vice-versa.

'You're two hours early. Oh God.'

'It can't be that bad,' I managed.

'It's a teenager's nightmare,' he retaliated. Now I knew there was something to worry about. The arguments about age with children nearly always go the opposite way. 'How old's your son?' says the inquiring, kindly pedestrian peering into the baby buggy. 'Four,' you say innocently, and try to continue on your way, with an insistent little voice carping in your ear, 'I'm *not!* I'm four and a *half!*' So my son downgrading his age by a couple of years wittingly and willingly, was very bad news.

'Well, come on, let us in, we've had a long drive, and little Guy's thirsty.'

'I'm thirsty,' said little Guy, bang on cue.

The moment I stepped inside the house I could fully understand my son's reluctance to let us in. In fact his stalling tactics were nigh on being a barring of the way. I dumped the bags in the gap between the front door and the sitting room – a space which in his younger Star Trek days, he would call the Air Lock and slam his bicycle against the wall having fulfilled a shopping expedition for me with a 'Mission accomplished' – and looked around my usually neat and tidy home with a feeling of great foreboding. The not-so-new green Axminster was carved up with the track marks of so many pairs of Doc Martens or similar tractor-like boots, that its normally velvety piled surface resembled a churned up field on which many army tanks had undergone quite complex military manoeuvres. The rest of the sitting room was comparatively mildly blitzed. (Comparative to what I was to find a few dazed seconds later in the kitchen, that is.)

All of the ashtrays were full to overflowing. There were empty beer cans on almost every available surface. All my beloved plants were drooping for lack of water, but of course he couldn't be expected to have noticed that. If he had in fact imbibed *half* the amount of beer that the empty cans indicated, he wouldn't have been able to see straight. I braced myself, took a deep breath, held my tongue, and headed for the kitchen, while my son, having rushed to silence the tin-can-factory impersonations coming from the stereo, now hovered nervously behind me. He is not the hovering type under normal circumstances. That, too, didn't bode well.

I doubt whether more washing-up could ever not have been done, and still stand stacked up. It was a *Guinness Book of Records* pile. I doubt whether there was a single item of crockery, cutlery or glassware left in any of my cupboards. Kitchen ditto – full ashtrays, empty beer cans. There, on the kitchen table was what would have been a very large bottle of whisky if it hadn't been empty, and beside it, sitting at the kitchen table in very fetching, very well filled underwear, was a very pretty blonde girl who I had never seen in my life. For four years it had been Claudia. I looked at her, she looked at me. Nothing was said. I looked at my son.

'There's nothing to say,' I said, and continued, 'There's nothing to say that won't make it worse.' I opened the door of the fridge it was empty apart from a packet of turkey for the cat and half a dried up lemon.

'Go to Malik's and get some bread and some milk.'

'I'm thirsty,' said Guy, coming out from behind his mother's skirts, with a smile on his face. Children have a barefaced enjoyment of other people's sticky predicaments, and I certainly was sticky. Rivulets of sweat too were running down my son's forehead. 'Some bread and some milk and some orange juice – take the money from my purse – it's in one of my bags.'

'Mum –'

'Don't say a word, just *go*.' He did. I've never known him obey so fast. Like the cat out of the cat door he was gone, leaving me with Miss Cleavage in the kitchen. Well, women notice those kind of things. Especially if you haven't got those kind of things. She stood up. The whole was as good as the half that had been visible above the kitchen table. The body was slim but curvy and the legs must have been the envy of all her friends. They propelled her somewhat tentatively towards me. I said slightly stiffly, 'Guy, take this glass of water till the orange juice comes, and go in the sitting room and watch the TV.' A sure sign of upheaval where I'm concerned, to have to recourse to the dreaded box.

I turned to his mother. 'Stef, take the scissors, be a dear, get out of the kitchen and dead-head all the flowers in the garden.' Obediently she went, dispatched to do gardening duty after a six-hour drive. We shared a knowing mother's look.

'I'll make some tea,' I added to her retreating back, which brought me to a dangerous visual proximity with what must have been a D cup – not that I have ever had any familiarity with that end of the range. I lowered my eyes and began attacking the washing-up. At least I could deal with what I was seeing there. Dirty Dishes didn't threaten my self-esteem.

'We had such good intentions...' The voice was soft and purry. Very kittenish. I wondered wildly whether she had any idea of the double entendre nature of what she'd just said.'But you *were* two hours early,' I felt like joining in. I wanted us to chorus it together.

'Shall I make the tea?' She reached for where I keep my tea things. I was, I admit it, unreasonably shocked that she should even know where my tea things were and as helpful as she was trying to be over the clatter of my washing up, I felt the gesture was inappropriate. Shamefully I reasserted my rights over my territory, however badly blitzed.

'No, I'll do it,' I said, more primly than I meant. 'We've got to wait for...' I made an effort not to call my son by his familiar baby name – I didn't know what level of intimacy they were on, in a manner of speaking. I mean as far as speaking went. But then by the look of the house they hadn't done a lot of that. 'We've got to wait for the milk to come back,' I said lamely. The legs retreated to the kitchen table where she lit a cigarette. I had given up smoking eleven months three weeks and four days previously.

'Why don't you take your cigarette upstairs? I'll give you a shout when the tea is ready.'

The washing-up upped, I headed for the broom cupboard and the hoover. Its rubber tube leaped out at me and fell to the floor, where it lay like a tired coiled snake round my ankles.

'Oh please let me do that,' she purred. A very big bead of my sweat dropped on to the not-so-new.

'No, really,' I said, 'it's much better if you go upstairs and leave me to do it. I'm much better doing it on my own.'

The prodigal son chose that moment for his return with the goodies. He just stood there clutching the plastic bag, looking at me. Not a great mover, my son.

'Here, you do this,' I said, thrusting the hoover at him and taking the bag of shopping.

'Um, she, er, um, she's – just going upstairs, to have a cigarette,' I added meaningfully, hoping that 1) he would insist that she go, and 2) realise that I had not a clue as to what this blonde vision was called. Claudia was dark-haired. I wasn't programmed for blondes. She must have guessed. She went. I made a mental note to myself that strong silent restraint obviously induced obedience and that I really must remember that the next time my Latin blood and emotions made to run away with me.

While he hoovered, more beads of sweat scattering in every direction, I filled a large black bin bag, and carried it, bulging with empties and dog-ends out to the bins which looked decidedly softened by the sun. I gave Guy his orange juice. He looked at me with such gratitude and big inquiring eyes.

'Is he naughty?'

I felt like saying in a tremulous voice, 'No, but I'm used to Claudia, you see. I didn't know that was over. No one told me.' But I just smiled, tidied up the sitting room, dodging the furiously energetic hoovering, and then went to lay the table to the accompaniment from the bathroom immediately above, of some pretty enthusiastic showering. A good half an hour later I called from the bottom of the stairs, 'Tea's ready!' and down they filed, one behind the other silent and chastened and dressed. They sat down wordlessly beside each other, their glances avoiding the three of us now assembled opposite them.

'Right, now,' I said. 'Shall we begin again? I'm Rowan's mother. How do you do? Would you like some tea?'

The places one visits aren't always in the present. Every year when Spring comes round (which is hardly ever, given the vagaries of our climate) on the official day, 21 March, I go back in my mind to a small street in Chelsea where I was living when I was expecting what turned out to be my son. There was a magnolia tree behind the railings of a house on the corner of the street, past which I often walked on my way back from the shops if I took the scenic route and avoided the bustle of the King's Road. It was my harbinger of spring, this tree. It paid no heed to official dates. Its deep pink buds tinged with white would remain firmly curled as a warning if there were frosts, worse winds and wet to come. It always struck me as curious that the flowers of this tree, when they thought it safe to appear, would do so long before the leaves. I liked this quirkiness.

I knew little then, even less than I do now, about gardening; confined to living as we were on the top floor of a ramshackle house, my sole horticultural exploits being the lavishing of love and attention on a couple of window boxes that I had planted with various herbs, only to see the brave shoots disappear one day down the throat of a hungry and opportunistic blackbird. My alarm, followed speedily by indignation, was the cause of much merriment on the part of my child's father, Roland, who felt that the blackbird had gone some way to putting my yearnings to escape London to a rural idyll into their proper perspective.

The year my son was born, spring was late and he was late. A week later than the doctors had said, and this in spite of my efforts to ensure that he would be a Pisces, by driving my second-hand mini fast and furiously over as many bumps as I could find in Richmond Park to no effect, as my particular bump stayed firmly in place. So I had to face the fact that whatever it was, and whenever it finally deigned to show itself, it would be an Aries. To add to this disappointment, the buds on the magnolia tree that year remained resolutely shut. Risible as it may seem now, my desire for a Pisces offspring, but I'd known a lovely man who was a Pisces, Sensitive and Artistic. Although astrology played no larger part in my life than the desultory reading of the horoscopes in the *Evening Standard* (if they were benevolent I believed them, if not the paper was thrown ungraciously aside), I didn't know a single Aries and had no plans to include them in my acquaintance.

The bump had other ideas. Rowan was born on 24 March. The horns of the Ram well-honed to interlock with matching stubbornness into the Goat of my Capricorn. But I was deter-mined to break the circle. To be for Rowan the mother I had never had. Resolute and well-armed with love, the bump took me on the biggest journey of my life.

Mothers and Sons

Few misfortunes can befall a boy which bring
worse consequences than to have a really
affectionate mother.

W. SOMERSET MAUGHAM, *A WRITER'S NOTEBOOK*, 1896

Like most young women I romanticised about being
pregnant, and then, like most young women, was horrified
to find that it was true. It was the early seventies, so my horror
wasn't in being unmarried – it was a far more basic issue.
Roland was training as a TV director in the wilds of
Manchester; consequently we were scraping a living on my
National Theatre earnings and what I could glean from the
odd television job. His flat was basic too. No bathroom, no
garden, we shared a loo with the floor below. A washing
machine was an unattainable luxury.

His horror came out as 'No.' Full of bravado I decided to
have the child, whether he was agin me or no. I was twenty-eight,
I wanted the baby, and felt in an inexplicable way I had somehow
drawn this child towards me. The 'Ayes' finally had it and
Roland stayed to face imminent fatherhood in much the same
state of trepidation as me. I filmed till the bump became too
visible – about five months – then spent the remaining four
months grovelling for radio work.

I worried a lot. Went up to Manchester on the train a lot.
Worried about the trains as a rail strike was threatened. Spent

my £25 maternity benefit on a second-hand sewing machine and sewed (the nesting instinct is a curious beast) a bedspread for our double bed. I spent hours pondering the logistics of the baby being in its carrycot in the sitting room if we were in the bedroom, and the baby being in the bedroom if we were in the sitting room. Past it being six months old and too big for this routine, I could not think. I installed, over the kitchen sink where everything was washed, including ourselves, a tidy-dry, where nappies could drip, until not dripping, they could be promoted up the line to make space for others. I worried some more. I was eleven stone three at the final count; shifting that bulk up four flights of stairs handicapped with shopping bags was hard labour. But mostly I worried about being a Mother. What was a Mother? Roland and I had both been left as small babies by our respective mothers and brought up by other people; not a situation replete with role models. It was a huge step into the unknown.

Rowan was born conventionally at 5.45 on a Saturday evening in March. British Rail obliged by providing trains from Manchester, so his father was present. He looked down at the baby and said, 'I wonder what he'll teach us?' I was surprised by him turning the parent-child relationship on its head, but it's a remark that I never forgot and one for which I have been often thankful. I secretly hoped that Rowan would grow up one day to be not just my son but my friend.

I looked down at this baby and felt as if I had always known him. And it was not a pretty sight; the Winston Churchill variety of baby, bald, ugly, and very grumpy. I felt none of the maternal urges that women are told they are supposed to feel. He was grumpy because I didn't have enough milk, and I was grumpy because I felt that I had fallen at the first fence of motherhood. But mostly I was worried about getting back to work to earn money to pay for this crying, puking, crapping machine. He wasn't the only one crying. A lovely Lebanese woman in the same ward caught me sobbing my post-natal heart out, and with unforgettable kindness hugged me and said, 'In the Lebanon, we say that every child brings its own fortune.' Beautiful, but small comfort, I thought. Now I know it to be true, and it has nothing to do with money.

I went back to work three weeks later, and he came too, as he often did when we couldn't afford help.

When Rowan was three years old, and the dreaded babydom nearly over, I cursorily asked his opinion about something and met with a very definite 'No!' I thought, 'There's a real person in there!' I was hooked. Intrigued and curious to observe this little life unfold. He went with me everywhere. We both quickly learned the effectiveness of Blackmail Technique. 'I will buy you whatever toy you want from this shop if...' We never went anywhere without crayons and paper, and I never worked abroad unless it was school holidays and he could come with me.

By the time he was five, after much mutual pain and difficult debate, I brought my ten-year relationship with his father (three years of it marriage) to an end. I left with the baby, his clothes, toys and my belongings.

That really was the step into the unknown. And the beginning of my acquaintance with insomnia. Was I bringing him up the right way? Was there a right way? There was no one to ask, no family, my step-sister and I being in the estranged state, and none of my friends had children. I had to be both mother and father. Was I overcompensating – coming down too hard on the father side? Or not hard enough? I didn't know. My only conviction was that he must know that he was wanted and loved. I never had.

The loving was the easy bit. The bottomless well that surged up and kept replenishing itself was a constant mystery and delight to me. It turned me into a different person. A person that I liked being. I liked doing for him, cooking for him. I liked reading him bedtime stories – never long enough and never often enough for both our likings. We played silly word games in the car to and from school; made up stories of characters with funny faces who did preposterous things. Haddiker Saxon, and Captain Beaker who did the opposite of what he was told. There was a time when a notice appeared on his bedroom door. 'Here lives Paul Green', which presaged months of him not answering to his own name.

The hard bit was the battle with time. Getting him to school before rehearsals and battling not to be the last mother to arrive, sweating, in jeans and T-shirt after rehearsals, painfully conspicuous amongst the Gucci scarves, and the Harrods waxed legs of the other mothers who didn't then have to dash off to a performance. 'Can you please come to speech day looking like an ordinary mother?' he said once. I was mortified.

Au pairs didn't help. More trouble than the child, the dog and the goldfish put together; their boyfriend problems, their unwanted pregnancy in one case, and their homesickness for Spain in several. Also the minute I walked in wearily through the door, there was no one to whom I could deflect their problems while I dealt with my prime concern; how the geography homework project gone, or worse the maths (bad news for both of us) and more importantly, who this person was today, that was my son.

Bad Marriage, Good Divorce is an easy formula but difficult to practise. We had agreed not to make Rowan a battleground for our own scars, so he travelled frequently between us. His father now lived in Los Angeles, and Rowan with the dreaded 'unaccompanied minor' label strung round his neck, happily chatting to the hostess, cast never a backward glance at his pathetic mother drenching the departure lounge. Then the house, my first home, bought with my own money, but for his convenience – on the tube line to school – near a park and within cycling distance to his father's Chelsea house, would seem a very empty place indeed. He had become the centre of my life.

We had few rules; eat up, shut up and hurry up, only one hour of TV a day, no talking when grown-ups are talking, no toys on the table at meal times, and when it's bedtime no mucking about because I've got lines to learn; if I don't I won't work, and if I don't work we won't eat. Was all this awareness of my pressures making him grow up too fast? I encouraged him to spend nights or weekends with schoolfriends who had 'normal families'. And I in turn ran a B and B for Jim and Max and Will in our home.

I tried to hide a lot of my concerns, especially when I was unemployed. But he'd only have to phone from a friend's house and hear me say 'Hello' to ask 'What's wrong, Mum?' One word from him too, and I would know exactly his state of mind. And still do. The battle with time and (un)employment often left me irritable with him and then ashamed of myself. I learned quickly to say sorry if I had unfairly taken out my day's grievances on him, and that showed him how to do the same. He wasn't sporty; kicking a football half-heartedly around Battersea Park we both gave up as a bad job. He had Will and Max and Jim and Heavy Metal. He would paint, read or write upstairs in his room, while I would write or learn my lines downstairs in mine. I asked him always to knock on my door before he came in, and I would do the same on his. He would come in to ask my advice or I would go and ask his. It wasn't always this Liberal Party. We did row. We're both very Latin. But it blows up big and blows over fast. I did smack him occasionally when he was small, but the devastation to my conscience wasn't worth it; television deprivation or being made to stay in his room till the rudeness, dumb insolence or sheer bloody-mindedness passed, proved a more effective means of getting the relationship back on the tracks. Or I would simply act daft and make him laugh.

Being a single parent wasn't often funny, but being a mother has been the biggest joy of my life – a privilege I only fully knew the value of when he went.

The Empty Nest

The beckoning counts and not the clicking latch
behind you.

FREYA STARK, 1893–1993

Of course he really left home when he went to university. Half my household equipment left home too. The sound system and cassettes, which were of course his, and his favourite blue mug, plate, knife and fork, which weren't. I drew the line at the blue quilt which I'd bought for his bedroom when we visited Vermont. I didn't want to envisage students in various stages of knees up or worse, sprawling, beer glasses in hand, all over $500 worth of the best American pale and dark blue patchwork. The bongos surprisingly stayed, as did the broken old blue office chair and piles of half-finished paintings and canvases which I then stacked on the landing. So I had a decimated ex-bedroom-cum-abandoned artist's studio, plus a rubbish tip to wade through and look forward to, as I crawled home through the rain-soaked roadworks on the M40, tears splashing on to my trousers, head abuzz with a dreadful sound loop that never varied in its monotony – 'He's gone, he's gone, he's really this time, gone.'

Of course there were the holidays, but I'd primed myself not to expect too much of them over the years, as a trip to visit his father in Los Angeles could, and often did, manifest itself at a moment's notice. He came home, as it turned out, often, and usually in term-time. Oxford is, after all, only an uncomfortable bus ride away from Victoria, and if he was rushed, well there was always a taxi to Shepherd's Bush (which would of course cost more than several uncomfortable bus rides), but then Ma would pick up the tab for that.

For twenty-four hours my kitchen would be turned into a non-stop café which also doubled as a Chinese laundry. Why Chinese? They never complain, they just get on with the job. All his washing would hang from every chair and radiator, and the never-ending supply of shepherd's pie, apple crumble, salads and fruit salads, washed down with the ever-welcome Guinness, would be greeted with whoops of delight from somewhere amidst the clouds of steam. My food bill would rocket, but then so would my spirits. No more poor-old-dear-living-alone hand-held basket for me – the two tins of catfood, a lump of cheese and a bottle of plonk. Forget it – it was back to the trolley piled high with all his favourite foods plus all the fresh fruit and vegetables he said he couldn't afford and the college refectory didn't provide. The upping of expenditure at Sainsbury's and the downing of the general state of my back from trolley pushing and ironing was nothing compared to the joyous rise in my general demeanour on rounding the corner of my not very distinguished street on the Wandsworth side of Putney, giving my usual whistle and seeing, a few seconds later, one of his bedroom windows shoot up and his head pop out.

I must confess to a sin more venal than the sight of a middle-aged woman whistling through two fingers in the street. When I said all his washing, I lied. I would keep a T-shirt back. I became a secret T-shirt sniffer. Now I know there can't be many people who would willingly put themselves in such close proximity to an unwashed article of undergraduate's clothing. But if you remember the smell on the crown of your baby's head, that special, *only his* smell, then you're in the right frame of mind, or rather nose. Pathetic, isn't it?

I don't want to paint too glowing a picture – often he would be furious that I had interrupted his work for nothing other than a welcoming shout, or if I intimated that I'd like help unloading the shopping from the car, he would bite back some resentful remark about the pressure of finals, and glower silently moments later at the front door. But glowers, silent or otherwise I could handle. At least they were attached to a face. At least I could hear the dreaded Caterpillar boots as he moved about overhead. I almost – though not quite – grew to be fond of the appalling ridges they carved in my carpet. I would often go to the bottom of the stairs in those last two weeks before finals and shout 'Lunch is ready', knowing that each time I was ticking off the times remaining for me to shout it. All this held no special significance for him, of course. I would still not be heeded till the third or fourth call.

But then, ultimately and inevitably, watered, washed, ironed and fed, he would go again, and I would be back to the crashing silence of living alone in a house with a top floor I didn't visit.

For the largest part of my life, his meals, his washing, homework, friends to stay, school visits out of London, ironing, missing buttons, teeth (missing or otherwise), verrucas, the bully in the playground and how the dreaded maths test had gone, had been my waking thoughts and daily preoccupations. No child of mine was going to have frozen food just because I was a single parent, oh dear me no – I have been known to make chicken in lemon and garlic after two shows at one o'clock in the morning – it took me years to find out his secret delight was a burger from *that* high-street chain. My then agent, despairing when I first got pregnant – well, he did have six of his young women clients in that state at the same time – began to understand *not* to mention a film offer if the shooting schedule didn't coincide for a large part with the school holidays.

Being a working mum didn't soften the blow one bit when he'd gone. No one to say, 'How did it go?' when I'd come in after work at 12.30 at night or, 'Oh well, it'll go better tomorrow, have a cup of tea,' after a decimatingly bad performance, or worse, a school's matinee.

Children of single parents often have to grow up more quickly to field parental bad moods faster than children who aren't in a one-to-one with a grown-up. I think it's called self-protection. As the storm clouds of stress and overtiredness would gather about my head I would often hear a 'I've finished my homework, Mum.' (I was Mum in those days, prior to which I'd been Mummy – the increasing shortness of my appellation obviously being in direct proportion to the amount of importance I held in his life.) 'Mum, so I'm going out with Max, see you, bye-ee.'

You would have thought I'd have been used to the goodbyes. Since he was seven he'd travelled the world alone by plane, mostly to visit his father, accompanied by nothing other than his Sony Walkman. He would invariably take the hand of the ground hostess especially allotted to children travelling solo, and trot off, still wired up for sound, with never a backward glance at his bravely sniffling mother who needed more than a hostess. She needed counselling.

Once, aged about nine, he'd flown out at the beginning of the school holidays to join me in Portugal, where I was working, and was outraged to find that when my few days of filming had finished we were to travel back together.

'S'not fair,' he said. 'I won't get on and off first if *you're* with me.'

The Gap Year should have helped. What a dreadfully accurate description of that time in parents' lives between school and university – a no man's land of time. Gone, but yet not gone completely. The biggest gap being in the parental pocket. Oh yes, we had the backpacking saga too. Don't leave home without one. Indonesia I think it was. For a month. A month of no phone calls – no contact at all. Just enough time for a single parent with no one to worry with, to go completely screwy with fears about all sorts of horrors, mishaps and unpronounceable tropical diseases – fears borne out, it would seem, by his eventual arrival at Heathrow aeons later, about a stone thinner and a delicate shade of yellow.

I wanted to shout with angry relief (like you do when they're three and you've lost them momentarily and then suddenly they're there) when the explanation for his hue turned out to be

nothing more dramatic (his words, not mine) than severe food poisoning for the last two and a half weeks, and the resultant diet of nothing but rice and bananas.

But given all these goodbyes, over eighteen years of single parenthood, nothing, but nothing could have prepared me for last Saturday. The day of The Final Move into His First Flat. Round came a Bedford Van (I shall, from now on, always harbour a particular dislike of Bedford Vans) and out jumped a tame builder. Down went the two tall bookcases, my Christmas present to him the year before last, when I'd said benignly, full of maternal grace and strength of character, 'For when you have your own home.' And now last Saturday he had it, and I was feeling anything but strong, and any grace I might have mustered to make this a special and significant day went right out the window.

'We've got to be quick, Ma. Alan's got to be gone in half an hour. Chelsea's playing at home.' It was left to me to connect these two facts. I mumbled something about not wanting it to be a dash and grab, but it was both. Dash and grab and devastation. Of my, I was going to say our, home, and me. I got left with, yes you've guessed it, the broken old blue office chair, the bongos, and piles of half-finished paintings and canvases, but I drew the line at the blue patchwork quilt that I had bought for his bedroom, in Vermont.

'But you said I could have it!'

'Did I? Well, I lied,' I said, managing to scrape some strength of spirit from amongst the debris of discarded books, piles of essays on Eng Lit Crit and Structuralism, amid which I was trying to maintain some dignity and authority. 'Please leave me something. I can't afford to have your bedroom completely redone.' It was, e'en I spoke, in the process of being painted sunshine yellow, by Dear Don the Decorator from Warwickshire. 'This old blue carpet with have to stay, so I need the blue quilt to tie in with it,' I whined pathetically, feeling very de-structured and on the verge of tears.

When he said, 'Oh, OK, OK,' there was that tone in his voice of, 'Don't you dare cry, Ma.' So I didn't. Not then.

'Probably thought it best to make it a short sharp shock,' was offered kindly in the accents of the Bard, from behind me as I stood, having dodged the tray of yellow paint, staring bleakly out of the window of what I was trying to reprogramme my mind to call my new study.

'What? Do you think all that rushing in and out' (they'd cleared the place in twenty minutes that, even with my poor maths, is about a minute for every year of my son's life) was just to save my feelings?'

'Probably.'

Probably it wasn't. Chelsea *were* playing at home, as it turned out.

So here I sit in my bright yellow room, that I'm trying hard to feel sunny about, with that blue patchwork quilt from Vermont on the bed, and an oil-paint-stained blue carpet that I haven't the heart or the gumption to clean. Oh, and the books and paper debris, the broken blue chair, the bongos and the piles of half-finished paintings?.

Well, the books went to Oxfam, the paper went in nuclear-war strength plastic bags to the local tip – that too, was the fate of the chair. The bongos went just out of earshot across the road to a six-year-old neighbour with very deserving parents. And the paintings? Well, I made a deal that I'd house the ones I liked on the walls of my now empty landing and new study in return for a freebie. And the half-finished canvases? I've stashed them under the bed in the spare room where they're invisible. After all I've got to get on with my life...up here on the top floor in the room that resembles a large and very empty bowl of custard...where there isn't even a T-shirt to sniff.

Into the Valley...
and Out

For many years Rowan's birthday and the eventual onset of spring, however reluctant, would trigger a memory of that beloved magnolia tree, although we left Chelsea many years ago for the wild and wayward shores of cheaper Putney. Wayward, largely due to the volatile and irregular nature of District Line trains to Wimbledon, and wild is my stock reaction to it as it rumbles past, shaking the foundations of my home.

Beginnings have always been hard for me. I don't know if it has something to do with being born at the end of the year, in the dark and unwelcoming days of December, as I've said, or whether it's just a Capricorn unwillingness to face the new, the inevitable change.

A few years ago Change and Newness burned their way into my life with searing speed and brutality, so vividly branding my memory that the beginning of spring now invokes not just a huge relief for having passed through those particular hoops of fire, and a gratitude for what grew out of the ashes, but a surprising willingness to revisit that particular place in my mind each year, to want to go back, to remind myself of where I've been. 'I came through, and shall return.' A need to acknowledge those significant milestones. Milestones of loss, loneliness and ill health.

In the Valley of the Shadow

Do not go gentle into that good night.

Dylan Thomas, 1914–53

But night is already at hand; it is well to yield to the night.

Homer, *The Iliad*, Book VII, c. 9th century bc

Something wasn't right. Things hadn't felt right for a long time. Something bad was happening, but I didn't know what. I was frightened, and as it turned out later, I had every reason to be. I hadn't slept properly for months. Worse than usual. Ever since I had taken sole responsibility for my five-year-old son and the multitude of au pairs with their multitude of problems, my sleep had been disturbed by an ever-wakeful ear, and a sometimes overwhelming sense of lone responsibility for us all. Fifteen years of single parenthood later, with no grandparents as crises back-ups, periods out of work, with only the £42 a week for my son, coming in from my ex-husband, and periods *in* work, when rushing out in the lunch hour to do the shopping, having done the cleaning, washing, and sometimes ironing in the morning *before* work, doing the cooking *after* work (which in the theatre can often mean at one o'clock in the morning) was the 'normal' pattern of my existence.

Sunday was the day for catching up with tidying the garden – I saw it as a chore as there was no time to enjoy it; helping my son with his homework; wading through the piles of correspondence and bills; and trying to fit in a 'family' outing of some kind to a museum, art gallery or a cinema, where I would often fall into the only deep momentary sleep I had.

If I was lucky enough to land work abroad, I would often accept it only if it coincided with my son's school holidays so that he could come too. That brought its own problems. Frequently I couldn't afford to take an au pair even if I had one, and filming on location in a foreign country, with a bored, tired child whom I'd had to get up at 5.30 a.m. to come with me to make-up, and then who'd spent the rest of day drawing, reading or as a last resort, watching television in a language he didn't understand, trapped in my caravan (if there wasn't a kindly wife of one of the crew holidaying with us who would child watch), was not the most ideal situation in which to work. But I did it. Often at the end of another exhausting week all I could say to myself was, 'You got through it.' Getting through it was all I could manage. I didn't laugh much. I didn't have much fun. I was so tired and in such a permanent spin that I didn't even see the treadmill I was on. I was either totally on the go, working down my list for the day, from one absolutely essential task that just couldn't be left, to another – or unconscious, in a troubled, unrefreshing short-term sleep from which I would wake seemingly more tired than I had been the night before, and drag myself irritably and short-temperedly through another day.

Very occasionally I would have a day off, usually through force of circumstances rather than design, and trying to stay still for even a day brought such terrifying awareness of the pains and aches in my appallingly tired body (my shoulders felt as if liquid concrete had been poured into them, my legs felt like lead, and my head was permanently abuzz with negative chatter), that I would be anxious to start rushing about doing things again, so that I couldn't hear what I now realise were warning signals. I felt like a little cartoon character with clockwork legs permanently running up a cliff, the summit of which had to be attained at all costs. What I didn't know, was that after fifteen years of running, the cliff was shortly going to be taken from under me.

It was an *annus maximus horribilis* that was to be my downfall.

My second friend had died of cancer in the July of that year, and unlike the first friend, who had shared her thoughts and fears about her illness and possible demise, and whom we, her circle of devastated and loving friends, had supported, with practical help, and sustained with emotional honesty and our own need to understand and face our imminent grief and loss as we helped her relinquish her hold on this world, this second friend was in denial every step of the way. Ill people must be allowed to make their own agenda, but it made her very exhausting to be with. It was difficult to know what to do to bring her relief of any kind. Apart from practical acts of help: driving her from Islington to Wimbledon, where my homeopathic doctor would try to alleviate the after-effects of chemotherapy, to which she had finally acquiesced as a last resort. Driving her as carefully as the congested London traffic would permit, as she sat, her frail frame like some delicate glass ornament, cushioned by a sheepskin rug, her body too thin to bear even the comfort of my leather car seats.

Conversation on this journey was fraught with dangers too. Every subject was a minefield, peppered with taboos that were not to be mentioned, let alone discussed. I found this hard to handle as I was godmother to her youngest child, a girl who, at twelve – not the easiest of ages – was facing the prospect of her mother dying at home. I wanted to reassure my friend that I would take up my responsibilities to this dazed, uncomprehending little girl in full. When I did finally pluck up the courage to mention it quietly – she was attached to an oxygen tube almost permanently by then, in the oldest, most forgotten part of the Brompton Hospital and she'd just scoffed with some relish the garlic prawns and raspberries and crème fraîche that I'd brought at her request from Marks and Spencer – she looked straight past me and said, 'I think I'll get my hair permed when I get out of hospital.'

She got out of hospital to die. She was my oldest friend. We had met at Drama School when we were eighteen, and with her dying I felt a large section of my younger self had gone too. We had never lived in each other's pockets, our lifestyles were very different – for a start she'd had a lasting marriage that she had cemented at all costs – but whenever we'd meet up, that initial closeness, born of the tribulations of being penniless students and zany good-time girls together, would return. We occasionally met for lunch to gossip about the present states of those we had known in our past, and share the many worries of being young mums and aspiring actors.

I didn't know that she had planned her funeral. None of us except her immediate family did. She only accepted that she was dying on the Sunday, and by the Tuesday she was dead. I was two days into a week's holiday in the south of Ireland, trying to rest and stabilise a rocky relationship, when the news came. We flew back to London immediately. She had requested that I read the 'Death is nothing at all' piece at her funeral. I was surprised and, in spite of my grief, flattered and relieved that she had wanted me to be part of this special tribute. It turned out to be a task that was almost too much for me to handle with anything like the professional technique I can normally draw and rely on in difficult circumstances, as my personal feelings crowded in and threatened to overwhelm me. I could only manage it by placing my hand on her coffin, where I saw *her* hand in my mind's eye, and praying wildly for her help to get through it. When I returned to the front pew, shaking uncontrollably, my son (her godson) sitting immediately behind me, having flown back from America with no sleep for twenty-four hours, put his hand on the back of my neck and stroked it. I was unable to staunch my grief and the unvoiced sobs racked my body. The sad remnants of her little family sat silent and straight-backed further along the front pew, and I was riddled with guilt at my unseemly lack of control.

The interrupted holiday in Ireland was also to have been a much-needed period of rest and recuperation. I had not long returned from filming in Ethiopia with a director who relished the Outward Bound aspects of shooting in hills that harboured bandits – our convoy was shot at once and a driver injured – and who found the blistering heat and the clouds of dust that the jeeps kicked up, just part of the day's fun. Most of the crew went down with dysentery at one time or another and the pot bellies of the props men went up and down like the rear ends of the famed Bushmen of the Kalahari.

I lived the life of a fastidious nun on location, going to bed early every night, never eating anything other than bread and vegetables, and handfuls of acidophilus tablets to keep the dreaded gut-rot at bay. My days had been a round of struggling not to mind the stinging sweat trickling down my itching, grit-coated, made-up face, and trying, in spite of the constant choking, whirling dust, to keep my sore, red eyes open at least a crack on the word, 'Action!' Trying, too, not to mind at the end of a twelve- or fourteen-hour day that there was no water for a bath in the simple little hotel in Gondar, as the actors would always get back there after the rest of the crew had gone through its meagre supply. They went through beer in the same way.

In spite of the Boy's Own Adventure nature of the whole shoot, I found it a disturbing experience being cosseted in the relative luxury of the Addis Ababa Hilton, when just outside the perimeter fence was a shanty town, where people lived in indescribable poverty, literally scratching a living from the dust, while we moaned about the failure of butter to appear on the breakfast tables.

There was a curfew in force which limited expeditions out after filming in the capital, but on hearing the sound of gunfire most mornings just before dawn, and being told that this was the EPRDF shooting thieves and burglars, I suspect not many of the crew felt this restriction too keenly. The Ethiopian People's Republican Democratic Front were shockingly young teenage boys sporting Kalashnikov rifles, which they displayed with great pride and a degree less safety than we needed to feel comfortable. It was only later that we learned that the Russians, occupied with the decline of the Soviet Union, were no longer supplying ammunition, in the same way that they had stopped building homes for the Ethiopians. Many roofless shells of buildings lined the dust tracks that were the main roads. A mockery to those who scrabbled for shelter in the mud of the winter rains.

Few of us enjoyed the food from the catering van, not just because it wasn't good – it wasn't – but because it was impossible to eat with bony arms outstretched through the gaps in the fencing that kept us separate from the rest of Ethiopia. We gave away food, batteries, toothpaste, shampoo, medical supplies, shoes, pens, clothes, and money. And went home to the relative safety of Europe with empty suitcases and full hearts.

Two days in Ireland amid lush green fields, where fat sheep gazed contentedly at me as I ran off the guilt of homemade scones, jam and cream, had done little to expunge the searing memories of the innate dignity of the stick-thin Ethiopian people. It had done even less for the rocky relationship, which I knew, but wouldn't admit, was irretrievably on the rocks.

The beginning of the week after the funeral found me back at work on the second series of a TV programme where the leading actor resented not only my friendship with his leading lady – a friendship of some fifteen years' standing, born of many roles played opposite each other in the theatre, and a great mutual warmth – but also her asking my help in rewriting some of her scenes. This culminated some weeks later in his successfully managing to have me written out of the third series. This hurt. Although I really should have felt flattered, I suppose, that he should have seen my little contribution as such a threat. I was much saddened by this, not least of all because it was also the most lucrative job I had every done. So it was goodbye too, to being able to put my hand into my cheque book to finance my son's gap year without thinking about it.

But fate stepped in and, without a day's break in work, I found myself back in the beloved classical theatre, at the RSC, playing Gertrude opposite Kenneth Branagh's Hamlet. Gertrude is a famously difficult role. It's bricks without straw. She's regarded as one of Shakespeare's leading characters, but in fact she has less lines than Rosencrantz. She is almost silent in the last half of the play. After the closet scene where Hamlet kills Polonius by mistake, thinking he's Claudius, and then tells her that Claudius killed Old Hamlet, and violently attacks her for being voracious and shameless in her sexual appetites, it's perhaps not surprising that from then on she's lost for words. So I decided to play her almost catatonically deranged. I had no idea how accurately I was holding the mirror up to Nature. Gertrude is torn by her son wanting to go back to university. My son had just started his first term at Oxford. Locating this core of Gertrude's pain, I exacerbated my own. This was the blue touch paper.

Meanwhile the rocky relationship got rockier. There was a worsening atmosphere in my home that was almost tangible but impossible to define. It would hit me every time I opened my own front door. My son was no longer there for my attention to be deflected from this. I realised things were not what they might be when, after teaching a particularly draining masterclass at a drama school near Oxford, with students, who largely, if I was brutally honest, didn't stand a chance in hell of getting into the profession, but were working themselves into the ground in cafés and pubs all hours to pay for their fees, I found myself, having pulled the car over on to the hard shoulder, sitting staring ahead of me at nothing in particular, but not wanting to drive the rest of the journey home.

Home was where the uninvited guest was, sulking, passive-aggressively refusing to communicate about the problems he knew we had. He was one of the 'if you don't talk about it, it will go away' school. But worst of all, he continuously and remorselessly pointed the finger at me. He said I was responsible for this feeling of ill ease. I thought not. He said I wasn't happy in my work. True. He said I was (my word) 'bereaved' that my son had left home. True. He said I was always tired. Painfully true, but resented by me. He said I was still mourning the loss of my friend. True. Like most bereaved people I was also full of guilt for what I could have done and didn't, and what I ought to have said and hadn't. He said I was menopausal. Debatable. I hadn't had any outward signs of it, but desperately wanted something physical to blame and something on which to attach the fault for these dreadful feelings.

About this time I had a very vivid dream about not being able to see my car. It sounds so trivial and undramatic. (My actual car was brand new, the first in nine years, bought with the labours of the two uncomfortable TV series and, luxurious as it seemed to me, it also seemed a high price to pay for having worked with someone so deeply dismissive and discounting of my contributions.) The car of the dream was enveloped in a menacing and impenetrable mist. However hard I tried I just couldn't reach it, and it was paramount that I did. Some unspoken imperative urged me on. The mist, as ephemeral as it appeared, was like a ring of translucent steel. Again and again I tried to approach it, but made no headway. My feet didn't move. The dream was pervaded with such a haunting despair that I found myself aware of my own distress while I was dreaming it and, awake, it clung to me like a demanding, ever-present shadow. I was unable to shake off the memory of it until many days later. I'm not a car person. I don't care what it looks like as long as it goes. Often if asked what car I had, I would say a mushroom-coloured one. But I'd read bits of Jung and knew that the car had replaced the image of the horse and carriage as a symbol of the Self.

A few weeks later, by then well established in a pattern of restless, disturbed nights with little sleep, I was returning home from rehearsals of *Hamlet* in a slow-moving traffic jam, when the match to light the blue touch paper was supplied. I sat motionless as I watched my six-month-young car sail into the car in front, which sailed into the car in front of that. My feet didn't move. Fortunately no one was hurt, but the damage was shocking. Broken headlights, bonnet buckled like a concertina. The front of my car was a steaming, shattered mess, and the back of the car in front of me was none too pretty either. I did what you are always advised not to do, I said it was my fault. It was. It wasn't so much the damage to the three cars that unsettled me, it was that I, ever-capable, ever-coping, organised, efficient me, had, like Hamlet, Done Nothing.

My fault had become the leitmotif of my existence at home too. None of this potent brewing turmoil was helped by the fact that my partner's ex-wife, after months of threatening him through his solicitor, finally succeeded in dragging me into court too. Divorced a good while, they had been haggling for some time over a financial settlement. She was taking him to court. And now she wanted to take me too. As a witness for *her*. A witness for the prosecution. The niceties of this legal irony were lost on me at the start. Initially I'd been outraged at the mere idea of it. I didn't want to be involved in something that was none of my business, and that had had nothing to do with me. But I was informed that I would be subpoenaed if I didn't appear. So, raging with resentment, appear I reluctantly did.

The whole messy business, which was eventually and not at all surprisingly settled in his favour, just as everyone expected, was based on her assumption that because I worked in television I must be a millionaire, and as he was living in my house (not a situation I had invited, or was happy with) he therefore didn't need any of their mutual property or money, as I must have enough to keep us both. I was at the time £5000 overdrawn. And even top salaries at the Royal Shakespeare Company are far from regal.

Our joy at his legal victory was short-lived. I celebrated by taking him, my son and my son's then girlfriend to a slap-up meal at Leith's. We had a bottle of Bordeaux the same age as my son. It was the last of my TV money and as it turned out, the last of the summer wine.

All the savings that for the first time in my life I had managed to accrue thanks to the TV series, had gone on making a house habitable, that my partner had bought in the south-west of France. No fool like an old fool. Having not wanted him to be in, or involved in, my property, I then got involved in his. Although he had said initially that he had bought the house for me – he doesn't speak a word of French, and had only managed a day trip to Paris before we met – his name alone remained firmly on the deeds.

In between breaks of more than five or six days in perfor-mances of Hamlet (a four-and-a-half-hour stint, nine hours on matinee days – we did every word), I would get on a plane to France, get off the other end, roll up my sleeves and paint the new shutters, dig up the garden, reseed the grass, plant oleanders marguerites and marigolds – the only plants that would survive the blistering sun of the Languedoc, and deal with gas, water and electricity companies and obtuse French builders who were installing a new bathroom, a new loo and replacing a sink, all of which needed decisions the minute I appeared. Indecipherable scrawls on small-squared paper about plastic tubing and overflow pipes, which I would have been hard pushed to understand in English, let alone in the nasal twang of south-west France, were thrust into my frown-wearing face. I bought a second-hand car, (we couldn't, I realised, afford both the air fares and the exorbitant cost of renting one), a new fridge, hoover, sheets, towels, and material which I brought back to England and sewed into matching curtains and bedspreads, which I would then take back on the next trip out.

As if this wasn't enough to win me the housewife/gardener/decorator/site manager of the century award, I decided in a rash moment to have the barn at the bottom of the garden converted into a plunge pool. It couldn't be rightly described as a swimming pool as, three strokes into it you would bang your nose on the other end. But it would be somewhere cool where the ravages of the summer heat which could reach the lower 40s C could be washed away. We were miles from the sea, and the inland lakes were not for bathing in. So out came another series of scrawls on squared paper, permission to open up a drain in the adjoining alley had to be sought from the local council, and a huge pipe had to be run through the entire length of the lawn. No easy feat. Bureaucratic French is even harder to understand than Plumbing French. My non-French-speaking partner was of course non-active in all this.

It was against this jolly backdrop – car shattered, Gertrude shattered, paint-stained and French weary – that, completely unplanned, I found myself, very calmly and uncharacteristically quietly, walking in through my front door one evening after another hard day toiling over the doomed Dane at the user-unfriendly Barbican Theatre, and I heard myself asking him to go. I had got to the end of my tether with this no-go, no-improve situation, and inside I was suffocating and screaming silently as I felt my life getting smaller and smaller under his possessiveness and refusal to face pain of any kind. The only sense I have been able to make of pain is to learn from it and grow. Kindly, well-respected professionally and honourable man that he was, he had spent his life in denial of two broken marriages and little contact with the children of either. This fundamental belief that I had about life, I felt could no longer be ignored or discounted. I was then forty-seven, and felt it imperative to stand by what I believed about life and the living of it.

He was astonished by what I had done, or rather the manner in which I had done it. So was I. I had never felt so calm. He spent a good while stomping about upstairs and packing very loudly – I suspected he was playing for time and hoping that I would change my mind, but I didn't. I just sat, unmoving, at the kitchen table waiting for the time to pass. I remember being rather shocked at how dispassionately I felt about the whole business. I waited for the bomb to fall. Eventually he left. I breathed out for the first time in two years. No bomb fell. I felt nothing but relief. I was now totally alone for the first time in my life. The cliff, without my noticing, had disappeared. But inside I was still running.

As a way of reclaiming my now empty home (although my son occasionally came back for university holidays if he wasn't visiting his father in Los Angeles) I decided I would, in one last whirl of extravagance, have my sitting room and hall repapered. I thought it wise to employ the husband of someone I was working with, rather than have a complete stranger in my home while I was in Elsinore. Wrong. In spite of what was written on his business card about being a painter and decorator, he was neither. He was a cowboy. The stripes on the paper weren't cut to match, the edges of the paper where it touched the ceiling were ragged and unfinished, there were great air bubbles trapped under it at points too numerous to count, and plaster had been dropped on the dado rail and simply painted over. In short it was a disaster area. I thought it would take six days. It took six weeks to sort it out. Six weeks of *Hamlet* every night, which wasn't free from its own share of disasters. The various sets of curtains that swagged the stage would often get stuck and refuse to move at all, which would either necessitate us playing cramped together in a much reduced space, or the Stage Manager would have to stop the show while the stage staff disentangled the mess. Once the fire iron got stuck and the show was stopped for twenty-five minutes. We got a much-needed break in the marathon, but we also got catcalls and whistles from an understandably impatient audience. Very unnerving. I would then come home to the comfort of my bomb-site, where a new carpet had been laid, neatly ordered by me to coincide with the seventh day, which I had originally deemed would be decorator-free.

A kindly builder from the Guild of Master Craftsmen tried to let me down gently, but even he couldn't stifle a guffaw of horror when he first saw the room, and after looking around in amazement for several minutes said that there was nothing for it, but to pull the whole lot off and start again. The whole lot being thirty rolls of hand-painted wallpaper from Osborne and Little. Well, I said it was an extravagance. It certainly was – to have to buy the entire amount over again in less than ten days.

The day the last of the shelves went back in – not to its original place as Mr Cowboy had forgotten to mark where they had been – was the day the match was struck, and that blue touch paper well and truly blazed. I got home after nine hours of *Hamlet*, replaced all the books, cassettes and videos on the shelves, took up the dust sheets, and hoovered, cleaned and polished till the early hours of the morning, my aching, tired body by now ablaze with exhaustion. If there had been someone there to see this insane overworking, they would surely have stopped the frenzy, as that was what it was. But I was alone and trapped, running round and round in my personally built wheel of self-induced torture. Somewhere deep down I must have had the conviction that I was invincible. Hubris. Pride was about to meet its fall. And the bomb was ready to drop.

It had become a joke amongst my friends that the moment they bowed out of any work, pleading tiredness, was the moment

I went into overdrive. The joke was about to be on me. I sat in my new sitting room, a builder's site no longer, and imploded. I sobbed and howled. The noise shook me at first, as I didn't know where it was coming from. It sounded like a wounded animal caught in great pain. I poured another and another glass of wine and felt worse. I staggered around the kitchen heaping invective after invective on decorators, partners, absent sons. Even silly Gertrude was not spared the free-flying flak. I took my swollen-eyed and almost incapable of moving self slowly, clumsily and hesitatingly up the stairs to bed. I lay awake most of the night. Alternatively I tried to stop crying and tried to pull myself together, and failed at both. I felt utterly uprooted, desolate and despairing. I was in free fall. My mind was jabbering nonsense, which I was powerless to silence, and nowhere could I find a position in which my body felt comfortable or at ease. Moving it was painful and very slow. It was as if it didn't belong to me. Indeed it didn't. I dozed fitfully, shudders of dying sobs punctuating my intakes of breath.

The following morning, a Sunday, the phone beside my bed rang. I went to pick it up and couldn't. I could no longer move. My head told my body what to do, but my body was powerless to put the order into action. I lay there astonished at my helplessness. The phone went on ringing and I went on not being able to do anything about it. Aeons later, by getting slowly out of bed and kneeling on the floor I managed to pick up the receiver, and the poor unsuspecting friend on the other end was treated to a slurred, choking, indistinguishable mumble of pain, that went on and on and on. I could no longer speak coherently or clearly. I yelped. Snot ran down my face. My eyes burned with crying. It hurt to blink they were so swollen. There seemed to be no connection between what I wanted to say and the thick, slow malformed words that came out of a mouth that had forgotten how to form them. Every kind and concerned inquiry from her brought fresh uncontrollable sobbing that hacked through my body, shocking and frightening me, that I was powerless to stop.

Years of living on borrowed time had come to an end. Years of not listening to the needs of my body and pushing it beyond the limits of endurance, had taken their toll. Years of the worries and fears of being a lone Mum, battling against all odds for me and my child, had worn me down to nothing and burnt me to a shell. I had come to a complete and utter standstill. Except I couldn't stand. I, the great Mrs Fix-It of all time, was utterly helpless. Ill and alone. From somewhere else in the room throughout that long day, I looked down on what was happening to me, and felt nothing. I had nothing. It was to take me three weeks in hospital, and three years after that, till I felt anything resembling well again. I could no longer wear any of the hats I had been hiding under for most of my adult life. I was no one's lover, no one's mother. I had no money, no man, no son, and no health.

It was also the best thing that could have happened.

Out of the Valley
of the Shadow

'Come to the edge.'
'We can't. We are afraid.'

'Come to the edge.'
'We can't. We will fall.'

'Come to the edge.'

And they came.
And he pushed them.

And they flew.

GUILLAUME APOLLINAIRE, 1880–1918

In hospital I was put in a wing that housed the post-natal depressives and the anorexics. I was neither. It was a joke. But nothing made me laugh. I cried as the nurses unpacked my bag. My bag with so few things in it. How could I have taken so long to pack so little? The overnight bag had taken hours to assemble as I had sobbed round my house, trying hard to remember where my toothbrush and slippers were. This simple feat seemed impossible to accomplish without wandering into room after room and then wondering why I was there. Every object appeared loaded with memories that were a fresh spur to my distress. My son's shoes left at the bottom of the stairs where I could pretend that he was about to come in, but he wasn't. A photograph of an old boyfriend which seemed a talisman of yet another failure. The cat who looked at me with mournful eyes – he alone had witnessed my hours of crying, and I had forgotten to feed him. My house itself which had always seemed such a sanctuary, now felt like an empty shell. All the years of effort that I had put into making it comfortable and pleasing now meant nothing. I didn't know whether I was crying tears of relief that someone had made a decision for me, or crying tears of fear that now things were really serious. Hospital. What would they say at the theatre? My poor understudy would have to go on. Well, at least she'd had a whole day's notice. It felt strange to think another body would be wearing those dresses that had been made for me and that I loved. And my son? What would my son say when he knew I was in hospital? They mustn't tell him. It would worry him. I mustn't worry him.

'Where's your nightie, dear? There's no nightie here...' Why did they want my nightdress? I wasn't going to get into bed, was I? It was the middle of the day. Noise of people in the corridor distracted me. I felt angry with those women who I could see, as the door to my room was left open, those young women with that tell-tale lump still round their middles having not long since given birth. What had they to be sad about I thought angrily. They had their babies. Mine had grown up and gone. I was alone.

The nurses brought me a meal on a tray and I cried. I couldn't remember the last time anyone had brought me a meal on a tray. That simple caring gesture had me choking over food that I couldn't and didn't want to eat. I had no appetite for anything. They tucked me up in bed and I cried. I couldn't remember when I had last had a caring, loving person insist and ensure that I rest or sleep. Except when I was a child. I remembered my dear foster mother, who by then had been dead seven years, and I cried some more. I wanted her back. I wanted her there. She would have looked after me. I felt like a child. An abandoned, unloved, unwanted child, which is what I had been before my foster mother had taken me into her care.

When the doctor, a personal friend, had decided that hospitalisation was the only solution to my distress, she had said, 'You have to go. You have no one to look after you.'

Those words had been the trigger for this seemingly unstoppable new flow of tears. They had viciously hooked themselves into me and gouged out this never-ending stream of pain. How could it be? No one to look after me? I'd spent my life being surrounded by people. Film crews, television crews, theatre companies. Now there was no one. Only my son. And he wasn't there. On the hospital admission form that the nurses had had to fill in for me, I had been asked for my next of kin. There was only his name to put down. What a small unit we were. So vulnerable. I had never felt this so acutely before. It terrified me. Just him and me. And he was gone.

I couldn't interrupt his second term at university. He'd had enough trouble adjusting to the regimented life of a student again after the gap year of freedom. His first term had been an uncomfortable, unhappy time. His initial reaction to the overwhelmingness that was Oxford, had been to want to pull out and quit. He was only just beginning to feel settled. I had no right to disturb that. And besides, what nineteen-year-old boy would want, or would be able, to cope with a mother whose every sentence was inarticulate with despair. I didn't even want him to know that I was in hospital. I felt that I had let him down. I had always been a fighter. I had battled for us both, and now I couldn't even walk.

No one to look after me.

Of course there were friends, but they all had their own lives and families. London is a big place. It could take two hours to get to Putney from Chalk Farm, and two hours back. I didn't think my friends who lived there could afford that kind of time out of their busy schedules. So I didn't ask. One of them did phone every single day though, and that was a great comfort. I hadn't been able to give much time to friends, bringing up a child on my own and working. Besides, two of my closest friends were dead. The third had moved out of London back home to Shropshire. My so-called family (with whom I had never lived – the little there was of it) was in France, and I hadn't seen my mother or my half-sister for years. My choice. Self-protection.

I seemed to have spent my entire life looking after people. My foster mother, at sixty-nine, had needed my help when I was twelve to do most of the shopping and to go into the town to pay the rates, and as wrong as it had seemed that I should be responsible for such important things, I had had to do it. There was no one else. Now I had no one.

My home had been full of my son's teenage friends, always wanting a bed or a meal or both, and I had been happy getting ironed sheets from the airing cupboard and making up beds, or being the centre of the household in the kitchen as I cooked. Hearing them stomping up the stairs and playing music and laughing, the house had been a busy, happy place. There's a saying in French, 'La femme est le soleil de la maison.' With my son going the sun had gone too.

They gave me pills to help me sleep and pills to help me walk and talk. When they wore off I could do neither. I would slur my words, which seemed so inexplicably slow in coming from my head to my mouth, and I would have to hold on to walls or furniture even to make a simple journey across the room. Sleep when it came at last, after all the months of wakefulness, was a drugged blessing, that silenced the raging torrent of chatter in my head, but left me incapable of getting from the bed to the bathroom in the middle of the night without help.

I was allowed no visitors. Except the one friend who lived in Putney and took over the care of my cat and plants, and took my nightdress home to wash. The handing over of that simple, intimate chore filled me with the frightening realisation of how frail I had become. I had to swallow my pride, aware that I was going to be in hospital longer than I thought, and ask her to bring me some more clothes. Shamefully, I snapped at her when she brought the dark green trousers instead of the sage green ones I had meant. We laughed about it later, but I didn't at the time. I was shocked that I had no resources to cover the rawness of my feelings. Why had I snapped at her when she had been so kind? This wasn't like me. But I no longer knew who 'me' was. Every simple task seemed to slip out of my grasp. My behaviour was as unpredictable to me as it appeared to be to others. I could barely manage a conversation with her at the end of the day, and walking with her from the floor that my room was on, down two flights of stairs to the reception area of the hospital, was out of the question, and beyond my strength.

And I had a new play to start rehearsing in just under three weeks. If I wasn't better they would surely give the part to someone else. Already my understudy had played several performances for me in *Hamlet,* and a reputation for being ill is the one reputation that nobody in my profession wants.

If I didn't work we didn't eat. How many times had I repeated that to my son, like some sort of catechism, over the years? I panicked. Panic came easily. It was always there, just lurking below the surface, waiting to pounce the second the effect of the pills wore off. I had to get better and get better quick. I thought I would be in hospital at the most for a week. The nurses were silent when I asked for confirmation of my departure. The most response I would get would be a feeble smile and a low shake of the head. I began to feel paranoid, as if they were all in league against me, and I began to doubt the wisdom of the doctor friend who had put me there. At the end of the week I still couldn't walk. How could I possibly work? The new script that I was supposed to rehearse as soon as I started back in *Hamlet* arrived by post. Mrs Alving in Ibsen's *Ghosts.* A huge role. A wonderful and unusually huge role for a middle-aged woman, but an emotional roller coaster ending in utter despair. I looked at it and felt tired to my bones. With it came the conscientious young director's copious notes on the Lutheran church in Norway in the late nineteenth century, and the position of women in Norwegian land-owning society. It could have been written in Martian. I could not make any sense of it at all. I could not focus my concentration. More tears of despair. The nurses and my doctor threatened to take the script and the notes away from me – 'You must have no stress at all.'

'But it's not stress,' I mumbled, 'it's work – I must work.'
Again those knowing smiles and shaking of heads. I felt such a
boiling anger, such furious resentment against them, against
myself, against everyone and everything.

I would sit in the armchair in my room and cry and cry, not
knowing why. I would watch the clear sharpness of the cold
winter evenings, reflected in the vast expanse of unreal blue sky
that stretched across my window, and feel as empty as what I saw.
I felt my home was a long way away from me. And I felt a long
way from everything and everyone. My past life seemed like it
had happened to someone else, a long time ago. All the love and
affection and attention I had had both professionally and
personally now seemed worth nothing. Where were they, all
those people now, I wondered. I felt abandoned and rejected by
everyone I had ever known. What was wrong with me? I didn't
recognise myself. Inside, I was awash with confusion and overwhelming fear about everything that came into my head or my
heart, and when I had the nerve to look at myself, while holding
on to the sink in the bathroom to wash my hands, the face of a
woman I didn't know looked back at me.

Eventually, of course, my son had to be told. I think the hospital
was presented to him as some kind of glorified health farm, to
alleviate the seriousness of whatever it was that was wrong with me.
It didn't work. When he came he was tense, withdrawn, resentful,
and monosyllabic. Inside, I yelped with pain. The one person in
the world I wanted to see, and I felt, although he didn't say it, that
he thought I had failed him. I thought I had failed him. It must
have been so strange for him to come down from Oxford and stay
in an empty house. Trivial concerns plagued me. There was none
of his favourite food in the fridge and the central heating was not
on. A cold, empty house. A house that was devoid of me. Ironically,
I was devoid of me. Inside I laughed an ugly, frightening laugh. I
was frightened to show him how frightened I was.

'What's wrong with you?' This was said like an accusation.

'I don't know.'

'Well they must have said what it is.'

'No, they haven't.'

'So how do you feel?'

What possible words could there be to describe to my nineteen-year-old son that I felt my world had collapsed around me, I had collapsed, my life felt meaningless and that I felt literally good for nothing and no one. My brain swam with words to use as possible alternatives to describe this overwhelming despair. None of them appropriate and none of them accurate. I drew myself out of this morass that was my inner world, and realised I had suddenly no recollection of what he had asked me.

'Sorry (oh how sorry I felt about everything), sorry, did you say something?...What did you say?'

'I said, "How do you *feel?*"' I fought back another surge of tears that his voice, tinged with exasperation, threatened to unblock.

'Tired.' I wanted to howl with laughter at the smallness of this ridiculous word. 'Tired,' I repeated, as if it would give it more weight and explain it better.

'Well, how much longer are you going to be in this...place?'

'I don't know,' and shamefully my eyes filled with tears and he looked away.

It was not a good experience for either of us. It was the first time he had ever seen me really ill. He didn't like it. And he didn't like me. Waves of disapproval emanated from him. He would cock his head on one side and give me long, silent looks behind half-shut eyes. I was too ill to realise that this was his defence. I felt guilty. I wished fervently that I was yellow with jaundice, or had an arm or leg in plaster, so that he could see where I hurt. So that I could see where I hurt. I felt like a malingerer. My heart ached with unfilled need. I shocked myself because I was glad when he was gone.

The script of *Ghosts* and the notes stayed unopened on the chest of drawers in the room, where they became surrounded by daily increasing bunches of flowers from well-meaning friends. The flowers meant nothing. I watched them droop and die in the suffocating central heating. I didn't change the water or pick off the dead blooms. Someone had sent me white lilies. I thought, rather ungratefully, that they made the place look like an undertakers. This macabre thought gave me an eerie sort of comfort.

Mother's Day, silly commercial nonsense that it is, came and went, and my son didn't. It coincided with his birthday. Another stab of guilt, that for the first time in his now twenty years I was not at home to share it with him. But somehow I had managed, through a friend, to order him a chocolate cake made in the shape of a university mortar board. It was waiting for him at home along with a bottle of champagne, in the empty fridge. He'd gone away for the weekend to visit friends, and I was devastated that he didn't even call. I passed other patients, other mothers, in the corridor (I was by now able to walk feebly along to the room where we could make ourselves decaffeinated coffee, which I hated but needed frequently to drink, to counteract the appalling dryness that the pills left in my mouth), and the bunches of flowers that they were clutching, undoubtedly given by their visiting children, pierced me like needles. He did turn up eventually, the day after Mother's Day, clutching a garish bunch of red carnations that must have cost him more than he could possibly afford. I worried where he'd got the money from. He pushed them rather shyly and ungraciously towards me. And I wondered suspiciously whether one of the few friends who were allowed to speak to me on the telephone had called him and reminded him of his omission.

I didn't dare voice my disappointment at his forgetfulness. The surge of emotion would have been impossible to control. After all, I wanted him to see that I was getting better.

'How was your weekend?'

'Fine.'

'Where did you go?' I didn't mean to colour the question, but it did come out accusatory. I realised suddenly that I hadn't known where he was. It was one of the few fundamental family rules that we had, that I must always know his whereabouts. In case anything happened. How could I have forgotten to ask? Supposing something had happened. Not to him – a possibility that he, like other young men, always shrugged off as so much mother-worry nonsense – but to me. Given where I was it didn't seem such a preposterous thing to ask.

'I told you. Northampton.'

'No you didn't...I don't think you did.' I tried to soften my response.

'Yes I did, Ma.' 'Mum' had become shortened to 'Ma' with the onset of university.

'Well...I...'

'You don't remember.'

That was true. I could retain so little these days.

'Did you like the cake?' A less dangerous tack. New subject.

'What cake?'

'The cake I've had made for you that's on the kitchen table.'

'Oh, I haven't been home yet.'

Of course. Why should he go home?. What was there for him *there*? He would be far more comfortable at his girlfriend's house. *Her* mother wasn't incapable and ill with exhaustion in hospital.

'So you haven't seen the cake?'

'No, I said I haven't been home.'

The surprise seemed suddenly to have been a tame idea. It had fallen flat. I had spoiled it all by telling him, I had done it wrong. Again.

He didn't stay long, and I made a dreadful pretence of being able to walk with him some of the way down the stairs to the reception area, which, instead of reviving his hopes of my improvement, left him aghast and irritated at the slowness of my pace, and made the possibility of my imminent release from hospital recede even further. I waved him goodbye with a false smile on my face then sat, collapsed on the stairs, put my head on my knees and wept with renewed hopelessness.

My head argued that it was unreasonable of me to expect my son to fill this aching gap in me for affection. He was, after all, at the age where boys do push their mothers away to make space for the women in their lives. He needed to relinquish the ties that bound us, and here was I, so needy that I was in danger of trying to tighten them. I hated myself for it. Right through his childhood I had always been able to put his needs first. For the first time ever, I began to wish I'd had a daughter. Surely a girl would understand? Even that thought felt like a betrayal.

I was rescued by a kindly passing nurse, offered an arm to lean on, roundly scolded for overdoing it, and escorted promptly back to bed although it was only seven in the evening. I was glad to be there. It wasn't till I was wakened some hours later to be given my pills to put me to sleep, that the full horror of what I had just managed not to achieve hit me. If I couldn't walk down two flights of stairs, how could I possibly manage four and a half hours of *Hamlet* – there were two flights of stairs just from the dressing room to the wings at Stratford. There were steep stairs backstage that led up to the 'play within the play' set, and the fight in the closet scene was rough and physically demanding. I often discovered I was bruised after it.

The worry weakened the blessedly welcome power of the pills. For the first time in ten days I woke in the middle of the night, panicked, frightened and alone. I rang the bell for the night nurse who came, and stood patiently while I treated her to an outpouring of these scrambled, tumbling thoughts.

'I've got to get back to work.' It seemed so stupid to be begging in the quietened dark of the middle of the night with tears pouring down my face, for a return to the normal world. Even as desperate as I was, I could see the ludicrousness of it.

'But you can't work, dear, can you?' She was a kindly Irish woman, who had done more than simply pack me off to bed like some of the other nurses, and had listened to me wail and whine on more than one occasion with remarkable patience.

'But I can. I've got to. Oh please make them help me.' I felt and sounded pathetic. 'If I lose this job I'll have lost a year of work, because we play *Hamlet* at Stratford, then I open *Ghosts,* which comes into the Barbican...' (my befuddled brain couldn't sort out times or dates) 'probably June next year.' I realised how ridiculous the machinations of the repertoire system of the Royal Shakespeare Company must sound to an ear that was familiar with none of it. And June next year sounded as far away to me as if it were a place on the moon.

'But dear, it takes time, you've been – you are – very, very tired.'

'I'm not, I'm not,' I sobbed. 'I haven't got... I haven't got time.' That certainly was true. I hadn't had time for years. I had been locked into a battle with time for as long as my son and I had been alone. It was a battle I had always lost, but never gave up fighting.

She put her arms around me, and I wished she were my mother. She smelt of starch and talcum powder, and I never wanted her to let go of me.

'You see,' I blurted into her shoulder, I've got...' Difficult to find the words to voice the unsayable. 'I've got – there isn't any one at home. My son's gone and the house is... empty.' This last was hardly recognisable as a word, it provoked renewed sobs and gobbets of slime and snot slid from my nose on to her clean uniform.

'I've got to get back to work. If I don't work, I'll go crazy.' Was that what I was? I had never dared ask. But now I'd said it. It was out. Another taboo word. Can't they give me some more pills?' I asked tremulously.

'How many are you on?'

'Two – pink ones,' I replied, feeling foolish.

She got up from the bed. I liked her all the more for having broken the cardinal rule about not sitting on hospital beds. She came back with my chart. I longed to see what was on it. I felt paranoid again that the doctors – several of whom had visited me and asked me each time for yet another version of the incidents that had led up to my being here – had written an assessment of what they thought was wrong with me, and that was knowledge that I felt was being wrongfully withheld.

'Two, that's fifty milligrams...'

'Is that a lot?'

'No, no,' she said in her lovely lilting brogue. It sounded a vast amount to me.

'Then can you ask them, please, to give me more? Will you please? Ask them tomorrow.'

'I'll have to leave a note for the doctor tonight. I shan't be here tomorrow.'

Irrationally, I wanted to shout, 'Oh please don't go, don't go, I need you here!'

'When will you be back?' I ventured. She looked at me in an odd way, a quizzical look on her face.

'Why tomorrow night, of course,' she said. 'I'm on duty again tomorrow night.'

I wanted to laugh with disproportionate relief.

'What will the extra pills do? How will I feel? Will I be all right?'

'You won't if you don't snuggle down now and go to sleep. I'll make you a hot drink, then to sleep you go.' I felt like a naughty child. It was a good feeling. A very small good feeling. The first good feeling I had felt for a very long time.

She came back with the drink, and another sleeping pill.

'Will those extra tablets make me feel woozy? Will I be able to talk? I must be able to talk. Will they stop me remembering my lines? They won't, will they?'

I seemed to spend my days and now my nights in this place, asking for things. Nurses came in with my meals during the day, when I was trying to meditate, without waiting for my 'come in' in response to their knock. When I said, 'Would you mind waiting for me to say, "Come in",' they just smiled at me, and went on doing it. It was as if what I said was of no consequence, because I had said it.

I got my extra tablets. I had been in hospital for just over two weeks. I was now on 100 milligrams a day. I felt as if I was looking at life down the wrong end of a telescope, but the aches in my body had magically disappeared and in the mornings when I woke, I felt something resembling being glad to greet the day. I couldn't remember when I had last felt that. I could stand and walk unaided and could talk at a reasonable rate without slurring my words. There were only four precious days to go before my three weeks were up. I knew the RSC had been pestering my doctor for a decision about when I would be well enough to work, although she tried to keep it from me, and when I asked her what she'd said, desperate for a date to be put on what I now saw as my release, she tried to make me laugh and failed by saying, 'I told them I'm not psychic.'

I could manage now, to walk slowly down to reception on my son's or my friend's arm. I was cross to see the drugs that I was on, advertised on huge hoardings in the reception area. 'For a doctors' conference,' the receptionist answered when I testily inquired.

'Oh, that's great PR for the patients who're on it,' I said. 'But I don't suppose that matters as long as the drug company sells it by the bucket load to the doctors. Makes me feel like a bloody guinea pig.' She smiled that professional smile and looked away. I wanted to scream, 'Don't *do* that! It drives me nuts!'

In the morning I would wander slowly down to the gym in my baggy tracksuit in which I spent most of my days and do a few minutes on an exercise bike. I was shocked by how little I could do, and how soon I felt worn out. Where had my strength gone? That unshakeable pool of stamina that I had always drawn on to get me through a show when I was overtired, was simply just not there. It had evaporated. Panic began to rise in me again, but somehow there was a barrier between me and it. The barrier of the drugs. A barrier of cotton wool. It didn't feel at all unpleasant. I had to get out.

'I have to get out,' I said to the matron on duty the next morning. It had taken me nearly an hour to get out of bed and wash and dress myself. I had put some make-up on and washed my hair. I felt triumphant.

'You're not going anywhere,' she said. 'We can't discharge you. That's up to the doctors.'

'No, I meant out. *Out*,' I said irritably. There are some shops, aren't there, further down the road? I'm going to the shops.'

'No you're not, young lady.' I hated the way people in positions of authority in hospitals patronised patients so.

'Well, I want to get out. Where *can* I go?'

She looked out of the nearby window. A glimmer of pale spring sunshine cast a shadow along the wall.

'Well, I don't suppose it would do you any harm to take a turn outside. Don't overdo it, now. Put a coat on. And tell reception where you are or if you feel it's too much for you.'

I wanted to run, and shout and scream with delight. But I turned slowly and mustered all my forces for a walk down the corridor to my room to get my jacket, which I knew would be a journey taken under her piercing, assessing gaze.

'Oh, and by the way,' I turned back to her. 'I'm sick of nurses barging into my room before I've said, "Come in." It's downright rude. And I think its damn insensitive to have all that drugs advertising in the lobby.'

As I turned to go I heard her say, 'You must be getting better. You're starting to complain.'

Choosing not to look at the drug advertisements, I opened the door from the main reception to the front driveway and garden, with an excitement that knocked at my chest and would have been painful, had it not been cushioned by the pills.

The cold spring air hit me hard. The world looked and felt new. I felt new. New and somewhat strange. How long since I had come here? I couldn't remember coming up that driveway. I couldn't remember who had brought me here. It felt like a lifetime ago. I stepped out and walked gingerly across the grass. My legs felt unreliable, and the grass looked unbelievably green. I had never seen grass that green before. Perhaps it was the drugs. Or perhaps I had never looked. There were spears of fat green-budded daffodils pushing up through the earth, and clumps of astonishingly white snowdrops. I stared and stared. I felt such an overwhelming surge of gratitude for everything I could see, that I wanted to cry. But these were different tears. They were tears of joy. I had never known what tears of joy were. I had thought them a cliché. But here they were pricking my throat, and stinging my eyes. Aware that I might be being watched, and that a crying fit would be a mark against me, I set off towards the main gate, making my way unsteadily across the lawn. It was cold in the shade of the trees, and although I shivered, I was too intrigued by all the different colours of the leaves on the evergreen bushes that lined the driveway to pay much attention. The gate seemed a long way off. The driveway seemed to twist and turn for ever. I had no recollection of it stretching that far ahead.

When I got to the gate after what seemed an age, I had to hold on to the wall. The traffic rushing by made me gasp with shock. The noise and the speed of it appalled me. Cars whizzed by, one after the other. My head reeled, and I worried that I would fall.

My legs were trembling. How could I ever have managed to survive in that noise, let alone drive in it? What I had taken as a normal part of living in London now seemed an impossibility. Of course I wasn't capable of driving, but how could I even face that maelstrom of noise and speed? It seemed inhuman. But I would have to do it, and do it in three days. I turned back and regained the peace of the hospital grounds.

I sat on the damp grass in the sun a day later, with my arms around a woman who was crying because her husband, who she had found was having an affair with a friend, the pain of which had caused her to attempt suicide, was visiting the hospital to discuss with the doctors whether or not he would take her back. 'Who are the crazy ones?' I thought. She had beautiful long dark hair, and was well dressed. She shook. Not just her hands which twisted and mauled a pretty lace handkerchief, but her whole thin body which was pressed against mine trembled uncontrollably. It was the first prolonged human contact I had had for weeks, yet it seemed somehow wrong that I should be drawing comfort from her distress.

She wanted to run and write a plea in lipstick on his car windscreen. I didn't think it wise, but felt ill-equipped to stop her. I just went on hugging her and said, 'Do you really want him back? He's caused you such pain.'

'Ye-es,' she howled. 'I can't be alone.'

The pills had taken paramount importance in my life. I was anxious that I would be given the increased amount to take with me. I confirmed with the night nurse that this was so, and went the next morning to the control desk, manned by her of the prison warder gaze.

'I've just come to check,' I said confidently, 'that I've got the increased prescription to take with me when I leave.'

'Leaving are you?' she replied disbelievingly, fishing out my notes from the shelf under the desk and scanning them. 'Yes, the dosage has been upped. Possible discharge Friday,' she read out, unconvinced.

'Friday it *is*,' I said meaningfully, and as I turned on my heel I played my ace. 'I was only here for the drugs.'

She played hers. 'You'll be back,' she said.

My son came in a taxi to take me home on the Friday. The speed with which the car was driven made me feel sick, although it can't have been that fast. My head spun with each vehicle that passed us. I held on to the door handle and tried to deepen my shallow breathing. I was so glad to be out. To be back in the world. But the world seemed a terrifyingly fast and busy place. 'I've been well and truly institutionalised.' I thought. My dear neighbours, Hedi and Mike, came out and waved as we arrived outside the house.

Home. 'Home,' I said to myself. I wanted to cry with relief as I saw it. I had been away so long. 'Home.' Inside I knew I was still a long way from home. I had trouble controlling my legs as I got out of the car. I smiled feebly and waved back.

'Are you up to talking to them, Ma?'

'No,' I said, and surprised myself.

On Saturday, very slowly and very deliberately, trying not to worry my son, or panic myself, I packed up my home for a year. On Sunday my son drove me, and a laden car, irritably and speedily to Warwickshire, to the dear friends whose stables flat would be my home for the season in Stratford. It was only when I saw their faces as they saw mine, that I realised how unwell I still was. They could ill conceal their shock.

On Monday morning I started rehearsals at ten o'clock for *Ghosts* and then was escorted at 4.30 by the company manager from the rehearsal room to the main theatre where at 6.30 I would start four and a half hours of *Hamlet*. This thirteen-hour day was to be my convalescence for the next six weeks.

Once the initial strangeness of finding myself back on the set of *Hamlet* was overcome, and I steeled myself to the sidelong glances that the members of the company made in my direction whenever they thought I wasn't looking, I had to trust that, once my dresser had kindly supported me from the dressing room down the stairs to the wings, the magic of Dr Theatre would take over, and the lines and moves would come flooding back as second nature. Largely they did. Only once did I get paranoid, when I saw a smirk on Laertes' face in the middle of Gertrude's

'There is a willow grows aslant a brook' speech. When he came near enough to the chair I had to sit on in the wings whenever I wasn't on stage, I asked him why.

He said, 'The line is, "There on the pendant boughs, her crownet weeds clambering to hang..." You said, "There on the crownet weeds, her pendant boughs clambering to hang!"'

Twice I thought I was going to die on stage. I leaned against the proscenium arch – a gesture I usually did in the first court scene, as a sensual enjoyment of Claudius's statesmanship – and I felt the whole theatre recede and move away from me. Again, when having been poisoned at the end of the play, and lying 'dead' on the floor of the stage, the whole theatre suddenly dropped away alarmingly from underneath my body.

I felt suspended above a pit, with nothing to support me. I had to wait till the kind people either side of me hauled me up and into place for the curtain call.

Death didn't frighten me. Not any more. I knew, in a way, I had already died.

Once the run of *Hamlet* was over, I was free to concentrate solely on mapping out Mrs Alving's tortuous journey of facing the failure of her life and her son's destruction. Learning lines usually came easily to me. But now I had trouble retaining more than six at a sitting, and would have to write them out in an exercise book to get them to stick. But I was happy not to be alone, or at home and out of work.

I had the late spring evenings to myself at the stables flat, but I had the comfort of knowing that Joe and Audrey were just across the way in The Hall. I was still being driven to the theatre as I was still not allowed, on the 100 milligrams of medication, to be behind the wheel of a car. I had, in times past, often walked from the flat, through the grounds of the estate, along the road to the cross roads about a mile away, and then up the steepness of Larkstoke Hill to view the sweep of the valleys where the four counties join. I couldn't reach the crossroads, but set myself a secret task of getting up the hill and off the pills before the press night of *Ghosts*.

I didn't make it up the hill until several months later. But I was pill-free by the first night.

It was, I realise now, a big step to take. And it was a step I took without my doctor's knowledge. But I took it. I wanted to do Mrs Alving. I didn't want 100 milligrams of Anafranil to do it. When I took the curtain call after the first performance of *Ghosts*, I felt as if I had climbed a vast and monstrous mountain, through hellfire. Which, of course, I had. On stage and off.

Over the next three years I took two steps forward and then three steps back. There were times when I despaired of ever getting back the energy I once had. In some ways I never have retrieved it. But it was a false energy, built on the quicksands of striving for perfection, overachieving, proving, proving, to myself and others that I was strong and good and therefore worth something. I no longer have that need.

Three years is a long time to be ill. A long time in which to learn patience. But time isn't my enemy any more. I am no longer 'hurrying on to a receding future, nor hankering after an imagined past'. I have time now. Time to listen to my body, and the tell-tale signs of overtiredness and stress. I listen to people more, too, and have learned to ask for help. I laugh a lot. Mostly at how preposterous I am. The child I had in my life has gone and in his place I have a relationship with a young man whose opinions and advice I seek and value, and whose character I relish. His separateness from me I see now as a blessing. I sleep deeply and well most nights now, and in the afternoons if I feel like it. If I feel like it. That simple fact of feeling like it is a gift. I don't mind being wrong, and I don't mind so much not working. I have other things in my life. Days off to visit exhibitions and art galleries, gardening, walking, writing, drawing, and cooking for friends, who I treasure now with a gratitude and an enjoyment I wouldn't have thought possible three years ago. I pray often. And give thanks often. I have many things in my life that I like. I have come home.

Home

So I came home alone. And home alone is where I've been for five years now. When the sun shines and I'm feeling well and working and the bills have been paid, it's a good place to be. Living alone, unemployed and unwell, is hard. Especially in a big city where neighbours can be transient. There are few of us in my street who have been here more than five years. One gets used to a new face in the street and then suddenly it's seen no more. Most of the big houses are now divided into flats and there are few families like me who have braved it out in the same home for more than a decade.

'Oh, you can't move,' said an ex-girlfriend of my son's, Claudia, whose company I still enjoy. 'All my teenage memories are in this house!'

I don't think I'm still here because this house holds fifteen years of my life. Traces of my son have been well and truly smoothed over now. It barely resembles the home he grew up in – apart from most of the furniture in the sitting room still occupying the same places – but that's more to do with the bizarre and unaccommodating shape of the room than anything else. I can understand many women moving into a smaller flat, as several friends of mine have done, when their mothering days were over. And I've been very near making that decision on many occasions but have always drawn back at the brink. The pigeons have gone from next door on one side, but the occasional fracas on the other still rumbles from time to time. At least I haven't got noisy neighbours above or below me, as I might well have if I moved into a flat. And I can't really see the point of all the upheaval that moving involves, to end up in something that's half the size of what I have now. I guess it's all down to finances again and that Capricorn unwillingness to change, unless it's absolutely essential, or worse, foisted on me. There are days when I take great comfort in chatting to the various well-known shopkeepers nearby, and other days when I think I know this area too well and it holds no more surprises for me. But that's nearly always more to do with my frame of mind than with this particular bit of SW15.

There's a saying in French that 'when the house is finished it's dead'. Well, fifteen years of living here, my bedroom still hasn't got that delicately etched pale rose wallpaper on it that I saw and wanted some years ago, and the grubby top landing still sports the ghastly woodchip covering that was there when I first moved in. And how I'd love a loo and a shower on the top floor for visiting friends, so the pleasure of their company isn't diminished as I stand corkscrew-legged on the landing waiting for them to vacate the bathroom. So I'm not short of domestic challenges. Or designs for better living.

There's the cat too. I couldn't possibly move him at his venerable age. It wouldn't be fair on him. This is his home too, and for the moment, until the next wave of yearning for pastures new hits me, it's mine too.

Living Alone

A man is *so* in the way in the house!

MRS GASKELL, *CRANFORD*, 1853

So I live alone. That phrase almost instantly conjures up pity and sympathy. Not least of all from myself. I have to work hard not to be overcome by the waves of self-pity that threaten to engulf me in the onrush of kindly concern from others when they hear me say it. Widowed? No. Divorced? Yes. But that was fourteen years ago so it doesn't really count. Recently broken up with someone? No. I have lived alone out of choice, since my son left home five years ago.

I was adamant about not wanting to live with a man on a day-to-day basis since my divorce. It had taken me a long time to heal, and even longer to find the guts and courage to stand on my own two feet, alone with a small child, and I didn't want that strength, if I'm ruthlessly honest, that shell of protection that I had managed to build round myself, eroded. I didn't want to feel dependent on someone being with me all the time. Of course, no man is an island, and no woman either for that matter – we all need each other. Not dependence or independence, but interdependence is the ideal state. People do need people. It's common knowledge that a baby left alone with no one to talk to it or cuddle it will grow up considerably ill-adjusted socially and unable to relate to people in an intimate way, as a result of this lack of human contact.

But, in spite of the pleasure of being significant in someone else's life again, it's a significance that can, I feel, be just as easily maintained by being occasionally together, and then at a comfortable distance with the help of British Telecom. The telephone and use of it (for people like me who don't like it) is a great indicator of a sharp rise in the loneliness graph. Lots of loneliness equals lots of calls.

If I had a daughter (which sadly I haven't, at least not in the literal sense, I do have a 'theatre daughter', Alex, a young girl actor after whom I look, coach and advise, berate and bolster), the one thing I would have struggled hard to provide her with would have been a home of her own, however humble. How many times did I find myself and all my worldly belongings, in my well-spent youth, on the pavement at midnight, because of some lovers' tiff. Or worse. How many times did I find myself struggling along in a relationship that had long since lost any glimmer of life, because I had nowhere else to go? The lies I had to tell myself and the Him in question, because I had nowhere else to lay my head. Of course there are many women who are trapped in situations economically, and maternally, where it just isn't possible for them to have their own home, should they so want it.

It does take courage to live alone. It's hard in these days of advertising the supremacy and desirous state of coupledom, not to feel rejected, unwanted, unsexy, or just plain discounted, living alone. Sleek cars are for cruising in à deux, fizzy drinks are drunk straight from the can with a mouth just beaded with the right amount of sweat on the top lip, as a magnet to the opposite sex. Use of this shampoo, or that conditioner will have some square-jawed, icy-eyed young beau, with his designer ruffled and greased hair, just slavering at the chops as you walk by tossing your locks. Now we know, those of us who live in the real world, that this just isn't the case. All the driving of my ten-year-old Honda Prelude has got me is a reduced number of appointments at the osteopath, because I chose a car for the lumbar support built into the seats. I don't drink straight from the can, because you never know where they've been, and knowing my luck I'd end up with a cut lip. Also I think it's bad manners. Quaint. But true.

And being a woman of a certain age, the only admiring glances I get for my hair are from my hairdresser, or girlfriends who are in awe of the variety of colours that my head has undergone in the space of one short year. We women of fifty-plus had a grounding in the feminism of the sixties, and learned, while we were cutting our equality teeth, to try at least not to define ourselves by whether we had a relationship with a man or not. Some thirty years into the course, I think I can probably state that I have acquired a beginner's badge.

No, it's not on the level of attractiveness or eligibility to the opposite sex (or the same, if that is your preference) that living alone hits hard. It's as simple as putting the key in my own front door after a hard day's work, and having no friendly, concerned voice call, 'How did it go?' or 'Never mind it'll go better tomorrow. I'll make you a cup of tea/Horlicks/pour you a glass of wine/offer you a shoulder to sob on, a razor to slash your wrists with…' etc, etc.

That front door, though, is in itself a symbol of triumph. I never owned a home of my own, before this one, where I have now lived for fifteen years, and waiting to acquire it till I was thirty-eight doesn't exactly put me in the successful infant prodigy or financial wizardry bracket. I had come out of a marriage where *I* lived in *his* house, and consequently never had the right to hang a picture or move a piece of furniture (except of course to hoover). He owned all the artwork and all the chairs and tables – there simply wasn't room for any more, and what's more he had a brilliant eye, and acute aesthetic taste for placing what he had. When I did finally move into my modest four up two down narrow terraced job, I played dolls' house for weeks. I simply couldn't believe that I wasn't going to hear from somewhere over my shoulder, as I rearranged pot plants, pictures and chairs, 'No you can't put that there!' I could and I did. Often. Just for the hell of it. Or rather for the sheer pleasure and the freedom of it. I like home-making and re-making. I suppose it's the transitory and insecure nature of my profession that makes me such a homebody. I like creating my own space.

And there lies the core of living with someone. Space. My goodness, did the upper classes of yore have it right! Their own dressing rooms. Who wants to sleep in a bedroom with his smelly socks and dirty underwear all over the floor? I've often marvelled at how most men, avid sports fans that they be, and active amateur tennis, cricket, football or golf fanatics, can be such rotten shots when it comes to placing clothes on chairs or in the dirty linen basket.

The answer which the rich also had, of course, is separate bedrooms. Ah! The bliss of it! Not having to grind your teeth with frustration or just plain hatred as he drifts into a deep sleep, three breaths after closing his eyes, while you lie awake staring at the ceiling, fighting not to stretch over and throttle the throat from whence are emitted, some three breaths after that, those wallpaper-shredding snores. No fights over the duvet, or whether to have the window closed or open either. But who in this day and age, apart from lottery winners, and the naturally mega-rich – if there is such a state naturally – can afford to have a bedroom each and one for meeting up in?

The logic of separate bedrooms speaks for itself. I feel the privacy of the smallest and most intimate room in the house should be protected at all costs. I'm not a prude. But it takes a strong man to stomach his beloved covered in white face pack, or soaking up to her nipples in strawberry-flavoured scum, or face tampax strewn all over the shelves; and the female cry against the residue of his razor; stubbly shaved-off hairs and grotty froth clogging up the sink, is universal from Clapham to Chile, and enough to turn any woman green as she spits into her mascara. Familiarity doesn't necessarily breed contempt but it can breed nausea. Mystery must be maintained.

Avoiding the humdrum has long been a topic for discussion amongst the betrothed in literature. As Millamant says to Mirabell on the subject of their proposed marriage in Congreve's witty Restoration comedy of manners *The Way of the*

World, 'Let us be very strange and well bred; let us be as strange as if we had been married a great while, and as well bred as if we were not married at all... [I wish] to come to dinner when I please, to dine in my dressing room when I'm out of humour, without giving a reason. To have my closet inviolate... and lastly, wherever I am, you shall always knock at the door before you come in...'

I suppose it's the inevitability of day-to-day living together, that gets me. The sheer grinding routine and habit of it, that dulls the freshness, and what should be the delight, of each new day. If you're bored and you live alone, you have no one to blame but the paucity of your own interests and the lack of an ability to amuse yourself.

I used to say to my ex-beau, whenever a plausible excuse presented itself, like having to get up to film at 5.30a.m., 'It's not that I don't want to sleep with *you*, it's that I want to sleep with *me* more.'

And there perhaps is the crux on which most relationships are originally based, and then ultimately flounder. People often stay together because of that old fear of being alone. Odd that isn't it? Video nasties and horror films sell by the million, but millions of people have the wherewithal to scare themselves rigid, right there on their own doorstep, without spending a cent or flicking a remote control, wherever they happen to be standing. Themselves, and solitude.

'The unexamined life is not worth living.' We use the presence of other people to staunch our fear of taking a good look at ourselves. We use the characters of other people to fill in the blanks that we find in our own. We project on to them the ability to give what we haven't got: self-esteem. And all goes well until that fateful day when they are more preoccupied with their own needs and wants and problems than ours. Then comes the crash. Anger with them and horror at facing how little we like ourselves.

You can't avoid how little you like yourself if you live alone. Then hopefully you can't avoid doing something to improve the situation. How can you like other people if you don't like yourself? Jean-Paul Sartre is often quoted as saying, 'Hell is other people.' I'd like to take issue with M. Sartre over this one. I think hell is oneself. Until you grow to understand, nurture and like yourself that is. Then your appreciation of others is sustained at a healthy distance and not fuelled by a voracious need. The best advice I heard a mother give a daughter was, 'Marry someone you love, not someone you need.'

I'm often surprised at how few people have managed to live alone for even the shortest length of time. They go from the comfort of the cradle to the chatter of school and the crazy freedoms of college into living with someone and then providing cradles for their own offspring. Is it any wonder that many marriages founder when children leave home? It's for most people the first time that they have ever been alone, and looking back on a life lived surrounded by others, can be a frightening business in the silence of isolation. Is it, too, the silence that we're frightened of? We go from the TV to the car radio, to the Sony Walkman to the dreadful music that they play in shops and lifts. Such healing can be found in silence. My dearest friends are the ones I can be quiet with.

I don't get invited to dinner parties often, I don't live that kind of social life. Also I'm an odd number – very difficult to place me round a dinner table when everyone is in twos. But when I do, if I'm feeling strong enough to battle the first round and overcome my sense of oneness, I see, often, couples who have long lacked any terms of endearment or gestures of affection. I don't inhabit a world where lack of affection is because of a withholding. Three of my closest friends all live alone. I guess we're like dog owners, and parents of small children – like attracts like – and hugs are high on our list when we meet. Only one of them is French, dear Lis, the nightdress washer, and for the other two English reserve doesn't come into it. We know a hug-needy person when we see one.

I go to the cinema alone sometimes, and I have treated myself to the occasional meal alone, mostly when working abroad. It's not an event I nurture on my own doorstep, I'd rather cook for myself. I indulge in all my favourite foods, and yes, I light candles on the kitchen table too. The one pre-requisite for a comfortable meal out alone is a good book. It stops you staring glassily into the middle distance, for fear of seeming to stare at other diners (I invent fanciful novels in my head about the couple on the next table, usually preposterous, if I'm book-less), but a book also prevents unwelcome advances, either vocal or visual, from a Passing Predatory Male, though I suppose at my age I ought to be grateful. The PPM has been the one reason I've avoided holidaying on my own since I got my fingers badly burned in one of the coldest spells Spain has ever known. With the prospect of a week of dinners in splendid isolation in a hotel restaurant – well, there simply aren't that many good books to go round without paying excess baggage. I came home after my fourth day. I know when I'm beaten. I thought I could be wind-chilled in Putney for a few pesetas less, and be alone more easily in the comfort of my own house, which, even with the present mortgage rates, comes nowhere near costing me £140 a night.

So the money I would put aside for holidays, if I had it, goes on my cottage in the Cotswolds, which I can't afford, where in less that two hours on the M40, I can transfer my lone London living to the soothing peace of country silence and the renewing beauty of fields and trees. Not that it stays silent for long. There's always someone popping their head round the back door for a cuppa, and always someone to say 'hello' to as I walk down the village street to the local shop-cum-post office which is a veritable hive of chatter and gossip. I attend the village church regularly – more 'hellos' and 'how are yous?' – and having renewed my small place in this community, I recharge my batteries by walking the nearby hills, and then sit of an evening by the crackling log fire.

> I am not one who much or oft delights
> To season my fireside with personal talk...
> Better than such discourse doth silence long,
> Long barren silence, square with my desire;
> To sit without emotion hope or aim,
> In the loved presence of my cottage fire...

(Kindling bought for fifty pence a box as off-cuts from the village hurdle maker.)

There in my cottage I receive comfort and nourishment for soul and body, and am filled with such gratitude for it and my overdraft.

Living alone I can write, read, draw, sit, sleep and eat, when I want to. I can get up in the middle of the night and guzzle a hot drink or just stare out at the night sky without a well-meaning 'Why are you getting up?' following me down the stairs. I can cook for friends when I want to and enjoy every minute of it, without my Jewish Motherness being activated into looking after people every minute of the day as I used to, when mother and partner. Like most mothers, I was good at mothering others, but bad at looking after my own needs. I didn't for a good while even know what they were. Since my son left I've had to learn to put myself back into the centre of my life.

Of course I get lonely. There are times when my interests fail to interest me, when my garden seems like all weeds and work and no pleasure. When the good book I thought I'd bought isn't. When an apple and a lump of cheese is all the cooking I can face. And when the silence in my house is more burden that boon. That's when I run up the phone bills. As I said, it's always a pretty reliable indication of my feeling lonely – the number of phone calls that I can make in an evening – and then sometimes as luck and my overdraft would have it, my friends are often out, away, working or just too busy to chat. But I think I prefer feeling lonely alone, to feeling lonely in the company of other people. (Stephen Sondheim, expressing his feelings about this subject in the musical *Company,* is fond of quoting Chekhov: 'If you're afraid of loneliness, don't marry'.)

When I was working on Broadway – one of the loneliest places in the world, centre stage on your own in a Broadway theatre – I remember hearing on the radio (a great friend and solace to those of us who live alone by the way) a Barbra Streisand song, with a line that came zinging out at me: 'It's a crime to feel lonely or sad.' I'd like to take issue with Ms

Streisand too. It isn't. It's just that we're all too frightened to admit that we do sometimes. Out of the closet all you lonely loners! It's only human.

In spite of my years alone I do think that a commitment to an ongoing relationship is the biggest challenge that any of us can undertake. So perhaps I will eventually look back on this time as a period of learning how to Be with myself, so that I can Be better when I'm in the company of other people.

The greatest gift that has been given to me from my years of living alone, is a very real and vivid pleasure in the company of other people. It's not that I didn't like people before. It's just that as a working mother and single parent I didn't have that much time left over at the end of a busy day, for anyone, perhaps least of all myself. I was always at full stretch. Now I have time. Time to Do less. And Time to Be more. Time to listen. Time to look. And Time to be grateful for the company of strangers.

Cats and Kindness

I think I could turn and live with animals they are so placid
and self-contained.
I stand and look at them long and long.
They do not sweat and whine about their condition.
They do not lie awake in the dark and weep for their sins.
They do not make me sick discussing their duty to God.
Not one is dissatisfied, not one is demented with the mania of
owning things.

Walt Whitman, *Song of Myself,* 1855

I am alone and quiet in my silent house. The cat sleeps curled
like a black comma on a stool exactly his size. He seems happy
enough. He sleeps a lot. During the day on an old tall chair, in
the evening it's the stool. He's old. Seventeen is old for a cat. He's
been with me here the entire time I've lived in this house. In fact
when I was thinking of moving last year, as I said, it didn't seem
right to move him. Cats are places people, not people people,
like dogs. They need their surroundings, I suspect, more than
they need us. So here we've stayed. I'm not soppy about cats
though. I like to feel I'm French, not English, about animals. The
French have a healthy rationality about house pets. Toto or
Loulou may be well loved, but it's under the table with them at
meal times, no begging for titbits, and farm dogs sleep outdoors
in kennels. It's always struck me as an extraordinary fact that
there is more ill-treatment of children in this country than

perhaps anywhere else in Europe, and yet our birthday cards have a sickly abundance of kittens tied up with ridiculous bows, and jumbles of puppies falling out of baskets. Show any of these real articles to a native of these shores, and you will elicit a plethora of sighs, oohs and ahs, that would be lost on a picture of a child with a runny nose and no shoes living in any of the urban wastelands or cardboard shanty towns that disgrace our big cities. When I did a poetry recital to raise money for charity recently in the village where I would like to pretend I live, the organiser, a well-meaning, good woman and one of the backbones of the parish, suggested that the money raised go to Romanian orphans. Of course I wouldn't dispute the desperate plight of these Romanian children. But why is it that charity dons a glow of glamour when its recipients are projected far from these shores? Do we feel worthier the further the money goes?

'What about giving the money to the old people in the village?' I suggested.

'There aren't any,' she said, adding, 'any who would take it.'

I couldn't believe it but I wouldn't dispute it. We'd already been once round the houses with my disinclination for the money to be given to the residential base for WI courses.

Me: 'Isn't that for rather well-to-do and middle-class women?'

Well-Meaning Good Woman: 'The WI was started for women in depressed rural areas...'

Me (not wanting a history of the WI – it's been going since 1915 and for goodness sake, I only had five minutes and a wig fitting to get to): 'Yes, but this isn't a depressed rural area, and won't non-WI people in the village resent collecting money to send women off on a weeks holiday to learn jam-making and appliqué?'

WMGW: 'We also learn to...'

I never found out what – but as a compromise the money went to replacing some stained glass in the church window. Not quite what my altruism had intended. But at least I've made my mark on the village. And as the church is mostly attended by the old, they get to benefit from it in a round about way. At least she didn't suggest we send it to the Cats' Protection League. Not

that there's anything *wrong* with the Cats' Protection League, but if we are to believe in the ladder of evolvement of souls in the reincarnation book, and our furry friends are just a rung below us humans, then surely we should get our priorities right? People before pets.

Of course we have an obligation to care for our dumb friends and for animals who can't look after themselves. I've been regaled with a myriad of stories in my time, as has everyone I'm sure, about the amazing dog that can open the fridge door, and help himself to his own food (and probably everyone else's) and the astonishing cat who helps herself to grapes from the fruit bowl. Why is it that people are surprised when animals can do what humans do? Shouldn't we be astonished that even a seventeen-year-old cat's backbone (that's 119 to you and me) is still so pliable that it can sleep with its nose tucked up in its feet, and can still clear a three-foot jump? I bet Jeanne Calment and all of her amazing 121 years couldn't have done that when she was alive and hadn't been able to since she was *très petite*.

But canines can't be trusted not to press the defrost button and felines cannot live on Vitamin C alone. Some time or other since *we* got up on our hind legs and moved out of the post-primeval forests, and the cat and dog came too (they knew which side their bread was about to be buttered on), sooner or later we had to wield the tin-opener for their benefit. Or the scissors. My cat won't eat tinned food. Not tinned food for cats. Well, would you want to eat the same vile-smelling mush day after day? What's for breakfast? Tinned rice. Lunch? Tinned rice. Supper? You get the picture.

And ludicrously, animals' tinned food is made to smell like what *we* would enjoy. The pet-food manufacturers sure have got their wires crossed. Everyone knows dogs, especially, like misshapen, bacteria-ridden lumps of grot which were aimed at the dustbin and missed. And have lain there, just under the skirting board, for about three weeks. Cats prefer anything that is not at dish level. If they have to jump or climb to forbidden places, the food takes on a magnetic extra savour. It's like the apples we used to scrump (can I hear the jeers of modern youth, who'd probably see more of a challenge in shoplifting a video?) hard, green and unripe, but better-tasting by far than the tame dish of Golden Delicious on the kitchen table.

I'm sure they spice up cat and dog food with all sorts of dreadful addictives. That's why those cats and dogs in adverts go bananas over yet another dish of brown lumpy jelly. Oh goody goody, another fix. Another high. More. More.

Have you ever noticed that dogs and cats eat real food, if they can get it, in quite a different way? There's a kind of sedate enjoyment about eating real food, that demands, even from them, another quality of attention. I'm not talking about the animals that think they are doubling as hoovers, whatever's on their plate. They've probably got worms, or something worse, if they always eat that fast. Or if they're still at an age when it doesn't matter what's on the menu, as long as it's chewy. The chair leg, abandoned slippers, the phone... This sedate enjoyment is probably preceded by a few moments of total shock. My god what's *this*... Sniff. It's not lumpy, it's not jelly. Sniff. It's what *they* eat! Slowly now, there must be a reason why they've dished it out to me. If they don't want it, it must be *off*.

Cats, though, are renowned for turning up their noses at humans' leftover food. Salmon terrine? You can't fool me, it's got chopped-up cucumber and crème fraîche in it. Yuk. No thank *you!* That's why I love cats. They're arrogant and independent. You've put that piece of material to protect the chair? Fine, I'll go and sleep on the sofa. Or better still the bed.

Yes, I know I said I wasn't soppy about animals, but I do let him sleep on the bed. Well, I figure if he's bright enough to have sussed it's the warmest, softest place in the house and he gets stroked and made a fuss of into the bargain if I'm in it too, then he deserves to be there, just through sheer enterprise. And cats are clean. He washes himself more than I wash myself. Mind you I don't sick fur balls all over the best Axminster when I've had a bath, but I have, in a wet rush, walked the Body Shop's best body foam all up the stairs to answer the phone.

If I stroke him on his stomach when he's not in the mood, he's just as liable to claw me as to purr, and I respect that awareness of his own physical territory, and am not a little frightened of his unpredictability. I suppose that capriciousness is the basis for the cat being allied with the feminine principle. In Jungian psychology the female side of the male psyche, the anima, is represented by the cat. The cat, too, is often twinned in symbolism with the moon, another icon of femininity and changeability. There is something deeply mysterious at the centre of the cat. Something Other. The dog can be known. But never the cat in entirety. That's also probably at the root of cats being linked with witches as their familiars, and often associated with magic. The dog is much more pedestrian. He'll always be happy to see you. Cats are more discriminating. They have to be wooed. I like that feeling of not being able to take cats for granted, or rather their affection for you for granted. The best of best friends are the ones who put you in your place if you've presumed on your friendship, or give you a hefty pat back when you've come off the tracks. Unpredictable but friendly. It's that mixture of wild and tame that is such a paradox, so mysterious and beguiling. It's not a great leap of imagination from the cat to the tiger. In the wild they taunt and tease their prey before killing it – a spectacle of awful fascination. There's apparently no mention of a cat in the Bible. Perhaps over the period when the Old Testament was written, the image of the pagan Egyptian cat god, Bast, was too close for comfort.

My cat does, after a fashion, 'sit' when I tell him to, when I've had enough of him pawing my stomach or my legs when I'm trying to read in bed. He's not a particularly intelligent animal, but he knows a lack of attention when he sees one, and will often try to shift my script out of the way with his nose. I suspect this feeling about intelligence, or the lack of it, is mutual. If I've forgotten in the hurry-scurry of the day, to feed him his evening meal, he just sits by the doorway near his dish looking fixedly at it, till I notice or nearly trip up on him. He doesn't even raise his eyes as I reach for the scissors, although his ears do twitch in the direction of the snipping noise. I love his cool. I wish I had it. Especially when I was younger. I have a dreadful feeling I was the labrador puppy type. Indiscriminate affection, a lot of approval-seeking licking and intrusive high spirits.

Yes, I have to take the scissors to my cat's food. He likes sliced turkey from Sainsbury's, and it has to be cut up small. Teeth aren't high on his list of daily implements. So turkey it is. That's breakfast. For supper it's tuna fish. We arrived at this diet by a process of elimination. He eliminated all the other food I served him with a quick disdainful sniff, a swish of his tail, followed by a lightning exit through the cat door.

Occasionally, if I've been away for a few days, I serve him guilt food. Prawns and chicken. The guilt food presented itself as a solution to my being with the RSC in Stratford for nearly a year, and him giving me the socks to go away with as it were, by disappearing on my return for days on end. Playing hard to get. Feline cold shoulder for a couple of days is all very well, but when I had to turn round and go back to the Bard's birthplace on the third day, all I ever saw was the empty dishes where the food had been. So I grabbed him, when he did deign to show, and gave him a good talking to. I don't mean diddums language. I mean, 'Hey you! I pay all that money for your food and I never see you! You just eat it and bolt! I have to go away because I'm working... and... Well I'm not having it! You're supposed to be my friend. So be my friend. I need your company'.

He narrowed his eyes and blinked in a dismissive way. Now I know he couldn't understand the words I was saying. Like the cartoon, where the cat owner is going into effusive verbal raptures over his animal and all the cat hears is Blah blah blah blah, and then his name. But he stayed. And now it only takes a couple of minutes when I come back from being away before he's purring again. Could it be prawn and chicken conditioning?

Well, the whole point of a cat is company and cuddles, especially if you live alone as I do. I wake up in the morning, come downstairs to make my coffee and while it's filtering I stick my nose in his fur. The house doesn't feel so empty when there he is, stretched out along the front window sill, exactly the length of the gap between the pots of plants above the radiator in winter, or in the patch of sunlight on the carpet by the armchair, whenever we have sun. There's a joke amongst film people that if you want to know the warmest place on a freezing film location, or the place on the set that's sheltered from the wind, find out where the sparks are. Well, cats are like electricians – the best spots are second nature to them. Feng Shui experts make a fortune out of selling knowledge about the best spots in a house. Save your money – watch a cat.

Also, cats are expert at feigning indifference in embarrassing situations. He recently fell off the window ledge while sleeping. Well, he is 119. You wouldn't be too clever on a space that's eight inches wide at that age either. He fell with a thump to the floor. Instantaneously he had this overwhelming interest in his left leg. Imagine the chairman of the board falling asleep and exhibiting, on waking, such a passion for a trouser turn-up. It would save a lot of embarrassed looks elsewhere as he came to.

On a tuna fish and turkey-buying expedition recently, I had a conversation at the supermarket check-out. It was an unusually quiet time, and consequently the atmosphere then can be vaguely, only vaguely, reminiscent of the old corner shop, when there's only forty-three people in the queue and not 507. The assistants like to chat on these occasions to the customers, undoubtedly to break the appalling monotony of sitting on those ridiculously uncomfortable chairs and listening to that infuriating 'ding!' as the machine reads the bar codes on the products. Or the even louder but lower 'bleep' if it doesn't.

'You sure do like tuna fish,' said a delightfully rotund lady with a wide smile, a Jamaican lilt and generous earrings that denoted that she was probably from the wilder shores of Brixton.

Oh God, I thought, this is going to be embarrassing. I'm probably spending more on cat food than she has to spend in a week on her children...

'It's for my cat,' I stammered.

'Your cat?' she guffawed. All forty-two people in the queue suddenly found me far more interesting than the bizarre diet in the basket of the person in front of them – fig rolls, diet coke, spaghetti hoops and turnips, and the man without his soya milk – his complexion looked like he drank soya milk, – suddenly stopped worrying about whether he could hoof it over to aisle fifteen and get back with the weekly tofu in time for his turn. All eyes were glued on me. Ah hah! – an event. Something to brighten up the appalling drudgery of schlepping round this mausoleum twice a week buying things we can't afford and don't want and didn't mean to have, but it was a special offer, so I bought two...

'Yes.' I could feel myself go scarlet. 'He's seventeen.'

'Oh, at dat age he deserve treat!' She beamed and I beamed back. I didn't have the guts to tell her I was vegetarian and the seven packets of sliced turkey in the basket – his weekly supply – were for the cat too. Sometimes it pays to masquerade as a carnivore.

So I too wield a tin-opener once a day. He has me well trained. He's the only cat I've ever really had. Someone gave my foster mother and me a cat when I was quite small, and being the disturbed child that, in retrospect, I evidently was, I spent most of the moments he was unguarded enough to allow me to catch him dropping him into the lavatory by the coal shed and watching him jump out. Jungians would have a field day over that one.

But this one I rescued from the needle which leads to the great cattery in the sky. His owners were headed back to the States, and he and his brother, who now lives next door (my next door neighbour, a lonely pensioner, stole him) came as a job lot. What they didn't tell me was they'd been hit with newspapers when they misbehaved. So consequently if anything remotely resembling paper was rustled (tinfoil noise being inevitable in the making of my son's sandwiches for his school lunchbox), these two traumatised cats would disappear under the nearest piece of furniture, and refuse to come out for days. So it's been one of my life's triumphs to win this creature round. It took two years. I've won him round enough to be able to grab him by the scruff of his neck and shake him with love, and hear him go on purring. But he'll still get up and go if he wants to. The cat who walked by himself. I shall miss him when he goes. And, undoubtedly, weep buckets. But I probably won't go out and get another. Cats are like decisions. We don't choose them, they choose us. Best let them come to you.

I hope, then, that I can remember these words by Jean-Paul Sartre, which by some extraordinary coincidence I just happened to come across while I was writing this: 'When we love animals and children too much we love them at the expense of men.'

Over and Out

I love to stay at home. When I'm home. Packing suitcases, for which I could compete for the gold olympic speed medal, is fine when my work insists I tour, or film on location, or when my yearning for the hills inclines me cottagewards. But when I have a wodge of time that doesn't include a travel itinerary, then I dig my heels in. The 'gardens', front and back, receive a lot of TLC, the broken banister gets glued again, that cupboard hinge with a decided droop gets replaced – amid much spitting and fuming and silent prayers to the patron Saint of DIY – and I cook. I love to cook. A day spent in my kitchen with the radio for company and a new recipe to challenge and try out on friends is my idea of heaven. No going through the emotional shredder of a performance, no being under scrutiny, just pottering about in my kitchen, humming tunelessly and avoiding treading on the unsuspecting cat, in harmony with my own sense of time. Balm to the soul.

I know all the cookbooks say that you shouldn't try out a recipe for the first time when you've friends to feed. But I would never have mastered Tarte Tatin if my dear friend Maurice Denham hadn't let slip his predilection for it one night before coming to eat at my house. My friend David's stoic veganism gave me the necessary spur to tackle a Potato Pithivier Pie that would otherwise have been omitted from my repertoire, and he would have been faced with yet another dish of spicy chickpeas and yoghurt. I guess I like the challenge of having to get the new dish right, there and then, because if I

don't there's damn all else in the fridge to feed them with. I
have been known to say that I wouldn't quibble if theatre
critics criticise my acting, but criticism of my cooking is serious
trouble. It's not true about the theatre critics of course. I
simply avoid reading reviews. Strength of mind isn't in it. It's
pure and simple self-protection. But criticism of my cooking
offends the very roots of my Jewish Motherness. If I were
Jewish. that is. That's a family rumour that's been fed partly by
my not knowing who my father was (I know it goes through
the female line, but even so...), but it's mostly a label that
suits me well as I overload the plates the second time around.
'Yes, I'd like some more, Ma, but not the Jewish helping,
thank you'.

The Earth Mother in me swells and grows with satisfaction
and contentment at the prospect of a table of people to feed.
Feeding four, I shop for eight. Feeding two, I shop for four,
and so on. I think it might have something to do with being a
war baby, growing up in a time when everything was scarce,
and noticing, even when I was quite small, that my foster
mother's pantry rarely had more than one or two things in it.
My cupboards are always full. Ditto the freezer. It might be
siege mentality: what if I ran out and there wasn't any more?
But mostly I suspect it's the squirrel instinct. Helped by an
innate, congenital flair for extravagance.

Food plays a big part in my life. I love to cook it, and I love
to eat it. Good food that is. I'm a food snob when I'm eating
out. And a pretend Rothschild when I'm buying for eating in.
In both places I'm a guts.

I'd have to confess to the venal sin of asking for certain
things to be taken off a dish if I suspect that the chief chef in a
restaurant's kitchen is Monsieur Microwave. 'Could I have the
deep-fried goat's cheese salad please?' All innocence, 'Is it
cooked on bread?'

'Yes.'

'Could I have it without?'

Crisis. I see before my eyes neat little rounds of pre-packed, polythened circles of goat's cheese, nestling on and inseparable from the same-sized rounds of bread. Untouched by human hands since they left the goat's cheese and bread clamping machine in the factory. All ready for a quick spin round the microwave.

I can't afford to indulge my snobbery and eat at the Ivy or the Caprice when I'm doing theatre work – the money just won't stretch to those dizzy heights. TV and film work will, but my preference for those places has got nothing to do with the clientele having largely a theatrical bias, it's simply that the food's so damn good. As is the River Café's – a meal there was a Christmas present from some friends who can afford to live in the South of France and eat in this works' canteen in Hammersmith.

I'm not good in crowds. My deaf ear may have something to do with it – it's hard to hear the person who's speaking next to you when the background noise is at Good Ear-splitting level. And being crowd-phobic, I have an in-built loathing of the tube. I'd rather get up an hour earlier and brave it by bus. Travelling back from a performance, nerves raw and self shellless, on the London Underground where no one can afford to indulge their need for private space, or their respect for anyone else's territory, even if they had it, is guaranteed to send me into an inwardly screaming panic.

So what a quandary am I in then, when good food is served in large places.

Brave New Food

The meek don't want it.

GRAFFITI ON A WALL

I have seen the future and it's rude. Not tits and bums rude. Pushing and shoving rude. Plus lots of attitude. I went last night with some much younger friends to a fashionable venue in London's West End. Now I count myself lucky to have younger friends, indeed my sense of luck could reasonably be described as pride. I'm proud that they should seek out my company and even prouder that they should deem it enjoyable. But often the age gap becomes what is really a taste gap, and last night proved the point.

My idea of a good night out, especially a Friday night out, is largely to avoid using any road in London that is remotely westerly in its direction, as much of the population in London that has four, two or six wheels tends to head West from about eleven in the morning. Secondly, although it's east from Putney, Friday night in the West End should be avoided whatever the cost. There is a kind of manic determination to enjoy oneself that pervades Fridays east of Green Park, and west of the Aldwych, and where they meet in the middle – bedlam. I'm not talking about groups of our foreign friends with the spirit of sightseeing upon them, talking in tongues and hung about with cameras, but about the avenging hordes of natives from our own shores (largely the banks, and Banks, of the Thames) who descend on Piccadilly Circus and Leicester Square, in dogged pursuit of A Good Time. Perhaps what they're avenging is the week spent in the office.

It's always struck me as curious that the English have to enjoy themselves in large groups. Is it that the puritan ethic still wreaks havoc at some deep level of the subconscious, and consequently going out to enjoy oneself is still a pastime fraught with such guilt that there's comfort and strength in being surrounded by like-minded sinners? Sin safely in numbers. Safe is the last thing any sole intrepid wanderer might feel trying to get from one side of the Circus to another on a Friday night – I'm talking pavements here. It's probably safer to walk in the streets. At least with the buses, taxis and cars being at a virtual and constant standstill, there's less likelihood of being mown down on the tarmac. On the pavement it's quite another survival course.

We parked the car only two streets away from the birthday-party rendezvous, a small side street within spitting distance of Piccadilly Circus. That in itself was nothing short of a miracle. Not the spitting. That's become an increasingly familiar health hazard of late, I've noticed. Banana skins are now old hat. You can slip on spit in some of the most exclusive quarters of the capital.

I've always been a lucky parker. There are parking-place angels whose help I invoke, and who never – well, hardly ever – fail me. I don't seem to have quite the same hotline to the lottery angels, or to the angels who preside over vacant and *cheap* country cottages with thatched roofs and roses growing round the door. But I'm working on those two. The one of course being concomitant on the other. Maybe there's a good luck angel who could encompass the workload of the other two and reduce my praying time.

The car safely stowed, its anti-burglar device activated, no, not the car alarm, my own home-grown, as yet unpatented deterrent – rubbish scattered all over the floor, the A to Z open and spilling out old bits of hand-drawn maps on scraps of paper, half-full bottles of water on the seats, a tatty umbrella, empty wine-gum bags, discarded cassette boxes, a back-support cushion, and a dirty chamois cleaning sponge stuck in front of the radio – enough, I would have thought to deter any self-respecting car thief, plus the fact that the car is ten years old and unwashed since my last visit to the country, and consequently covered in bird shit.

That was the easy bit of the evening. We fought our way through the next fifty yards of pavement. People were just milling about seemingly with no sense of direction. It was difficult to see a way through. Had the entire population of the metropolis been drawn to the centre as if by some unseen hand, I wondered, and then been struck by mass amnesia? My unvoiced question was answered only a few struggling feet and digging elbows later, when my son, who knowing well my dislike of crowds disengaged the hand he had put in one of mine to haul me from A to B with as little fuss and protestation on my part as possible, announced, 'That's it.' He indicated with a nod of his head what I could just discern to be a small doorway ahead of us, around which the massing hordes seemed to be at their thickest and most buzzing. Inwardly I blanched, and had it not been for the affection and esteem in which I held my birthdaying friend, I would have turned tail and fled there and then. Well, given the crowds, tried to turn and stagger.

'Come *on*, Ma,' said my son, accurately sensing my flagging enthusiasm and giving me a push at least metaphorically. No self-respecting twenty-three-year-old wants to be seen in the West End on a Friday night holding his mother's hand. Even I, crowd phobic that I am, could see that.

I was right about the people in the doorway buzzing. It was abuzz with resentment. The resentment of trying to get in and being prevented. And it was only 7.45 p.m.

There were several tall, very beautiful black men standing inside the entrance. Bouncers, I thought, only they didn't look very aggressive. That was left to a rather small, square white chap who made up in attitude what he lacked in height.

'Yes?' he questioned us, in a surly manner that had hidden in its depths the sense that we were somehow in the wrong for having had the temerity to come through the crowd to the front of the queue. Between us we meekly mumbled our friend's name and the details of the evening. 'They're already here,' he said tersely. Wrong again. Well, they had said half-past seven and it was 7.45, but it was the West End and it was Friday – didn't he know?

As we went to walk past him, he almost barred our way and said, 'Have you been here before?' Actually he didn't say it. Again it was that subtle mixture of resentment and blame.

'Yes,' said my son, bluntly – which was true. He had. I wanted to say, 'What on earth has that go to do with us being here now, being invited by our friends? Would you not have let us in, if we hadn't been here before?' But I could hear that my son's patience fuse was getting shorter.

'Go *on*, Ma,' he said, rather irritably.

So on I went, down several flights of stairs (behind young women talking loudly, tossing their long newly washed hair, obviously in a great hurry), to find myself in the semi-dark, which, when my eyes had become accustomed to the murk, I discovered was in an open space that resembled a railway hall edged with several kiosks, one selling magazines, another the place where we were to leave our coats. I took my coat off and stood for several minutes while the two young women behind the counter engaged in what was obviously a very intense conversation about something or someone in one of the two vast rooms that gave on to the hall. Eventually one of them looked at me in rather a quizzical manner, I handed her my coat which she took roughly, her eyes and her mind still elsewhere. She just stood there and so did I. I ventured,

'Do I get a ticket?' She looked at me in a most bemused fashion. I was about to say, I don't mind not having a ticket, really I don't. If this is the new way you do things, that's fine by me. I'm sure I could recognise my coat at the end of the evening, you see, it's got a brooch on the left lapel...

'Yes,' she said, inflected with such a naked despising that no one could have failed to get the subtext – 'Of course you get a ticket, you idiot.'

I followed my son, duly chastened, to a vast palatial room interrupted by pillars picked out in gold leaves at their tops. I can never remember if the ones with leaves are Doric, Ionic or Corinthian. This was not the moment to clear up the lack in my classical education. Hundreds, yes hundreds of people were having supper. The noise was astonishing. Thankfully no music, just people talking and eating. The chatter echoed round the vastness. The walls, which I could just distinguish in the distance, were painted purple and hung with several ornate gold mirrors and what I supposed must be bits of modern art – one had neon lights that flashed numbers on and off. There were tables with starched white tablecloths and little blue nightlights burning on them everywhere, as far as the eye could see. And dozens of waiters weaving in and out of them, carrying silver trays high above their heads.

I simply couldn't believe I was in London. It reminded me exactly of the faded grandeur of some of the palaces I had seen in St Petersburg. Those stately lavish icons of a monarchial past, that dripped chandeliers and priceless works of art inside, and yet outside, crumbling and disintegrating, were propped up with scaffolding. In spite of all the gold leaf, I felt there was an air of decline about the place, coupled with the grim determination for enjoyment that often accompanies decline. I remonstrated silently with myself for becoming fanciful, put it down to hypo-glycaemia, and was more than relieved when my son spotted our friends, way over by the far wall, and guided me to their table.

A waiter, in shirt sleeves, appeared almost immediately. We had hardly time to say our hellos, and exchange our birthday wishes, when this very personable chap – the first indication we had had that anyone who worked in this establishment was remotely patron friendly – Chinese or Japanese I guessed, but with an American accent, appeared to take our drinks orders. Things were looking up. The orders placed, another shirtsleeved waiter appeared with a basket full of different kinds of bread, of which the raisin and nut was so excellent I had to eat three slices one after the other and wash them down with a not bad at all glass of red Zinfandel.

Another chap appeared, black-suited and unsmiling, to take our orders. We weren't ready. He became momentarily more unsmiling, then disappeared. The menu was atlas size and there was a lot of competition between my taste buds, my hunger, and my head. Eventually my taste buds won on the first course, salmon fillet stuffed with potatoes creamed with chervil and topped with a dollop (minute at it turned out) of caviar – my choice here probably due to my heightened sense of Imperialist Russia – and my hunger won on the entrée, sea bass. The food orders were then duly given to him of the non-smile, who was reminded by the birthday girl that our party was still two short, a fact that was met with stony-faced silence – blissfully she was too happy to notice – and he again disappeared as silently as he had come. Then the wine, a red Pinot Noir from Oregon was chosen, via shirt-sleeved waiter number three, and arrived instantly, unlike the two remaining friends, who were either embroiled in a fight upstairs to get in or had been held up at home by their eight-month-old daughter refusing to go to sleep. I knew which I would prefer.

'It would be awful if it wasn't for the food,' shouted my son from the other side of the curved shell of a sofa on which the four of us sat. I was astonished at how accurately he had read my mind, and how benevolent he was being. He was by then, I think, on his second gin and tonic. The noise had increased in volume, and with dread I could just hear loud music beginning to challenge the level of the conversation between us all and those around us. I had another slice of bread and took a swig of Oregon's best. It was superb. I nodded and smiled benevolently back.

The first course arrived via he of the black suit and the black look. I should have known better.

'Would it be possible to have some more bread?' I asked innocently.

'More bread?' he repeated disbelievingly. I had obviously transgressed some unspoken house rule. He did his silent disappearing act again. The disapproval was palpable.

The food looked and tasted wonderful. The risotto, penne, and prawns in ginger all met with grunts of pleasure which fortunately went unremarked by our near neighbours, whose own levels of laughter and good humour had risen considerably. It was like eating in Grand Central Station with the catering done by the Caprice. The plates were whisked from under our noses the second we had finished. Amazingly good service, I thought, much cheered by the victuals and the liquor.

The birthday girl – Hedi, my Hungarian neighbour – remarked how like the old cafés in Budapest the place was, cafés where writers and artists would meet and talk.

'France too,' I added, thinking of the cafes with painted murals and elegant mirrors that edged one side of La Place du Capitole in Toulouse. I looked around me. Most of the clientèle were under thirty-five. In fact I realised I was probably the oldest person in the place. They were all fashionably and expensively dressed. The tight black miniskirt was much in evidence, ditto vast expanses of leg, bare shoulders and lacy see-through tops. Not many artists here, I thought. Where did all these young people work? That they worked was not in question. The prices of the dishes would be well beyond anyone not working. I knew. I wasn't. Neither was my son. The bill would pinch a bit.

Hedi and Mike's missing friends arrived as our main course did. The baby, not the bouncer, was to blame. They had the presence of mind to be seated as quickly as possible under the basilisk stare of he who bore the food with the undertaker air, and ordered just one course – whether by desire or the necessity of causing minimal fuss I didn't know.

The birthday girl's husband, he of the excellent taste in wine, and a need to live dangerously, devoured his steak and pronounced it excellent, as was the sea bass, the lobster and whatever it was that my son had. Oregon's blushing grape had me too well in its power to notice. I was at the beginning of a love affair that I intended to pursue whenever the confines of my purse would allow, and the increased horizons of my local wine merchant permit.

A good meal was had by all. Dessert? No. Birthday cake had been ordered. There was a momentary kerfuffle at the table as the plates were cleared away and the birthday cake mentioned. Troubled whispers and consternation amongst shirt-sleeved numbers two and three. Black suit must have been summoned, because suddenly He was there. Or maybe he was employed for his psychic powers. It certainly wasn't for his PR. Or maybe it was. He stood unspeaking, looking down on us while one of his minions suggested we might like to eat our cake in Dick's Bar. He obviously didn't need to communicate by anything as mundane as the words used by the rest of us mere mortals.

'No,' I said, the reason for the super quick service suddenly becoming horribly clear. Emboldened by sea bass and Oregon's best, I said quietly, 'They want us out so they can squeeze another table in. No, you paid for this table, Michael.' Michael was beginning to look unsure about our continued residency. Was this another rule of the Brave New World? I was suddenly overcome with feeling old-fashioned. 'No, Michael,' I said. 'No.'

We stayed.

The chocolate birthday cake was a marvel. A melting fondant coating, and a squishy creamy interior that sandwiched the two halves together. The others had decided previously to go on dancing somewhere after. 'Adrenalin Village,' they pronounced with relish. Well, that did it. I decided I would go home. I'd had quite enough adrenalin for one evening. I knew when I was beaten. Or I thought I did. That was before we decided to make a visit to the ladies' loo as an intermediary stop before I faced the renewed hordes upstairs.

The loo had a queue. What a great British tradition the queue in the ladies' loo is, and this was no exception. A silent line of women standing obediently one behind the other, looking vaguely into the middle distance, vaguely disconcerted about having to be in a place for which the purpose was evidently clear and vaguely rude. We obediently joined the queue and observed the rules. All the young women there had a polish and veneer of worldly sophistication and self-assurance. The shine was glass-hard. And the silence crystal sharp. I thought of the comfortable middle-aged chats I was now party to in ladies' loos... That's a nice dress. It really suits you. Thank you... Does this ladder show?... I've put on such a lot of weight since I last wore this jacket, does it look awful?... Have you got a safety pin? Do my grey roots show?

Is it that getting older gives us a common enemy, the increase of wrinkles and the increase of waistlines, provoking a mellowness that comes with that acceptance, making us accomplices in mutual adversity and sisters under the skin, as well as because of it? Why did these young women see each other as enemies at one extreme and competitors at the other? For surely that was the reason for their non-communication? Where had all those years of sixties sisterhood gone? Was the battle still to get a man at all costs, and see any other attractive female as a threat and an obstacle to that end? I felt being older gave me the right to look around and observe these disconcerting, unfamiliar younger members of the species – my new found friend from Oregon, too, probably had something to do with my sense of courage.

A young woman came out of the loo with hair as spiky and black as Cruella de Vil, and as it turned out, an attitude to match. Pointing to the table, on which was arrayed a collection of cosmetic aids (something unseen by me in a ladies' lavatory before – perhaps it was by way of recompense for the hefty bill, and even heftier service, I mused), she said to the round-faced, kindly Oriental woman whose job was obviously to preside over this silent gathering, 'This hair spray has run out. Get some more.' And then added as she turned to the washbasin, as an afterthought, 'Jimmy.'

Well, that did it. I turned, unthinking, to the young woman behind me, a pretty blonde in an ice-blue dress that added to her glacial demeanour and said, 'Why are people so rude here? I've never been in such a rude place in my life.'

I expected her to freeze me out. Surprisingly her face broke into a wide smile, the ice maiden melted and said, 'I know. It's *awful*, isn't it.'

The whole atmosphere in the lavatory changed. People relaxed and let go of their projected self-possession. I think even conversations were struck up. No more stuck up. Goodness me. Women talking to each other. I was glad to be going home.

Having fought to get in, we had to fight to get out, but this time I was more enthusiastic. Having been in, though, didn't apparently bestow on us the right to be treated politely on the way out. There was no Good Housekeeping seal of approval stamped on us for having graced this emporium with our presence and our money. My son, keen to make he of the squat appearance (who was now virtually manhandling the swollen numbers in the doorway) aware that he was only accompanying me to the car and would be returning – and they would let him back in, wouldn't they (glutton for punishment he) – had to state his request several times before the bouncer, obviously more keen on bouncing than on listening to polite inquiries, deigned to turn his very valuable attention on us. Meanwhile I turned to one of the beautiful black men and said, 'It's awful here. Why is everyone so rude?'

He smiled and said, 'Yes, I know, it's awful.'

We were right. It was awful.

My son said as we reached the car, 'Will you be all right to drive, Ma?'

'Of course I will,' I said, 'I've only had two glasses of wine.'

But I was wrong. I wasn't all right to drive. Only a few yards out from my miraculous parking space a taxi carved me up, edging his way, I thought unfairly, in front of me. I wound down my window and was very rude. I then drove aggressively out of a congested West End.

Stay away from the young. They're a corrupting influence.

Of course my grumpiness at noise, crowds, bad waiters and slow food in large spaces could be put down to my deafness, or the one leitmotif that coloured all this year, that I've been avoiding even mentioning in much the same way that for ages I neatly forgot that I was deaf when it suited me. While we're talking age and crumbling faculties, I can avoid it no longer. I'm menopausal.

Apparently there are tribes in the dim dark recesses of Africa or South America, for whose women the menopause is greeted with rapturous joy and celebration. I remember reading an article about how several European male anthropologists had to defend themselves continuously against these tribal women of a certain age, who jumped all over them, without so much as a by your leave, with offers of gaily, daily abandoned sex. They were somewhat crestfallen when the chance to celebrate their freedom from the previously obligatory results of intercourse were politely declined.

The anthropologists found no evidence of night sweats, hot flushes or mood swings, except, perhaps, their own. It would seem from this, and other studies (see *The Change* – Germaine Greer is, not surprisingly, very vocal on this subject) that the negative effects of the menopause, both psychological and physical, are a Western blight, stemming largely from the West's attitude to women who are no longer deemed viable as mothers, fanciable as sex objects, or marketable as an adman's target.

Middle age at last declares itself
As the time when could-have-been
Isn't wishful thinking any more...

Yes, well...

Already I am no longer looked at with lechery or love.
My daughters and sons have put me away with marbles and
    dolls
Are gone from the house.
My husband and lovers are pleasant or somewhat polite,
    and night is night.
It is a real chill out.
The genuine thing.

But instead of going under all this negative publicity, isn't
there something that we ourselves can do? Can't we celebrate
this age, take a leaf out of our jungle sisters' book and embrace
(once we've got over the temporary problem-state) our
problem-free state?

You know what you want when you're middle-aged. Or
better, what you don't want. You've had a chance to grow
comfortable inside your own skin – you've been wearing it long
enough. The struggles and the discomforts, not always resolved
or healed, leave it a little wrinkled. One learns to accept the
ridges, inside and out. 'There is beauty in an agèd face.' You
look like who you are, who you have grown to be. You know
who you are, and free from the rages and torments of identity
stricken youth, you, connected inside, can spend a lot more
time thinking inwards and doing outwards. Putting back some
of that which you've been lucky enough to take out. Or if
you've been luckier, some of that which has come your way
without your asking. You have ideas about the world and your
place in it, both of which will hopefully go on being challenged
and changed. You have to take more care of yourself to ensure

that the energy is there to face those challenges. But self-nurture creates its own affecting aura. Each day, after a certain age, when many much-loved friends are no longer in the body, comes as a gift, no longer a right, and as such can be received with thanks. Time has changed its attitude to you, knowing that you won't be rushed, knowing that you will make time for the things that you deem vital for as much harmony as possible, and your perception of its changing has changed you.

My dear friend Maurice Denham, who recently celebrated – and that is the word – his arrival at his eighty-eighth year, doesn't subscribe to the recital of the catalogue of failing powers. When I asked him what were the good things about getting older, he replied without a second's hesitation, 'You can say what you bloody well like.'

Menopausal Madness

Rule youth well; for age will rule itself

FERGUSSON, 1641

The afternoon of human life must also have a
significance of its own, and cannot be merely a
pitiful appendage to life's morning.

CARL GUSTAV JUNG, 1875–1961

I'm menopausal. Are you shocked? Well I am. I must belong to
the millions of women who thought it wouldn't happen to
them. Like death. I'm immortal. Or in this case, eternally young.
I thought. Of course the fact that I can mention it at all is an
indication of the outspokenness of my generation of women. Or
is it? Us feminists of the sixties who are frank about our bodily
functions, unlike the women of past generations who kept all
those female 'problems' quiet, and suffered in silence, bearing
the ravages and torments that their bodies inflicted on them to
themselves, thinking that it was their own peculiar personal
problem. We share ours. Or do we? We've come out of the
closet, or rather the bathroom, and have told it like it is. Or have
we? I've been amazed, talking on this subject (I was in danger of
calling it an issue – it does seem that way for some women) by

how many of my female friends do a neat sidestep whenever the 'M word' is mentioned.

'Well, I've never had it. I went straight on to HRT.'

'Well, I've got it, but I don't know what all the fuss is about.'

'No, I'm fifty-four, and it hasn't happened yet. Isn't it amazing? My boyfriend/husband/lover is really fed up…' This is said with a smile of such condescension and pity for those of us for whom natural menstruation is a thing of the past, so to speak, that it's difficult to maintain benevolent sisterhood feelings in the face of such smugness. Get the subtext? Any woman who has periods is normal. Any woman who hasn't isn't.

'Yes, I suppose so, but I don't have mood swings, night sweats or hot flushes.' Well, bully for you, as we used to say in hockey, when we were girls and our hormones flowed free. It's this last group who maintain the male medics standpoint (a standpoint based on no control group, mark you) that a 'normal menopause' is one without any symptoms at all.

Well, I've got the lot. Or at least I did until I took HRT (Helps Relieve Tension). When I say I take HRT, I am to HRT what Egon Ronay is to restaurants. To date I am on my fifth kind. I'm a stayer, you'll give me that. I suspect most women won't stick at it for that long. Talking of sticking – that was the second type I tried. The patch. Ever attempted to keep a sticking plaster on in a sauna at over a hundred degrees? (I have to cook at that temperature occasionally to ease my bad back. Oh the joys of a failing physique.) Also you've got to be in a pretty stable relationship for him to cope with running his hands over your butt and finding something resembling an elastoplast. What do you say to someone you haven't known that long? 'I'm going to Ethiopia and it's a yellow fever jab,' or 'I hurt myself when I was out cycling/walking/doing the garden?'

Heard the one about the husband who went abroad on a business trip and rang home to find his wife wasn't feeling good. The days went by and he felt on top of the world as she diminished in vigour and languished in the lounge. You got it. Or rather he had. When he got home they found he had her HRT patch stuck in the middle of his back.

So out went my patch. Or rather off it went. If there's anyone who's been feeling unaccountably well in the sauna of my gym, would they please let me know.

Prior to the patch, I was given the high-dose pill which equals low-dose self-esteem and minimal clothes choice. I ballooned to a size fourteen – I'm normally a size ten – and so out went the possibility of wearing most of the clothes in my wardrobe. Now I'm not a Kate Moss clone, and would dissuade any healthy sensible girl from imitating a stick insect, but I do work in an industry where a film camera puts five pounds of weight on you before you even open your mouth to consider that bag of chips/crème brûlée/three rounds of toast and marmalade. That's the other thing about it, it gives you an appetite of a horse – several horses. This is probably the moment those of you who are anti-HRT deem timely for a discussion on how the darn stuff is made. Well, I've got news for you. You can get homeopathic HRT. I haven't got it, but you can get it. And it has nothing whatsoever to do with our equine friends.

So the high-dose pill went the way of the patch. Well, not quite. I didn't leave it somewhere in the gym. It's probably, as I speak, whizzing round in my washing machine, making my whites feel just brilliant. There was an interregnum of no pill at all. My weight went down, but my colour went up and my depression scaled alarming depths. It's difficult to maintain cool, let alone look it, in front of a theatre full of people, doing a recital, i.e. without the benefit of make-up or wig to distract from the fact that your neck has just flushed livid scarlet, to be followed only embarrassing seconds later by a flush of real embarrassment that matches it and could stop traffic. I was acerbic to shop assistants and tyrannical on the telephone. If my son hadn't left home to go to university, he would have left home to escape the whiplash of my tongue. Wet T-shirts abounded in my house, and not of the kind that would win holiday-camp competitions. Mine were drenched with night sweat.

I spent hours sobbing uncontrollably over nothing at all, and in the same afternoon would find myself jumping up and down for joy like a demented child, again over nothing at all. Now there are those amongst my acquaintance (not my friends, please note) who would say, 'So what's new?' What's new is, I don't like this helter-skelter and I want off it. And that was before I clapped eyes on the little old lady in our village in Warwickshire who died from osteoporosis. I don't want to crumble, slowly and agonisingly, and be foul to those I hold dear in the process. Or more foul than I usually am.

So then I tried the no-period-at-all pill. Very popular with the ladies in Maida Vale apparently, because I had to make two trips to a chemist there when recording a play for the BBC at its Maida Vale studios, only to find that they were out of stock both times. When I did eventually manage to acquire it, I discovered that it was in league with balloon-aid. So I've been up and down weight-wise and irritability-wise six times to date. This puffing up and down like a pouter pigeon plays havoc with the measurements that TV wardrobe departments have of me. 'But you used to be such a skinny little thing,' they say, their mouths full of pins as they busy themselves finding seams to let out on the clothes that they've hired, based on the old pre-HRT measurements. (I fantasise, not altogether benevolently: 'TV wardrobe assistant hospitalised through forced ingestion of dressmaking aids.')

Now although I'd given up smoking (past tense), I'm a vegetarian (past and present) and I meditate (present and pretty continuous) and do yoga (intermittently, in short sporadic bursts at home because I can't, at the moment, afford the new year of gym fees) – I wouldn't like to give the impression that I'm a health-kick fanatic. It strikes me that if modern science is willing to spend piles of dosh on research to make life easier and more comfortable, it is self-defeating not to make use of their finds. It's often the smokers and the heavy drinkers who are first to boast that they've never taken an aspirin in their life. I do. Plenty. It seems pointless to suffer. Also, I have a very low pain threshold and a very high volubility when *in* pain. (I had a man friend, from the Borders, a Souter from Selkirk no less, who had a grand wit and would remark, '*She* gets pre-menstrual and *I* get tense.' We didn't last long as a duo.)

My foster mother, God bless her, who lived till she was almost ninety-six, survived till that ripe old age on a heavy diet of phenobarbitone, sleeping tablets and pills for hearttroubleandbloodpressure – which I thought of as one and the same illness throughout my childhood. Of course she never smoked, and having signed the teetotallers' pledge at Methodist Chapel in her girlhood, never drank. Well, she kept a bottle of brandy in the sideboard in the living room, but purely for medicinal purposes, of course. To be taken as required – when she felt bad; when the Suffolk easterlies blew cold and shrill; when she was worried about finding the rent; or the rates; or had had a bit of a to-do with a neighbour...

There's a lot to be said for keeping the body in its natural state and free of drugs. But don't those proselytizing health fiends get you down? Not for them the choc ice at the pictures (all those E numbers and additives!) or the devilish delicious darkness of that early morning espresso made with hot milk as the French and Italians do (stimulants! Lordy, lordy). But there's not much that's natural in the life of those of us who have to live it in the big cities. Car fumes, traffic stress, clock-watching stress, eating lunches on the hoof, public transport stress, because it's late or, when it does deign to arrive, because it's full. It's like the macrobiotic diet (and like all good children of the sixties I tried that one too). All that brown rice and locally grown vegetables and fruit might be all right in the rarified atmosphere of a Tibetan mountain, but when you're running for the number eleven bus and there won't be another for half an hour, you need something more substantial in your innards.

Now don't get me wrong. I've had my share of alternative medicine. I regularly go to be untwisted at my beloved osteopath; I've had acupuncture for almost everything under the sun – frozen shoulder, tension, the perennial bad back; I've had reflexology that was so beneficial I wanted to marry the reflexologist I felt so restored and pampered, but she was married already.

HRT's a bit like God. It provokes very strong opinions For and Against, and like God, I would say you have to make up your own mind. Or listen to your body and let that decide. Seems to me it's plumb silly to be allopathic *or* naturopathic. A little bit of everything that's available and apposite would seem to make sense. Get the needle if it avoids a pill. It'll give your liver a rest from dealing with drugs, so that you can have another glass of wine.

Of course the middle years bring a special sting to women. No more children. Or no children at all if you've left it too late (both these states may be regarded by some people as a blessing). But it's hard for women whose children, and maybe even whose husband, have left home – the former in search of education or employment and the latter in search of sex with younger women. Hard to watch the said husband begin a second family when that possibility is denied us. Not all women define themselves through their ability to mother. But this is often a time too, when 'society' says, 'You're finished, it's over. We don't need you as a mother/mistress/example of attractive femininity/job applicant/clothes model, etc...' And you say to yourself as you look in the mirror, 'Well it won't get any better, even after a good night's sleep.' You find that you are simply no longer visible to the majority of men. (Not that all of us define ourselves through our ability to attract the opposite/same sex either, but we all like to be liked, we all like to think of ourselves as reasonably attractive.)

One can argue the lack of PC-ness and democracy in the looks department, but it's a fact of life. Most men look right past anything female over thirty-five as a rule. In this country that is. But get off a plane in France or Spain and you're back in the running, of being run after. 'La femme d'un certain âge' has great kudos in Latin countries. Whoever heard anyone say that Jeanne Moreau, Stephane Audran or Catherine Deneuve were past it? Are our men frightened of mature women? Women who are perhaps financially independent, professionally secure and who have opinions of their own, that they don't have to render palatable to a frail male ego by batting their eyelids? There is beauty in a lived-in face.

There's a wonderful story about the great Italian film star, Anna Magnani. Hauled to Hollywood for a screen test, she was taken into make-up, where the make-up artist proceeded to eradicate as best she could, the bags and wrinkles around Miss Magnani's eyes.

'What you do?' came the question in that inimitable gravelly voice, before the session had got very far.

'Well, Miss Magnani,' came the response, in best LA euphemisms, 'I'm just making you look good.'

'No! You no touch my face! My face is my life! You no take my life!'

Don't let us, either, give way to the American way here. Don't let ageism rule. No nips and tucks for us. It seems that whatever cosmetic surgery removes in terms of unwanted flesh, bags or wrinkles, it replaces a thousandfold in the ability to lie about having had it! I mean no one can look *that* good, Joan/Liz, at sixty-two, even on HRT!

It'll be a red-letter day when we have female news readers as old as the oldest males in that metier. Where has that kind of equality gone? Did we ever have it? What happened to the swathes that were cut through choc-box prettiness by Sissy Spacek, Meryl Streep and our own dear Glenda? It seems the stereotype is back with a vengeance when you consider Sharon Stone, Michelle Pfeiffer, Julia Roberts – need I go on? Did those values fought for so hard in the late sixties and seventies go out as the recession came in? The production purse strings in Hollywood are held largely by men. Cue for re-entry of stereotype. God bless Olympia Dukakis for looking like most women do at her age. And hang on in there, Emma, don't let them get at you for not being sexy in their terms.

What is the obsession with youth? Apart from marketing jeans, fizzy drinks, CDs, make-up, aftershave, fast cars (and envy) to a yoof that largely hasn't got the money to buy them, it's only recently that some bright spark in the advertising industry has realised there's a market out there of middle-aged women who can, now that their children are gone, afford to buy quality things for themselves. But where has the reverence and respect for old age gone, that all 'primitive' cultures were based on, and some Asian and Eastern cultures still protect? Elders weren't called that for nothing. They'd lived. They'd experienced life. They knew about things. Their opinions and advice were sought after and adhered to.

It's indicative, even in our archetypes, that there's a gap in our thinking waiting to be filled: Maiden, Mother and then Old Crone? What about filling that gap between fecund maternity and doddering, dismissed old age with The Wise Woman? Perhaps we wouldn't be so mad, us menopausal Ms's if our opinions were valued and our experience and knowledge of life cherished. So I'm off to take a pill before I turn into a Horrid Ratty Tyrant. Or before I have a repeat experience of what I became familiar with between courses of HRT. Feeling that life wasn't worth living. It showed on my face and in my dealings with people. I like life. And I like people. On the whole. The pill won't give me eternal youth, and anyway I wouldn't want it. But I do want to feel well, and to feel well-disposed towards my fellow creatures. So until this helter-skelter that's going on in my body is over, I'm Happily Receiving Treatment.

I'm Sorry, Could You Say That Again?

My deafness I endure
To dentures I'm resigned
Bifocals I can manage
But God how I miss my mind.

ANON

There was a dreadful buzzing in my ears. I mean there had been a dreadful buzzing in my ears – well, a buzzing and a bleeping and a screeching and a ringing from a pair of headphones that they'd made me wear for what had seemed like an interminable hour in a stuffy claustrophobic booth. But I was no longer in the booth. I was sitting alone in a rather bleak, grey, institution-like corridor, and I could still hear the noises. It was pointless my asking if anyone else could hear the noises, as there was no one else to ask. The corridor was empty, until a man in a white coat came towards me clutching a sheaf of papers. 'Can *you* hear those dreadful noises?' formed its question-like plea in my mind, until I recognised him as the source of the disturbance. No, I don't mean he was walking towards me emitting sounds like a latter-day dalek, he was the man who'd switched the noises on.

'Now,' he said shoving the pile of papers covered with indecipherable graphs and curves at me, 'there's nothing wrong with your ears, but you're deaf.'

A medic of considerable wit and tact, I thought. I thought that clever thought later. At the time I was bereft of anything other than a rather defensive repetition. 'What do you mean, there's nothing wrong with my ears, but I'm *deaf?*'

'Well, there's no obstruction in the inner ear, your eardrum's intact, and the bones carry the sound well.'

O-level biology classes whizzed through my dazed brain. Could I recall that diagram with all those twirly bits – the cochlea, was it called? I remembered there was an anvil in there somewhere. I did remember I'd coloured it in a beautiful red stripy effect, or had that been my diagram of the eye? And the stripes were behind the cornea? How I wish I'd paid more attention then. It wasn't easy to pay attention now either.

'The bones, drum and inner ear are fine,' I repeated like an automaton.

'Yes, but the aural nerve is damaged. Have you ever received any blows to the head?' Pass, I thought, you're not a psychiatrist. I sidestepped his question and looked blankly at him. Or an infection, in childhood that wasn't cleared up?' he added helpfully. The fine coil-like spring...'

'Oh, *that's* the twirly bit!' I said triumphantly to his blank face.

'It's damaged in the middle,' he continued professionally, choosing to sidestep my inanity, 'which unfortunately means that you can't hear sounds in the middle register, which is the area most human voices operate in, but you can hear very low or very high sounds'.

Oh great, I thought, I can't hear the human voice – a perfect impediment for an actor – but I could hear, say, a mouse squeak, or a drum being banged. I hadn't up to now spent a lot of time in the company of either rodents or manic bongo players. Not since Hedi's son inherited my son's cast-off jungle drums. Did this mean a radical change of lifestyle?

'It might get worse with age, of course,' continued my prophet of doom. 'In fact the deterioration that is shown here,' he riffled through the papers and showed me a graph with a downward curve so steep it would have given any managing director instant cardiac arrest, 'would be quite normal in a person of say sixty-five.'

The child in me, ever eager to please and be approved of, tried to beam with relief at the word normal, but the grin stuck half way. I was forty-two.

'The left ear is considerably worse than the right.'

A picture flashed into my mind of a future totally inclined to the right. Not a favourite direction of mine. Well it would keep my osteopath happy for years straightening out the kinks in my spine and my neck. If I didn't keel over and fall flat on my face before I reached the treatment table.

'A hearing aid would be beneficial...' Another picture, equally grim, of a whorl of ghastly see-through tubing that was meant to look skin coloured, but in fact never looked quite clean, issuing from my deaf ear. I'd seen them, those mediaeval instruments, hanging not so discreetly from behind the ears of *old* people. No sir, not for me!

'Of course, you might need two.'

Pardon, what did you say?

'There are hearing-aid specialists...'

That was when I switched off. Switched off the good ear that is, and ran for it, at least in my mind. And I kept on running for several years. That's several years after I'd been fitted with a hearing aid. I carried it around in my handbag like a dinky piece of optional costume jewellery. I never wore it. Oh dear me no. Hearing aids are for deaf people. Reminds me of the alcoholic I knew whom I finally persuaded to go to an AA meeting and who came back with the smell of alcohol on her breath. When I pointed this out she said, 'God those drunks were so depressing, I had to stop on the way home and have a drink to cheer myself up.' Or my foster mother's response on being asked how she liked the old people's home: 'Well, it's all right, I s'pose, but it's full of old people.'

Deaf? What me? Not me.

Snug in it little blue velvet box, a thimble of pink plastic, with the tiniest of batteries, a delight of modern technology that had been made specifically to fit so sweetly, and barely visibly, I was assured, into my *good* ear. Yes, that was a surprise. 'No point in having it in your *deaf* ear, is there?' said the specialist jovially.

'It'd only magnify what you *can't* hear!' I swear there was a suspicion of a guffaw in his voice and a smirk on his face. But no, surely not. It couldn't be good for business, to mock the afflicted. 'Of course, *two* hearing aids would balance the sound perfectly,' he said, beaming. And your bank balance, I thought, and left the shadow of his smile.

I remembered the saying in French, 'The blind man is happy but the deaf man is sad.' The deaf certainly cause a lot of laughs, as I was to find out. Yes, the actor in me would certainly be sad if everybody else got the laughs, I thought grimly.

Coming in from work, forcing myself to sit down and join in with ten minutes of the hour of children's programmes that my son, then only twelve, was allowed to watch (the basic pre-requisite of a good parent then was to know at least what a ninja mutant turtle looked like).

'Gosh, can't you hear the telly, Mum? It's up ever so loud!' Snigger, snigger.

Then the volume on the remote control is pressed and normal sound floods into the room. Very funny.

Years later the new neighbours next door banged on the wall one night when I'd broken the habit of a lifetime and was watching the largely untouched TV in my bedroom.

'Is it loud?' I called upstairs to my son, deep into GCSE revision aided by heavy metal, both on his teeth and on the cassette player.

'Deafening,' he shouted back.

'What?' I said.

'What?' he said.

'Just a joke,' I muttered to myself. But he didn't hear. 'And turn that racket down, you'll go deaf!'

'What?'

'Oh forget it.'

But it was becoming increasingly hard to forget.

Going out to dinner with fellow actors, in fine, high spirits after the tension of a first night. Eighteen or so of us at table. A long joke unravelling down the other end. The table rocks with laughter. Pause. My cue. I whisper to the person sitting next to me, 'What did he say?' Actors are trained to know about timing. The moment had gone. And with it the joke. Getting an actor to step into a dead moment – or, as we call them in the profession, a black hole – is like getting an animal rights protectionist to cheer at the sight of a fur coat.

Then there was the time I worked with a director who had a gargantuan mouth-muffling beard – a grizzled Father Christmas number that curled into his lips from above and straggled sideways into it from below. I was sunk. I'd been approximating what I thought he'd said, nodding my head sagely, when I had only the vaguest notion of what he wanted me to do, and praying that, given the circumstances of the scene, I would guess correctly. But this was on location in Jamaica, outside, on a beach, where the winds can be very skittish. I was a good distance from him, and when it was obvious to all those near me that I hadn't a clue what I was supposed to be doing, and a kindly soul nearby related it all again, patiently and clearly but in a Jamaican accent, I had to come clean and the running had to stop.

'I can't hear.'

'What's wrong with you?' the very angry director with the grizzled Father Christmas-type beard shouted. 'I'm shouting!'

I wanted to retort, 'There's nothing wrong with me, but I'm deaf.' I think I actually said, or shouted, back, 'I have trouble hearing.'

There *it* was, out. Or half out. And out of my bag finally came the hearing aid. Not then though. Not for work, oh dear me no, I can't hear the atmosphere with a hearing aid in my ear. It's like talking with a finger stuck in your ear. You try it. Or like talking from the bottom of a fish tank. Don't try that one, unless your fish are on vacation.

That Jamaican episode was fourteen years ago.

Since then I've been through many variations and gradations of truth: 'I have trouble hearing.' 'I have a bad ear.' 'I'm hard of hearing.' 'I have a deaf ear' – till finally I arrived at the red-letter day when I heard myself say, 'I'm deaf.' No PC-ness here. Let's have the nerve to call a dead nerve deafness. I practised wearing my hearing aid at home to begin with. My house was a revelation. The central heating boiler sounded like the engine on an ocean-going liner. All clanks and clickings and whirrings. How had people managed to talk above this noise? The clock on my mantelpiece had a *tick*. I walked around it and stood looking at it in astonishment. Now that I knew it had a tick, it was developing a totally new character. I was like a fascinated child. I ran my hand up my right shoulder. I could actually hear the noise the material on my sleeve made as I did it. Extraordinary. I went out into the street to get something from the boot of the car. Simultaneously, a plane went overhead, the District Line erupted into life beyond the opposite row of houses and a lorry came down the street. Pedestrians in Putney were treated to the sight of a middle-aged woman, doubled up in agony, bent into the boot of a car, clutching her ear. I knew I wasn't expert enough yet to turn the volume down. I couldn't even remember which way the dinky little switch was supposed to be turned. I retreated yelping into the house, my good ear whining with the cacophony of noise. I had my hand over the dinky little thing, so was experiencing major feedback at first hand. Out it came. That was enough of that.

Now I wear my aid all the time when I go to the theatre, as a member of the audience, that is. Not when I go to work. Remember the atmos. It caused my son great consternation to be sitting next to a woman frantically twiddling the volume button on this oh so small dinky device. The volume dial is about a quarter of the size of a grain of rice.

'They'll think you're cleaning your ears!' he said embarrassedly, indicating the people in the row behind us. Odd, when and how parents' and children's roles get reversed.

What an indictment of modern actors, having to wear a hearing aid in the theatre. I expected to wear it if I went to a lecture, or was listening to a sermon – those people weren't taught how to speak. But if I sit more than ten rows back in the stalls I can't hear, and that's with my hearing aid *in*. When I teach (sans aid) I stand a good way away from the student doing the speech and say, 'If *I* can hear you, then the people in the back row of the gallery can hear you.'

No tea and sympathy, please. I'm in quite select company professionally. Dear Dame Peg was apparently deaf, I believe Stefanie Beacham has just outed her deafness and there are several other actors, whom I won't name, who have hearing problems. Not the sort of hearing problem I've learned to cultivate since burying my own prejudice and admitting my own deafness. The sort of problem brought on by a 'Ma, can you lend me...' Total instant block. Factor 20. It's very effective. I laugh.

It's not often deaf people laugh, except when they're with other deaf people. It's like the best anti-Jewish jokes are told by Jews, anything else is not acceptable in this PC age. Did you hear the one about the bloke walking down the street with a lemon in his ear? Another bloke walks up to him and says, 'Excuse me you've got a lemon in your ear'. And he says, 'You've heard of a hearing aid? This is a lemonade.' Not very funny, deaf jokes.

Three of my closest friends are deaf. I don't know whether like attracts like. We were friends first, then we discovered we were all deaf. It's a hoot whenever we all get together.

'What was that?'

'She said...'

'No, what did *you* say?'

Maurice's bad side is my good side, I think, and Hedi's bad side is Maurice's good side, she thinks. So we really all ought to sit opposite each other, but even I, as a failed maths O-level candidate, know you can't have three people opposite each other. Lis can sit anywhere, as she wears her hearing aid all the time. I only remember that when I go to kiss her, cover her good ear inadvertently for a fraction of a second and her aid emits a high-pitched shriek. I can hear that. She laughs. I can also see her wince.

Deaf people wince a lot. Not because of loud noises, or hands on aids, but because we get treated like idiots. What did you say?'

'I said...'

'I'm sorry, I still can't hear you.'

'I *said*...'

Cue for English-to-Foreigner speak. You know, that very loud and very slow talking, brain to idiot mode of communication.

I remember seeing recently the most heart-rending advertisement for the Royal National Institute for the Deaf. It ran the width of a huge hoarding. It had two ears on either side of it. From ear to ear was one very simple and concise sentence. It said, 'Just because we're deaf, doesn't mean we don't have anything between these.'

Quite so.

I've just realised – with something akin to the shock of eventually being forced to accept that my bad back might be improved with a new mattress for my bed, (Outrage! I've only had that mattress for... what is it? Ah, yes, twenty-five years) – that my hearing aid, its box now almost worn of all its blue velvet and kept shut with an elastic band, is well past its sell-by date. There are even dinkier jobs available with remote control buttons where you can lower the background noise, very useful for large noisy rooms full of people where a hearing aid is sadly absolutely no use at all. It just magnifies all the sounds, and can't discriminate between someone who's standing next to you talking, and someone turning the pages of a newspaper several feet away. But these cost over a thousand pounds. And I need a holiday. But I do need a new hearing aid.

I think I'll take the holiday. My problem is admitting I have a problem.

Playing Away

I never did take that holiday. Not then anyway. I'd had my fingers badly burned once before, not from too much sun, but from a surfeit of single person supplements that year I did venture to the Costa del Sol alone. Now no one who knows me could imagine that I am serious about what I just wrote, let alone serious about doing it. The Costa del Sol? Yo? Yes, I did go, but not when it was seething with lobster lookalikes drawn from every corner of the British Isles. Oh dear me no, I'm far too clever for that. I went in February. No claustrophobic crowds then. There were only four other people in the hotel. Two couples of course. So I never ventured into the dining room at night, for fear of playing gooseberry. I had room service. Cold salad, just slightly preferable to cold paella, which is what it would have been had I ordered it. I grew old waiting for room service to appear. Old and chilly. And that was inside. Outside it was Arctic.

It was so cold I had to wear a thermal vest. It must be the pessimist in me that had made me pack a thermal vest in the first place. Or perhaps it was the small still voice of sanity that had warned me as I booked the luxury hotel high on the hillside (away from the crowds, of course) that heat is simply not available anywhere in Europe before May. But we are stubborn, us Capricorns, as I've said before. Stubborn and stupid. I also packed three bikinis and a swimsuit.

The pool in the hotel was empty – apart from a collection of leaves that had been raked into a pile, the rake and a pair of stepladders. I pulled my jacket and scarf tighter round my throat as the wind bit into my blankly staring face and made my eyes smart. I've never much liked swimming anyway. I crane my head out of the water at a ridiculous angle to keep the water out of my deaf ear, for some obscure reason, so then I end up at the osteopath with a bad back. And swimming's supposed to do you good. Like holidays are.

Having explored the entire village on the first day, a stroll which took me a mere hour, down and around little alleyways edged with white-washed houses that must have looked stunning in the sun, but under the grey clouds scudding overhead had a veneer of bleakness that was more redolent of Yorkshire than the Mediterranean. Having lit a candle, unusually enough for myself, in the musty, silent, wax-covered hilltop shrine to a little doll dressed in gold complete with crown (I must have guessed even then that my holiday was in dire need of Divine intervention) I thought better of walking to the next village which I could see round a curve in the hillside, as the path I was on disappeared abruptly at the edge of a motorway. The Spanish are not renowned for their cautious driving and, as if I needed proof, I took the village bus down the hill to the town that I could see in the distance sprawling along the very built-up coastline. Suffice it to say that the one postcard I sent to a friend said, 'I have seen hell and it's called Fuengirola.' And I was lucky. Hell was closed. So none of the flashing neon lights advertising casinos, discos, cafes, amusement arcades, night clubs, shopping malls, hamburger bars, ice cream shops, candy floss stalls (candy floss – en España? Madre de Dios) were in fact flashing. Which was a blessing. And there weren't a lot of those around. In spite of my lighted candle.

After an uncomfortable walk along what I could only call the promenade – it did remind me of Blackpool – my only companions being little ladies with tightly curled perms walking tightly curled poodles, or Yorkshire terriers with bows in their hair, battling to stay on all spindly fours against a very skittish wind, the volatile blasts of which had the odd fisherman that I passed fighting to unravel a long net, I finally won the heated argument with myself, which was the only warmth I had come across. I decided to cut my losses and head for home.

Easier said than done. Of course I knew I would have to forfeit the apex ticket I'd paid for and fork out extra in order to escape before my allotted span. But I had forgotten the kindly woman at the check-in desk at Heathrow who, probably being a bit of a theatre fan, had recognised me. Chatting away merrily about this and that, she had blithely forgotten to tell me about – and kindly forgotten to charge me for – the suitcases that I had with me, which were, to my astonishment in an echoing mausoleum of an airport, in miserable Malaga, considerably overweight. They contained, of course, sun dresses and flimsy evening outfits for dining and dancing (who *was* I planning to dine and dance *with*?).

Overweight was one thing I wasn't after three nights of salad, washed down with one of the two locally bought bottles of red Marques de Caceres as I desperately tried, and grumpily failed, to follow a Spanish quiz show, a soap opera and the news on the TV in my room. This little question of twenty-two kilos overweight was not being overlooked by the unsmiling monosyllabic dragon at the check-in desk that barred my escape route. So excess baggage I forked out for. And I had bought nothing. I was returning empty-handed. Except for that second bottle of wine. It's still in my wine rack in the hall. It has a stick-it note on it that I wrote in a unique and unusual moment of wry humour about the whole escapade. It says, 'This bottle of wine cost me 8000 pesetas.'

Somehow the idea of drinking an unnecessary return ticket, used only one way, a single-person room supplement and twenty-two kilos of unnecessary, unworn holiday clothes, sticks in my throat and makes my eyes smart.

But they do warn us, us single people. If you want to go on holiday alone you have to pay a supplement.

I did brave Capri sola some years later on my friend Claudia's advice and encouragement: 'Yes, it is the kind of place you can visit alone. Yes, you can walk. It's all walking, no cars allowed past the centre. Yes, you'll be all right at night in the Albergo, no couples there – it doesn't have a restaurant'... But after five days of watching the never-ending parade of couples linked arm-in-arm to the beach, from the beach, around the town under the navy blue night skies, and five days of large lunches taken in the safety of family restaurants, replete with loud children and very Italian stares at a woman speaking very bad Italian, having the temerity to insist on a table for one, and five evening meals of Campari and orange before and after an ice cream, taken in rotation at one of the many cafes that border the square, I began to feel queasy. My enthusiasm paled under the suntan I'd acquired on a beach packed with bronzing sardines. It was the only time that I can remember feeling relief at being in a crowd. We were packed so closely, us sun worshippers, that it wasn't apparent I was alone.

I did meet a friendly German woman who was also trying to avoid worse blisters by buying, at the same time as I was, a stylish pair of locally made gold loafers with rubber studded soles and heels – perfect for gripping the slippery cobbled alleyways that rose steeply in every direction from the centre of the town. We struck up a friendship that kept me going for the last three days. She'd been going to Capri on holiday for twenty-five years. Booked the same room in the same hotel and knew everyone. André, the rather tall, polite head waiter with an undertaker's pall and demeanour who ran the best café near the beach, whose parting present to me was almost a smile and a bottle of his wife's homemade Limoncello. The guitar-playing father and son who sang folk songs in the Capri patois at their night club, songs that made your feet tap and your heart lurch and yearn with every Neapolitan dip and swell of the strings. Music that made us sit entranced by a language we didn't understand till the early hours of two mornings. We

walked back through the almost deserted alleyways, two
middle-aged women alone, but safe and smiling. Hearts and
heads full of music. Not a lot of places left in Europe where
that's possible. But surprisingly the local mafia keeps other
people's crime down to a minimum, or the bottom would drop
out of this very lucrative holiday market. Also there's nowhere
to run to on an island.

The crisis of confidence over holidaying solo came thankfully to an end recently, if only temporarily, when my son
became mature enough to recognise that time spent with his
mother was no threat to his independence, and meeting at
Heathrow didn't mean that either of us were planning on his
moving back home. It helped, of course, that I was footing the
bill. The two most effective methods with offspring are money
and blackmail. They can be used separately or independently,
according to one's bank balance or speed of mind. I used both
on the occasion that I suggested we holiday down the Nile.

It's difficult to write about a trip to Egypt in the aftermath of
the slaughter at Hatshepsut's temple in 1997. The blood is still
fresh on the stones. As the terrible news drenched all the
bulletins on radio and TV, flashes of what the marauding
eleventh- and twelfth-century Crusaders had done to Muslims
over two hundred years kept disturbing my mind.

My hairdresser – a well-read and intelligent woman who had
planned a trip like ours and had talked of nothing else for
weeks, and to whom I had lent my well-thumbed suntan oil-
smudged guide book – like millions of others, cancelled. But as
I write, only weeks after the tragedy, two of my friends are out
there. As a couple of intrepid backpackers from Australia said
to a newspaper reporter the day after the massacre, 'Yes, we're
staying. If we go home, they've won.'

Ankhs and Angst

It was Einstein who made the real trouble. He announced in 1905 that there was no such thing as absolute rest. After that there never was.

STEPHEN LEACOCK, 1869–1944

I have just been shaken and stirred. I took my son down the Nile for a week. It was a thinly disguised birthday present for him, but in reality I was buying his company for seven days and nights, and his thoughts and reactions every evening as we chewed over the abundance of magnificence that we had seen during the day. As the sun slipped over what might have been the yard arm of our cruiser, had it had one, we discussed Egyptian art, Dynasties (the pre-BC and TV kind), patriarchal religions and whether or not we had succumbed to Pharaoh's revenge. It was a somewhat desultory conversing, despite the highmindedness of the topics, with what was left of our sun-fried brains before they slipped into our third gin and tonic-induced amnesia. We never drink gin and tonic, and not having an English gene between us, the race memory of the days of the Raj can hardly be blamed for our untypical addiction. Egyptian wine is awful, and that's about the only thing Egyptian that is.

Of course, we're not the first to be captivated and entranced by that extraordinary country. The likes of Amelia Edwards (1873) indomitable adventurer, and David Roberts (1838), exquisite Scottish watercolorist, lost their hearts and minds to the place when most of the temples we saw were up to their capitals in sand or struggling to survive the Nile floods. The yearly life-bringing inundation that has kept the country alive since way before Moses and way after Cleopatra was celebrated in many a religious ritual and portrayed on many a temple wall throughout the whole of Egypt, but more locally and gratefully by the farmers who still scratch a living amongst the banana groves and date palms in the astonishing lush strip of vegetation that borders the Nile, while the rest of the country that stretches away on either side of the river is sand, sand and yet more sand.

The flooding is now controlled by the not very aesthetic Aswan Dam – one notices the baldness of modern engineering with some shock in a place that abounds with such natural beauty – but the farmers still draw the waters of the Nile with the help of a shadouf, a pole with a bucket on the end of it, supported and counterbalanced by two wooden struts. A sight older than Christendom itself.

Amelia, confined in corsets, lisle stockings and long skirts, lavished buckets of coffee, no less, on the statue of her beloved Pharaoh Rameses II to remove the white cast residue left by less caring Egypto-fanatics on his face, and David abandoned his woollen waistcoats and tweed trousers for the long flowing gowns of the locals, to capture, in temperatures that baked his paper before he could apply paint to it, the unbelievably bright greens and reds and the gold star-spangled sky of the Temple of Isis, painted originally during the New Kingdom some 1567 BC. Both of these stalwarts somehow managed to keep their heads without the benefits of air conditioning, not long after Shelley had immortalised the gigantic remains of the monument to Rameses II with his: 'My name is Ozymandias King of Kings, look on my works ye mighty and despair.'

We didn't despair much. We marvelled at the colossal crumbling remains of the two statues to Memnon that punctuate the desert between the Valley of the Kings and the Valley of the Queens; it was difficult to marvel at anything for long in the tombs at either of these places, as the colours and crowns and ankhs and muscle-bound men with large eyes outlined in kohl, and the sensuous women with their long elegant feet and exquisitely plaited hair, followed on one after another in dizzying succession. But the implacability of our guide Mohammed, who was as round as he was long, was remarkable as he kept up a constant stream of information and hieroglyphic interpretation in the face of some very strong competition from the loudest of French guides South East of the Eiffel Tower, backed by the chatter of some umpteen hundred other tourists in umpteen other tongues.

Tutankhamun's tomb left us speechless in its brightness and fresh beauty, a feast for the eyes and the mind only, that cameras were rightly forbidden to capture. We were awestruck by the Terraces of Hatshepsut's temple – she who wrested the throne from her nephew and kept it for an astonishing eighteen years, dressed like a man, replete with the delicate linen skirts and regulation god beard of the Pharaoh. I was unsettled and disconcerted by the Stalin-like size of the temple of Horus at Edfu, but that may have been induced by the gut-churning ride over bumps and dips in what could have been a road, through the people-, chicken- goat-, donkey- and 'Baksheesh, baksheesh!'-infested market, in a brightly painted and none too stable horse-drawn calèche.

We were silenced by the dawn breaking over the Sahara on our way to the gigantic rock-hewn statues of Rameses II that front the Temple at Abu Simbel, but that could have had something to do with the fact that we had to get up at 3.15a.m. to get there before the sun started to burn at around eight, and that a young man with a suspiciously gun-shaped bag got on the bus in the outskirts of Aswan and proceeded to sleep, stretched out on the back seat near the very African-smelling loo, through the entire journey. Even when the bus broke down in the desert, on the way back, he never stirred through the good deal of banging and clanging it took to get the fan belt off and the replacement back on. During this exercise the water level in our bottles became an object of unspoken fascination and quiet concern for those of us left on the bus, as the rest of the convoy whizzed past, one bus thankfully stopping to ponder and peer (as did the camels on the other side of the road) and to eventually pick up our few senior citizens, who had begun to wilt in the 110 degrees, and for whom the delights of the nearest mirage had long lost its attractions as the pull of lunch began to make itself felt.

It was a refreshing change to catch the morning breezes, sailing on a rickety motor boat to the temple dedicated to the goddess Isis, on a little island dotted with trees and oleanders at Philae, and to see endearing humanistic reliefs of Isis breast-feeding her son Horus (a virgin birth – there is nothing new under the sun) – a fundamentally mortal occupation, in strict contrast to her ability successfully to reassemble the hacked remains of her husband Osiris.

Ankhs, the keys to life, were everywhere – on columns, on walls and held in almost every Pharaoh's hand. Our keys to life were the cool flannels and warm hibiscus or lemon drinks offered to us each day on our return to the cruiser, sand-blasted and sun-dried from our morning expeditions into the oven that becomes Egypt after the end of April.

As the week progressed, our walks through these extraordinary shrines to endeavour, engineering (albeit slave powered) ingenuity, Pharaoh power, artistic vision and expression (the achievements of humankind's earliest civilisation, apart from the Chinese) became increasingly silent. Even the little pockets of people who had begun to group themselves together both on and off the cruiser, walked and looked wordlessly. We, the Brits, were still on all fours in caves while these gigantic monuments and gardens were being hacked out of the unyielding desert rock. It was a sobering thought. Possibly the only one that was, as each evening after dinner, washed down by copious beers, gins and vodkas (only the brave or the foolhardy, or in the case of my son, the terminally young, would imbibe the local ouzo – a drink that he described as having the foretaste of aniseed and the aftertaste of latrine), the fuel-injection specialist from Gloucester, the publican and his wife from the East End, the retired accountant from Maidenhead, the businessman from Aberdeen and the trainee solicitors from Guildford, would end up emulating our not-so-eminent forebears, in a variety of attempts at Arabian dancing to bongos and wheezing pipes that had the gracious and polite Egyptian crew and staff smiling discreetly into their Coca Colas. This was our cue to exit rapidly, G and T in hand, on to the relative cool of the top deck, for our regular dissertations on the nature of civilisation, the development of theology and other such lighthearted subjects, not forgetting the incident that provoked my son into renaming a certain tomb that of Nefartari, which had him in stitches and me in danger of repeating the experience.

Each night there was a different entertainment on board. Violin and viola playing Mozart, Chopin, Beethoven, although seemingly incongruous, we could stomach – amazing how current the word stomach was in everyone's conversation, especially as the number of seats vacant at dinner increased as the days went by and several of our fellow travellers fell by the wayside and or clung to their beds. But the night of the dressing-up-as-Arabs party had me out the door before the dessert was even on the table. 'Oh you spoilsport!' was thrown in my direction in the lightest of West Country burrs, which I silenced with a not too gentle, 'It's no holiday for me. I dress up for a living.'

We avoided tea in the Old Cataract and Winter Palace hotels, and by all accounts the regular guests avoided those of our package tour who braved it out, only to find themselves in splendid isolation as the residents, to a man, got up and left as they arrived.

Lord Kitchener's botanical garden on Elephantine Island looked as if it hadn't had a decent trim or a good water since he left. But we were charmed by the silence of the fellucca in which we sliced across the water, dipping and curving, with a hint of a breeze in the vast white sails overhead. And noisy and persistent as it was, it would have taken a heart of stone not to be touched by the raucous singing of 'She'll be coming round the mountain when she comes,' from some half-dozen or so children paddling around in little wooden homemade boats with square bits of board as oars. 'Luvvly jubbly!' was interspersed with the now familiar cry of 'Baksheesh! Baksheesh!'

I did succumb to a street seller here, in spite of all my promises to myself not to, based on my stepfather's rigorous training when I was an adolescent in North Africa. I was walking alone through the rather neglected garden, trying hard to avoid several abject-looking monkeys trapped in a pitifully small cage, and trying unsuccessfully to photograph a brightly coloured humming bird with its long beak, drinking deep from a scarlet hibiscus flower, when he seemed to appear from nowhere. He was an old man with a kindly, gentle face, a beguiling smile and the softest sell I'd ever come across.

'Sandalwood beads for your daughter? She will make her husband happy. She will have a good marriage.'

He must have picked up the hesitancy in my face and read it as reluctance. The afternoon sun had wrought its worst. I was fighting to find enough English words in what was left of my brain to explain that I only had a son, and he, I hoped, wandering around on the far side of the island, was far from naming the day.

'For you,' he said, changing his tack, 'for another happy fifty years of marriage.'

The sun had obviously aged me beyond description and I was way beyond any explanation of divorce. I smelled the beads. They were delightful. I gave him what I could decipher without my reading glasses as five typically dog-eared and filthy Egyptian pounds. He smiled some more and stroked my arm tenderly, so unlike the pushy pinchy market sellers. I was entranced. It was only later in England that the girlfriend I had given them to noticed that they were beans, and that the smell of sandalwood had long since faded.

Our Mohammed, like most guides, was very protective of us whenever we were near a market, and we had, at the outset of the trip, been given strict instructions about the rules of bartering, the implication being that most of his fellow countrymen who weren't crew, were unscrupulous and merciless grabbers, out for all they could get. So it was rather surprising when, having gone through the usual counting routine to establish that all members of our party were in fact safely on board the fellucca for its return journey across the Nile to our cruiser (my son and I, unusually, for once not being the last to board) that Mohammed himself started the hard sell.

'This is my friend Mohammed,' he said, pointing to a small grubby boy who was balancing precariously on the stern of the boat, 'and he is selling bookmarkers.'

Several of these not particularly attractive specimens were passed somewhat half-heartedly round the boat. They were garish strips, modern prints of pharaohs and gods, encased in not very good quality plastic. It was hard to see anything in them that could induce one to give them as presents or want to keep them oneself. A few silent, bemused moments passed when only the lapping of the water could be heard, and the distant squawk of the cranes in the botanical gardens. Then, it slowly dawned on us, one by one, that the boy had no hands. Dozens of book-markers found their way into rucksacks, handbags and duffel bags, and dozens of Egyptian pounds made their way into little Mohammed's pockets, a procedure that he managed with consummate skill.

'Brighter than my son who is the same age,' said our Mohammed as we pulled away, all of us more silent than ever. 'He knows he can't do normal work. He says he's saving to buy a shop in his village.' No one dared ask the question that must have been on all our minds. 'He was urinating by the river bank,' Mohammed went on, 'and there was an uncovered electric cable.'

Quiet Muslim care showed itself on another occasion as we were going through lock gates on the West Bank. The cruiser was dangerously near grounding, an event that every captain dreads, and rare though it is, apparently provokes instant resignation. A small boy, after several rapidly shouted instructions in Arabic, stopped walking along the river bank, expertly caught the rope thrown to him from the bridge of the cruiser, deftly tied it round the base of the nearest palm tree, and to much applause from the passengers who had witnessed this, stood wreathed in smiles, rightly proud of his magnificent achievement. Our Mohammed, as one of the crew jumped on to the bank to secure the boat more safely, discreetly threw a plastic bottle with some money in it to the boy. His disbelief followed by delight were as tangible as the orange sun that was turning the Nile a silvery pink as it was disappearing behind the distant palm trees. The smiles grew into the broadest that any of us had ever seen. Even smug Rameses II with his 200 wives, ninety sons and sixty daughters was put in the shade.

Nothing, of all the spectacles that we had witnessed could have prepared us for the majesty of Karnak, the biggest space ever constructed for worship, albeit only by the chosen few; no common or garden proles were allowed in, only priests and Pharaohs. With its awesome 134 columns of the central temple, it could have housed Westminster, St Paul's and Chartres several times over. Avenues of rams' heads; headless sphinxes; obelisks to war victories that pierced the unfailing blue of the sky; yet more walls and walls full of hieroglyphics of oblations to the various gods with their falcon heads, lion manes, snake hoods and water buffalo horns, intertwined with the ever present Nile lily and papyrus shoots; the increasingly monumental signatures of the various rulers who had insisted, in their turn, to carve a future memory of themselves over what had gone before. It was hard to breathe.

It was at this juncture that, overwhelmed and perhaps in danger of being sated by the dwarfing power of it all, I began to long for a church. A cool nave with a flagstone floor, the clean pure lines of a Norman arch, but most of all for a place where the human is venerated, and the Divine within the human. A place where the journey can be inwards to peace and serenity. Somewhere that gives us a glimpse of how we can live life better. Not just places mythologising death or built out of fear, insuring the safe passage of the body and soul from this life to the one after. A place that reminds us of Love. The best of all spiritual messages.

I was not to be disappointed. On our last day I had to confess to a lifting of my spirits at the sight of a crucifix scratched on the entrance of the Luxor Temple. It was less laudable that the early Christians had literally defaced many of the visages of the gods, and had, somewhat superstitiously I thought, also erased their hands for fear of further pagan wrongdoing. But then the Greeks had had their turn at graffiti centuries before. One of Rameses II's legs at Abu Simbel is covered with it. Even Balzac, who surely should have known better, scratched his name in the stone inside this temple. That's the thing about Egypt. It makes you want to leave your mark on it, because the mark it makes on you is indelible and unforgettable. Go. And you'll want to go back.

Just when you (I mean me really, but I'm feeling too guilty to admit it) might be beginning to feel edgy about leading and liking a lifestyle redolent of that of Joan Collins, albeit on a severely reduced budget (for JC that is; for you – I mean me really – it's a pyramid of luxury), along comes a little dollop of something to remind you that you're far from those dizzying heights of permanent, leisurely expenditure. The dollop in question could be unemployment, of course, but few sane actors, or any of us social outcasts, the self-employed, would take a holiday down the Nile knowing they were coming back to nothing coming in. A severely reduced budget indeed. Unless they like living life on the knife edge of angst. I don't like edges.

But angst comes with the job. And without it too.

Working as an actor also has its own built-in levelling process, much more mundane – less edge than angst. You could be starring in a Broadway show with your name in lights and a stretch limo to pick you up and take you (and the entire Piaf company in my case) home. But when the contract's over, the limousine goes with it, and you face the morrow and the uptown bus, with a few dimes in your pocket like every other human being. Apart from the ones for whom limos are naturally, by some freak of birth, a permanent uptown bus.

A few years ago I was astonished to read that the suicide rate was much higher amongst actors in the then Soviet Bloc countries, where being an actor was a highly regarded state and one of permanent employment. It seems that those of us in the West thrive on the big dipper of 'Now we have it, now we don't'. Perhaps we need that helter-skelter of attention, neatly followed by neglect. Or maybe we're just angst freaks.

It seems we need that shot of adrenalin off-stage, too, and the incipient insecurity of our futures certainly provides it. This unsureness keeps us in touch with, if not always humility, then often gratitude. Gratitude for what we have when we do, once more, manage to have it. And not having it for a while, can be looked at as a kind of boon, if we have the right eyes in – it doesn't remove us too far from the struggle of most of our fellow human beings who are also trying to make ends meet. Most of drama is about those people, not Kings and Queens, although those poor dears of course have problems of their own.

No, the post-holiday dollop could be a dose of Charity. Not other people's for you, but yours for other people. Working for nothing. Arguably better than not working for nothing.

Professionally it can be quite challenging too. The Charity do. Not just the frequently impromptu nature of the beast, in all its nerve-fraying one-off-ness, but the venues themselves can be quite a Waterloo.

Hard to really 'motor' Sharon Old's poem *Ecstasy*...

As we made love for the third day,
cloudy and dark, as we did not stop
but went into it and into it and
did not hesitate and did not hold back...

standing bathed in the light of the east window of the church, for which you are raising funds, faced by pews of stern-faced, rigid backbones of the community. Hard to throw away, and not just duck, Philip Larkin's 'They fuck you up, your Mum and Dad, they don't mean to but they do' under a free-hanging, life-size Christ on the Cross, dripping blood, as I did for MS in Wolverhampton.

Of course most church audiences are freezing cold so you can't really expect too much of a response anyway. And a lot of people who like poetry don't like church. So they're not an entirely comfortable captive audience either. Anything risqué is a big risk in a church. And anything spiritual can be instant freeze in a theatre.

George Herbert's 'Love bade me welcome but my soul drew back, Guilty of dust and sin,' didn't exactly wow them at the Wolsey in Ipswich. That was for the Samaritans. But I suspect that most of the audience were Theatre Club or Am Dram, and were in search of something a little more robust, and in line with the spirit of the evening.

In September things start dying,
Then comes cold October mist,
November we make plans to spend
The best part of December pissed.

The Samaritans present needed their forgiving natures.

Memorial services for actors are the hardest, of course. Not only are you coping with your feelings for the dear departed if they were dear to you, but you will be experiencing the worst possible kind of audience ever: your professional colleagues and their collective judgement. If you've just been roped in because at the last minute the youngest son couldn't face it, or brother Geoffrey never made it from Princes Risborough, then you're coping with feeling a phoney as well, as you feel your way through unfamiliar material. And having to acknowledge afterwards, to grief-stricken relatives, that you didn't really know him *that* well, is another performance.

Tabloid gossip and night-club punch-ups apart, neither of which I care to partake in, or witness, actors on the whole have hugely generous hearts. Last season at Stratford there was a last minute, at the half-hour call, whip-round for a young actor who'd had his new bicycle stolen. By curtain up he had the wherewithal for a replacement bike. And it was the youngsters in the company who started it. Those earning just above the Equity minimum of £250 a week, with two homes and often children to run.

Only those ardently dedicated to the memory of the much-loved Tony Quayle could prise people out of their homes on a wet Sunday evening to raise money for David Niven's Motor Neurone Disease charity of which Tony was head. As with the memorial gala for Colin Blakely, both theatres were packed.

Actors rarely boast about what they earn, as for most that's precious little to boast about, but when it comes to the money raised for, or rather squeezed out of, other people. £850 single-handed in a single night for the village hall! £1500 for Multiple Sclerosis! £2000 for the Samaritans! That's nothing to the £7000 in one evening at the barn in Bourton-on-the-Hill for the Cancer Research Campaign at Birmingham Hospital. But then I was only setting tables, stacking chairs and binning used paper plates. Poetry had nothing to do with it. Some opera singers sang. And charged us for the dubious pleasure. Unheard of for an actor to charge for a charity do. That's the whole point. You do it for nothing. Or a chance to dare to do the thing you've never dared...

£12,000 raised in a night by the Bristol Old Vic Theatre School gala for the adored Nat Brenner. And you got to hear Jeremy Irons singing an Eric Clapton number, 'Darling, you look wonderful tonight'. That was my idea, as I knew Nat loved the song. What I didn't know was that I wouldn't be able to control how much I loved Nat, and ended up sobbing in the wings, into Tim Piggott Smith's kindly proffered DJ'd shoulder. And laughing unmanageably at Jean Marsh and Eileen Atkins, all togged up like Shirley Temple, tap dancing to 'On the Good Ship Lollypop'. That's the whole point. You do it for nothing. Apart from the damage to your central nervous system. What could be a better way of acquiring a shot of adrenalin, daring to try the untried and having to overcome the post-holiday blues?

Charity Do's and Don'ts

In charity there is no excess

FRANCIS BACON, 1561-1626

And the greatest of these is Charity...

1ST CORINTHIANS 13, 13

Charity do's. Those bloodcurdling events at which actors, and sometimes musicians – though their union is altogether tougher about working for nothing – trundle their evening wear around the country to give their services for free in a show of hastily rehearsed and tensely performed (Oh God, what comes next?) poetry, prose, or song at various theatres, church halls, churches, and grand country homes, in order to raise piles of dosh for well-deserving organisations. It's hard not to feel like an impostor in the latter venue. Ever sat amongst the Chippendales, the furniture I mean, overlooked by the great and good of the family's ancestry staring down at you from expensively framed oils, and wondered how you were going to find the bus fare home? Or worse. How you were going to field the well-meaning but discomfiting question from the over-attentive host, 'Oh, an actor! And what have you done?' Athene Seyler's apocryphal retort instantly springs to mind. When faced with this question by a radio interviewer who obviously hadn't done his homework, she inquired sweetly, 'This morning?'

The Good Cause Rep is what Tim West wryly calls us. From the high standpoint of my overdraft I think it's a pity that the habit of doing Actors Benefits as they did in the seventeenth and eighteenth centuries has died out. I bet Garrick, Kean and even dear old Dora Jordan acted their socks off when they knew the entire night's takings were going into their own pockets.

Now don't get me wrong. We don't short-change the audience because we're working for Mr Stoll or Mr Moss, or even those grand old dames, RNT or RSC. I've never known any actor consciously decide to go out and give less. Our present work is our advertisement for future work. You never know who might be out there watching. Apart from 'What are *they* like?' (that means *you* the audience), most of the other backstage backchat is along the lines of 'Who's in tonight?' The film producer Tony Garnett had a framed truism on his office wall many years ago, '"The show must go on" is a phrase invented by the management,' but even so, I've known actors perform with cracked ribs, sprained ankles, migraines, bad backs and worse. Not for us the 'I'd better have the day off work – I think I feel a cold coming on.'

No we're not skivers. Nobody in our business wants to be known as a no-show at the drop of a virus. There's nobody in our business who doesn't want to be there. That's the joy of 'following your bliss', as world mythologist Joseph Campbell would say. In old-fashioned parlance, it's a vocation. In the vernacular, it's sheer madness. And charity do's must be linked somewhere in the murky subconscious with a death wish. Or at least a wish to lose several years off one's old-age pension.

It's the stress, you see. It's worse than an awards ceremony, where you didn't ask to be nominated or put into competition unwittingly and unwillingly with some of your best mates. Where you've had to get all dolled up in your evening wear, with a very fed-up companion in his penguin suit (charity do's and awards ceremonies have this in common) and you're not able to eat a thing because your stomach has turned into a churn, and not able to drink more than one glass of alcohol in case you make a complete prat of yourself in a drunken, and more than usually unintelligible, acceptance speech in the unlikely event of your winning. Well, ditto charity do's.

You probably got the script two days before, if the poor sod who's organising it managed through months of people dropping out at the last minute because they've got a film part and then their replacements dropping out even later because their telly shoot's overrun.

If amongst all this insomnia-making and life-threatening organiser's agony they got a script to you several weeks in advance, you can bet the bottom dollar that you don't have in your pocket, that the current version you're about to do at the church hall or stately home,. in six terrifying hours' time, is *not* the one that you happen to be holding in your sweating, trembling hands. You've probably never clapped eyes on your partners in fear before either, which doesn't add a lot to the sense of general ease. Is she as grand as I've heard? you wonder, about someone frightfully famous and clever who's packed them into the West End for years. Is he going to be as querulous and as irascible as his reputation? you ponder about that rather daunting, frightfully famous and clever TV star. But terror is a great leveller, when we're all under starter's orders from the moment we walk into the church or theatre or grand country house that's going to be the venue for your under-rehearsed and exorbitantly priced antics later on.

You leave your evening wear in its plastic hanging bag from Sketchleys, draped over the nearest seat, rescue your battered, hard-backed file with your much underlined script in it from your holdall (which contains your LSS – your life-support system: Carmen rollers, mouthwash, soft contact lenses only ever worn for charity do's which consequently take most of the break between rehearsals and the performance to fit in to your eyes; an extra pair of stocking tights in case, the odd safety pin in case and copious supplies of make-up that you will never use, have never used) and head for the nearest cup of coffee, if such a luxury should be on supply from the well-meaning friends of the well-meaning host.

If you've only ever done one charity do before, unless you're in a theatre, you know better than to ask whether there are dressing rooms. A ladies' loo, that never saw a heater, let alone a broom, more like, is where you dress. But once you're changed into the recital gear, you're not going to be spending any time wherever it is you've done the transformation from jeans into Jean Muir (bought second-hand or bought cheap from a TV production you were in when a size ten used to fit) because apart from the interval, you're going to be 'out there', in front of *them* the entire evening, performing something you've never spoken out loud until this morning – and that, probably, after a hundred-mile drive – unless you're one of those actors who do it out loud to themselves, and I'm not. I'd embarrass myself terribly and criticise my delivery so badly that I'd never get past the crisis of confidence or the second line, whichever came first.

So there you all are, eyeing each other nervously, and speaking in unsure, quivering tones – could be the mileage or the overdosing on coffee – looking at the pristine, unmarked-up, unfamiliar script with horror, as you realise someone else has got all the funny bits, and someone else has got a chance to show off all their regional accents. You've got the bits that are left over, which are usually impenetrable sections of Dryden's most obscure verse because the subject matter fits with the subject for the evening. You smile bravely through the lump in your throat and remember that it's for a good cause – 'it is the cause, it is the cause my soul' – if you're compos mentis enough to remember what the particular cause is. You then promise yourself that wherever that little demon is in you which says 'Yes' when you get one of those 'I was wondering if you were free on…' calls, you will locate it and strangle it at birth. There is a soft core of us, who are a soft touch, who seem to find it congenitally impossible to say, 'No.' Word goes round the business about who it's a waste of time to ask. There are some. In a business rightly renowned for its generosity and open-heartedness there are those who never say, 'Yes.'

Those of us who do are not so high-minded that we don't stoop to do trade-offs. I did a mega one with Nigel Hawthorne some years ago when we were doing *Shadowlands* in the West End. That was eight shows a week, two on Thursday, two on Saturday, and with a 'Yes' to a charity gala, bang goes that Sunday off, the only chance to remind yourself what your family looks like, reduce the pile of bills and letters that threaten to engulf the bottom of the stairs, and attack the mountain of dirty washing that threatens to creep out of the laundry basket and engulf the top of them.

'OK, I'll do you a Piaf song to help with your hospice in Stevenage, if you do me a Shakespeare sonnet in the Middle Temple for the Globe.' It was a deal. £65,000 was raised for the hospice in one evening. And the Globe ended up £63,500 better off, all expenses paid. A good deal. A good deal more than most actors can ever think of earning.

You can swallow the doing it for nothing bit. But it's when your bits, hastily read the day before, start going AWOL that you feel the lump in your throat. Bits are cut, bits are moved round and, worse, bits are passed from hand to hand. 'I don't want this Wordsworth! Can't make head nor tail of it, and I love that Siegfried Sassoon of yours – may I?' The director's face goes an even paler shade of grey: 'But I arranged it specifically so that the voices alternate.' Harmonic niceties go by the board in the free-for-all scramble that's the defence of one's patch.

Your face goes an even darker shade of puce while you hold your breath, and hold in a stream of invective, while you hope against hope that the West End magnet won't get her way all the time.

'Oh well, *he* can have the Wordsworth and *she* can have the list of wartime atrocities.' Another show-stopper heads your way. You wrestle then with far from charitable thoughts.

But when all of us Christians are out there facing the lions, unity's the thing. We stick together. The smell of fear is indigenous to charity do's. It's spread regardless of class, creed or billing. Its a great bond. The straight actor is at best a pack animal. Unlike the stand-up comic, who travels alone. Or the

WOMANKIND

BENEFIT PERFORMANCE
May 3rd 1998 7.30pm Q.E.H.

INTRODUCTION
Professor Deborah Sharp

Heart to Heart
poems performed
by
Jane Lapotaire

CLOSING ADDRESS
Professor Ursula King

RAFFLE DRAW

Cambridge Arts Theatre Disabled Access Appeal

Cambridge Arts
Theatre

A Reading of Poetry
by
Jane Lapotaire

Sunday 1 December 1996
7.00 p.m.

at the Theatre, Peterhouse
by kind permission of the Master and Fellows

Denne Gilkes Memorial Fund
President: Dennis L Flower Chairman: Guy Woolfenden

An Evening of

Favourite Poetry

with

Jane Lapotaire

The Shakespeare Institute
Stratford-upon-Avon

Sunday 13th April 1997

Denne Gilkes Memorial Fund Registered Charity Number: 502269

HEART to HEART

An anthology
of love's pains
and pleasures

Jane Lapotaire

Devised by
Chris Green and
Jane Lapotaire

Saturday 25 October
at 7.30 pm

Saint Mary's Church
Ilmington

Programme £6
in aid of the village hall

comic actor who wishes he did, when someone less experienced, qualified or kind, steps on one of his precious laughs. Hoops of fire are easier to face when you all face them together. That's the irreplaceable bond that theatre actors share, that is simply not the same when faced with a television or film camera. Then your fear is that your best shot will go on the cutting room floor, because the set designer thought *his* best shot was something quite other. Or the cameraman liked his lighting best in another. Or the assistant director thought the crowd behind you were best in another. And there's nothing you can do about it. Film and television work is out of your hands.

When the evening's over and the audience are clapping wildly, gratitude perhaps not entirely untinged with relief for those who were in the know about last-minute scripts and choices, or in on the shambles that was the rehearsal, and your hosts are even wilder in the profusion of praise and thanks for the vast amount harvested in one evening, your hands stop shaking, and you are glad that you did it. Your Jean Muir is a sodden sweaty rag, as you shove it anyhow into the tip that is your holdall, amidst whoops of delight and 'We did its!' in the broom cupboard of a dressing room, while you clutch a slice of homemade quiche and a glass of warm white wine, and try not to think about the long drive home.

Someone should do a gala for actors who do galas.

Endings and Beginnings

Heading towards the end of a year, other things may have come to an end, though not necessarily because of a particular date. I find all this millennium stuff and nonsense. Did any of us alive now think at age eight, or even thirty-eight, goodness me I'm going to be alive in the year 2000? I'm sure most of us weren't aware of it until quite recently. Until we were made aware of it by the all-pervasive market forces. Order your New Year's Eve 1999 champagne now. It's a critical milestone for capitalism.

Unless something cataclysmic happens to us personally, on the day, the HP payments will continue on 1 January 2000, as will the rift in the family, the search for a job, and the battles for better health. The cycles of birth, growth and death are no respecters of particular days, they have their own built-in timers, which can bring shocks or surprises, nice or nasty.

It's never easy to admit that something one used to value has come to an end. Especially as the years roll by, ending something has a resonance of The End that we all find difficult to face. The ego really tightens its grip when faced with death.

'Death? No thanks. Not for me.'

We often struggle on for years in outgrown relationships, jobs that we no longer do with zeal or relish, old patterns of thinking and detrimental habits (yes, I've started smoking again) largely because to face change, to be rid of the old, to face the new, is frightening. Or worse – to face the vacuum between the two.

Friends for Life

A Friend
To talk and laugh with mutual concessions; to read
pleasant books; to jest and to be solemn; to dissent from
each other without offence, to teach one another
somewhat, or somewhat to learn, to expect those absent
with impatience and embrace their return with joy.

ST AUGUSTINE, 354–430 AD

A friend is someone whose company you actively seek.

ANON

I've just lost a friend. No, that's not a euphemism for someone
having passed on, deceased, died. This is an ex-friend. I'd
known her for twenty years. Surely that's a time lapse equivalent
to having given up smoking? – you would think that by then the
habit had stuck. Well, it had. Stuck. The friendship. There was
no growth, no change, no journeying on, enjoying our differ-
ences or learning from them. There was also, now, no shouting
match, no airing of points of view, except rather calmly by letter.
Two me – one her. So far. But I see no future in it. A tepid,
dwindling correspondence perhaps, that mirrors so exactly the
dwindling that took place quite rapidly and recently between us.

But the friendship as such is finished. And I finished it.

And I am left with a sadness, and a feeling I can't quite deny or ignore, that to be unable to continue a friendship founded on such long knowledge, is somehow a shortcoming. Or is it?

We learn early on that friends are for life. Free from the constraints of a sexual relationship and all the tortuous webs that that kind of intimacy weaves, we run to our friends when distress, divorce or any other kind of direness looms. As someone from Stratford once said,

But if the while I think on thee dear friend
All losses are restored and sorrows end.

We had known each other well. We had lived together for six months with my then small son, aged nine, in her one-roomed flat. In fact we had all slept in the one room, taking turns to sleep in two put-you-up beds and a double in strict rotation. My son missed out on the double bed through lack of size qualifications, for which my friend more than amply compensated. School necessitated him being asleep at a reasonable hour, which curtailed our watching television, no great hardship for me, but it also restricted our chat, unless we retired to the rather cold and unwelcoming kitchen that she shared with two other flatmates, two gay men.

She had fallen on hard times financially, having been forced to resign from her job through the personal spite of a personnel manager, which meant she couldn't claim dole. As my son and I were initially homeless on our return from America, and had paid through the nose for a minuscule one-roomed flat of our own, while I trod the streets of a November London in between performances house-hunting, it seemed wisest all round for us to move in to her, for me to pay her bills and for her to offer babysitting services, which she did with great joy. I cooked for us all, which alleviated her terror of the kitchen. She had the time and the inclination to play games of Cluedo and Monopoly with my son while I, clueless, threw money around on real properties, having what turned out to be completely unsuitable houses surveyed. The two in question consequently had to be abandoned as potential homes and I had to start again at square one. But there was tea and sympathy and N to return to and air my troubles with. And she had me for moral support, food and finance.

It worked well. We were all happy. Everyone benefited. It cemented a friendship that had been going for five years, but then only on a cinema outing/dinner basis. We got to know each other well. There's no space for hiding foibles when you are living in one room. We laughed a lot at the impossibility of the situation, and chivvied each other often. I shooed her out of her own kitchen when I was cooking and she moaned at me for my refusal to participate in her TV addiction. I had a car, so trips to the launderette and local shops saved her feet and her carrying. When my son finally moved into our new home, my first ever house of my own, N was there to share our first day and our delight.

Over the following years our friendship became closer, and N became family. Birthdays, Christmas and all special days, it was taken as read that N would be there. Even her move back to her home town, refusing the chance to buy her London flat at a ridiculously low price, as the words 'mortgage' and 'bank manager' didn't fit in with her non-establishment vocabulary (although her refusal had, in my opinion, a slight tail-between-the-legs air about it,) didn't seriously dampen the closeness. I missed her going, of course. We spoke often on the phone, shared problems and laughs as we had always done and, as often as my work would allow, I would drive the three-hour journey to stay with her. We carried on our chivvying – she at me for doing too much and running myself ragged; me at her for not doing enough to keep her on top of her life. She hadn't noticed how her family treated her as a joke. Anything cack-handed, anything clumsy was called 'doing an N', and she seemed to go along with it. I didn't know why she didn't mind. Or if she did, why she did nothing about it. I would have minded dreadfully being the family victim, but at the time I didn't see this for the sign that it obviously was.

I carried on my sporadic financial support – her new job was not well paid, and she was not anyway good with money, and I would cook for her in her new home and shoo her out from under my feet in the kitchen there too. Her new home was my country retreat. I'd yearned for one for years before I acquired the cottage. She'd indulged my passion for wide open spaces, and I'd indulge her taste for special treats. She would sit in my car eating the picnic I'd prepared, happily listening to a radio station she couldn't get at home. Warm and cosseted inside, she'd smile with pleasure as she watched me disappear into the distance to walk the nearby hills. She was my best friend.

She wasn't happy in her job, the only one the small town could offer. It was a new departure for her, something she wasn't trained to do and, I felt, was ill-equipped to do emotionally.

'You, looking after delinquent children?' I joked. 'How will they know the difference?'

In spite of her size, she is a frail, sensitive woman, a Pisces, given to a lot of dreaming and not a lot of doing. She would writhe when I had a go at her for not doing something about changing her job as I could see the havoc it was wreaking. And she would smile and say, 'Oh, I know. I know. You're right. You are good to have a go at me.' That was my role. Having a go. Only the best of friends will tell you when you've gone off the tracks, when you can't see that you're out of order. I know. I still mourn my dear friend Caroline who used to say, 'That's such crap, Jane!' and she was often right. And even when she wasn't, I loved her all the more for putting herself and what she believed on the line in the face of my different views.

There was a terrible hole for me in North London where N had lived, but given the displeasure of the new job, all in all she seemed happy to be amongst her childhood friends, with family not too far away, and she was far enough away from London to smile wryly with relief and shake her head wonderingly at all the years she had endured there. She didn't want to come back to the grime, the noise and the pushing and shoving, and whenever she did come to us for the odd weekend, as her bond with my son was very strong too, she made not a little noise about how much she hated London, and would smile wryly about how I could manage to endure it.

My endurance wasn't always constant. I badly needed her to visit me sometime later, when the going got bumpy. I wasn't always able to be the coper I then thought myself, running a house, juggling a child and a succession of problem au pairs, working long hours when I had work, worrying myself sleepless about my mortgage when I didn't.

I asked her to help.

She didn't come.

Years later she confessed that she had come to London that time but had stayed with another friend. That took a bit of swallowing, but I swallowed.

The bumps in my life got bigger and when my son left home to go to university, as I've said, finding I had no reason to keep my fists up for the two of us any longer, my exhausted, burned-out body had its say, and the borrowed time I'd been living on ran out. The big bump to my pride was those three weeks I spent in hospital. She didn't visit. I was too ill and too worn out to notice at the time, but inevitably it came up later.

'You should have shouted louder,' she said. It was agreed that I was not good at asking for help or at describing how bad things were. I decided I would learn to ask for help. But again she needed mine before I had a chance to put my new voice into action.

A car accident two years ago rendered her immobile for several months and finally and relievedly, separated her from the job which she had grown to loathe and which had taken its toll on her spirit, her health and latterly, from what I could deduce, all her friendships. Conversation with her had become increasingly monotone as she did nothing but complain about the job; all suggestions about possible alternatives were met with sighs and inaction and or another glass of whisky or lager.

I gave her tapes and books from a support group that I'd been attending, full of positive rethinking of one's life and one's attitude to it. It had taken me a long time to be humbled enough to seek help, and even longer to admit that I was seeking it. Bewildered by finding myself living alone, my son having flown the nest, and marginalised in my profession simply because of being over fifty, I'd known that change was coming and thought I had prepared myself for it. But nothing I'd done could have prepared me for the shock of finding myself and my life so different to what it had been for so long. It's not for nothing that that shock is called the mid-life crisis. It's a time for taking stock, for finding the courage to face the past, the strength to let it go, deciding whether the future that's left is to be lived in the same way, and if not, doing something about it. They never warn you, these self-help courses, that the one casualty in your new positive thinking may well be a friend who doesn't hold you in the new-found, and hard-fought-for, esteem in which you now hold yourself. You're no longer able to discount yourself to be party to other people's discounting. Each self-help course should carry a could-be-fatal-to-friends warning.

N is twelve years older than me, and as I watched her slip down the slope of total inaction about herself, her future and her life, I realised that she had never done any stocktaking. She'd drifted or run. She had run from London, to her childhood home. Perhaps the tail had been between the legs after all. I decided to help with what had been of help to me. The books and the tapes were greeted with great delight, and determination to put them into action, which lasted several days. And the exercises she could have done to straighten out her thinking, were soon passed over in favour of another can of lager or the TV. You can lead a horse to water... 'Only the person who has faith in himself is able to be faithful to others,' I read somewhere. We began to get scratchy with each other.

As soon after her accident as my work would allow I drove (with another of her friends as a surprise) to visit her in hospital, replete with hastily bought Christmas presents for her, a good three weeks early. I sat hunched over her broken plastered foot, trying to reheal it with Reiki and love and care for a couple of hours, then drove another three hours back in winter gloom and rain and fed and housed the other friend on the way.

Since the accident of course she hasn't been able to visit me, even though she's been walking without a stick for the best part of a year now. So I've been doing the transporting of friendship, food, presents, the odd bit of money and buckets of TLC, even though I was barely handling the residue of tiredness and under-par health that followed in the wake of my hospitalisation, that's taken me several slow years to begin to put to rights.

Then my new voice came into its own.

I shouted loud for help last October. Too much work and too much stress all came at once. I was working on my one-woman show, rewriting and rehearsing at nights and rehearsing Katherine of Aragon during the day. *Henry VIII* was to open at the Swan in Stratford three days after I'd finished the run of my one woman show in Bristol. I was familiar with the signs. Loneliness and exhaustion is a powerful mixture. I just needed someone at home at the end of a long day, someone to be there when I finally and wearily dragged myself in through the door. I rang N.

Long pause after I'd stated my case.

'I can't come. I'm still waiting for the claim money to come through from the accident. I haven't got the train fare.'

'I'll give you the money for the train fare.' I often did.

'I can't afford to live in London.'

'I'll buy the food.'

'I can't. I really can't. I'm having a terrible time. My head's not in a good place. I'd be no help to anyone.'

So she didn't come.

I was upset. I was needy. I'd asked for help and got none. Somehow I knew that a corner had been turned. I'd turned it and I was walking away. Our paths had diverged.

She used the word 'betrayal' of what she'd done when she wrote her letter. I didn't feel anything as strong as betrayal, just horribly let down, and a pervading sense of finality.

She wrote too, that she couldn't cope with my 'having another go at her'. So my role was redundant and my robust nudging now obviously misplaced.

I didn't find myself over the ensuing weeks thinking that the friendship had been misplaced. I didn't deny it, or feel cynical about it. I didn't want revenge or reprisals. I did ring her once, overwhelmed by the tiredness that I had dreaded, to say that I felt gutted by her behaviour, and I was dangerously near to being angry. I got the answerphone, which was probably just as well.

The words of somebody very famous kept going through my mind. 'You should forgive not seven times seven, but seventy times seven.' We'd only had three major crises, but I knew it was over. I am no saint.

'Do you miss her?' another friend asked when I talked about the problem.

'Not really,' I was surprised to hear myself reply. 'She won't face pain.'

And I believe that's the only way to grow. By living through it and coming out the other side. It seems such an irony that during all her other troubles, losing her job, moving home, the anguish of that unsuitable work which destroyed the little security she had within herself, that I was there, trying to encourage, trying to help, trying to give her something to hold on to through the darkness, and now that it's all finally caught up with her, I'm walking away. I've walked away. Sad.

Another friend said, 'There are some people in life who are just takers.'

I'd never thought of N that way. I'd been happy to give. But the giving was running out. A friendship has to be a two-way exchange. The giving was being thrown into a bottomless pit. A pit that never improved or even changed shape. 'Love is not Love which alters when it alteration finds.' I had been looking for alteration. Or perhaps growth. So I looked long and hard at my help. Had I been trying to fix her, or just help her help herself? Should I have swallowed hard and just gone on, in spite of my sense of finality about it all? Should I have stayed on board, swallowing hard the other 487 times for forgiveness?

Would a 'sorry' have helped? A little sorry goes a long way. Both options surely would have resulted in inevitable resentment which would have poisoned, little by little, the little we had left. 'A broken friendship may be soldered, but it will never be sound.'

So then I had to look to me. What had I got out of it recently? A hard question to ask, but a necessary one. And sadly, I knew the answer.

Friends for life indeed. For Life. Life, that force which heralds change, and makes us change and grow. And on the journey, it would seem, sometimes we grow apart and some friends fall by the wayside. It is sad. A lot of things we're told in childhood that don't come from books, are fairy stories. The reality is somewhat different...

So now I find myself with a space. A space where a friend once was. But in that space other seeds may shoot.

Men

Someone must fill the gap between platitudes and bayonets.

ADLAI STEVENSON, 1900–1965

When I look back on the pain of sex, the love like a wild fox ready to bite, the antagonism that sits like a twin beside love, and contrast it with affection, so deeply unrepeatable, of two people who have lived a life together, it's the affection I find the richer. It's that I would have again.

ENID BAGNOLD, *AUTOBIOGRAPHY,* 1969

Of course there is an obvious gap in this book. To give them their due – and they don't get many – the press office at the RSC in Stratford and a tabloid newspaper, which for health and reputation reasons (mine) had better remain nameless, did try mutually, albeit not consciously, to put this omission to rights.

'They'd like to do an interview with you,' said a somewhat intrepid junior from the press office, 'about the men in your life.' That gave me pause. I pondered, not for too long, what the newspaper's motives could possibly be.

While I was playing Piaf I was hung on a neat journalistic hook of 'same childhood'. In spite of my continued assurances that I was not, like Piaf, four foot nine – I, at five foot five, just played her with my legs bent. Neither was I born on a pavement. My foster mother would have been most upset to hear Allingham House – Ipswich's wartime nursing home – spoken of in such a manner. I had not been struck blind at the age of five and been cured of it, as Piaf was somewhat miraculously, by the prayers of the ladies of the night in whose brothel the early years of her childhood were spent. I had never sung on the pavement for money, the nearest being my vocal warm-up in the car park of The Other Place at Stratford which often elicited from Geoffrey Freshwater, a warm-hearted RSC stalwart who played Piaf's agent, the odd penny thrown on the ground to stop me singing. I never had been nor ever would be the greatest female singer in the world, earning at one point just slightly less than what Frank Sinatra was carrying home in sacks. But the hook stuck.

Until I became a single parent. Then the hook was moved along to another slot. 'They can't dish any dirt on me,' I said to my son, rather pathetically, when he was old enough to understand and old enough to question why he was dragged into every interview. 'That's the only thing "they" want to talk to me about, it's hard to get them off the subject, and me sometimes for that matter, sorry.'

The pathetic quality of my explanation was coloured by a very real fear that the simple uttering of the phrase would send whoever could be bothered scurrying into my past with their dirt shovels. These particular instruments are now a continual subject of national debate, as far as the privacy of people who are unfortunate enough to fall into public view through no fault of their own are concerned, or people who have public jobs like actors, whose 'market value' and the theatre's pull for 'bums on seats' are increased by exposure in the press.

I pondered whether the single parent hook was now deemed past its hung-by date and whether the search was for something more salacious.

'Yes,' I said a few days later, eliciting smiles from the press office, not a frequent occurrence, 'I have four men in my life.' The smiles broadened.

Left to right: Professor David McLellan, Donald Hale, Canon Neville Boundy and Maurice Denham OBE

I had decided to give my son a wide berth.

'There's a Professor of Politics at Kent University in Canterbury. There's Don the odd-job man who drives my show van. There's my dearest Maurice Denham who'll be eighty-nine this year. And there's the Reverend Nev Boundy, Cotham's parish priest in Bristol, and chaplain to the theatre and the theatre school.'

The smiles had begun to droop.

'And they are all MY FRIENDS,' I said in capital letters.

I never heard from the press office on this particular subject again. But I did rather wickedly try to press home a point, mostly for my own satisfaction I suppose, when next I encountered the intrepid junior in one of the dark labyrinthine corridors of administrative power front of house at Stratford.

'What about that interview about the men in my life?'

'Oh,' she said, looking rather sheepish. 'They never rang back when I gave them your list.'

'I wonder why,' I said, truly wickedly, as I wasn't wondering at all.

The only ponder that then ensued was whether I would now be hung on a middle-aged female past-my-sell-by-date hook. To avoid that prong, and perhaps to pander to the salacious just a bit, there is a new man in my life. He is the most gracious, elegant, courteous gentleman I have ever known. He is excellent company, single and, unusually for a friend of mine, very rich. And I have lots of far from platonic plans to get to know him better. That's the London offering. But there's one looming on the horizon in New York too. Ditto credentials, except that he's a writer.

But just for the record: as far as Men In My Life are concerned, I have one son, no brothers or uncles, and have never known the name of my father. So knowledge of the male of the species on the family front has been in rather short supply. I've been married twice, divorced twice, have had two live-in lovers in London and lived in with another in New York, and have absolutely no intention of talking about all the bits in between.

I would like my heart to soar again, and more mundanely someone to make me a cup of tea or run my bath and offer me a shoulder for my head, but it's my older women friends I really value.

Their courage to face pain, grow inside and learn from it, and to pass it on with wisdom when they have surfaced, and humour when they have been beaten down by it. It's taken me fifty-three years to realise that men are totally different to women, and I must have spent thirty-three years battling for it not to be so.

Treading the Boards with the Bard

It may seem perhaps perverse to have left writing about my work in detail until last, given that it influences my days and is the means by which I live. Apart from teaching and writing. When my grubbing around for work as a journalist bears fruit, then my days are centred round my laptop, with the comfort of knowing that if I snarl up at the cottage in Warwickshire, then help is available in the form of the highly skilled Di, who comes from Leamington Spa and who, with great patience untangles the folders and files that have been triplicated in error, unravels the spaghetti that is my mind after two hours of fruitlessly studying the techno-speak in the instruction booklet – not a word of which I have understood – and slowly and carefully makes me practice what she's done, accompanying it all in words of one syllable that even my machine-resistant mind can understand.

When my services are required at the Performing Arts Department of Washington University, the Oxford School of Drama, the Bristol Old Vic School, the Globe, or any of the other places where I'm lucky enough to have a group of poor unsuspecting students in Shakespeare's thrall, then I go into performance mode. Teaching demands the same energy as performing, in fact often more. There has to be a continual outpouring of energy to fire the students, constant encouragement to get them off the ground and the words off the page, and a conscious working towards an atmosphere of trust and affection in the rehearsal room, so that they can be released from their own constraints physically and psychologically, and dare to try. The rehearsal room is where we get it wrong, where we go down all the possible avenues of thought and action that the text indicates, to find what is the most effective means and the most truthful end to portray the play to it's best advantage, and not to mind that if in the process, as often happens, we make fools of ourselves. Laughter is a great healer, and a sense of fun a great incentive to experiment. If it's all heavy going, too serious and over earnest, we might as well have taken those sensible jobs in banks and offices that were seen as preferable by our families to the precariousness of working as an actor.

Bernard Shaw, never short of words, said, 'We teach what we need to learn.' I hope my students get as much fun from me as I get from them. I learn the same lessons over and over again. Every student is, of course, unique, with his or her own set of physical or vocal shortcomings and often at the beginning of their training they see Drama School as a place from which they will eventually emerge magically rid of all these handicaps, into a shining new trouble-free zone.

Of course it isn't like that. Drama school just opens our eyes to the problems and gives us some technical know-how as how to manage these shortcomings throughout the rest of our working lives, so that their limitations and their influence on our performance is reduced to a minimum. A small proportion can be eradicated with awareness and work. I started drama school with a vocal range of about four notes. I think that along the way I have managed to acquire a few more. The girl whose voice may be stuck in the head notes of a thin soprano whine may be freed to locate the rich chest range previously hidden from herself, if she discovers that she was Daddy's favourite and used those tones throughout her childhood to get her way. Most of Shakespeare's heroines require an assertiveness that is to be found in those chest notes. The young man who is an apt and able interpreter of text may find that his nervousness about performing locates itself in rigid tension in his shoulders, so he is in danger of playing every part like a tortoise half-hidden within its shell. A few exercises to free up that area, and a psychological knowledge of why he should need to hide within his shoulder-blades, may give him the courage to face the fear inherent in us all when performing, and the relief of knowing that his fear is not particular or unique. I still, in an eagerness to get it right and to want to do it quickly, lean forward from my pelvis. An action that, some thirty years later, still has Rudi Shelley's Viennese tones ringing in my ears, 'Jane, why do you come round the corner with your nose first and your ass last?' In order to avoid this unfortunate posture, which can play havoc with my voice, as it can't be properly supported from the diaphragm in that position, I use the one rehearsal just before the first run-through consciously to check my physical alignment. Of course, spending most of my working life in the classical theatre means I am usually swathed in long skirts and held in by corseting, which does a lot to support and much to hide the fatal flaw. Short skirts and high heels are my Waterloo.

The actor is her own instrument, her voice, body and mind all indicate what state of awareness and understanding she is in. There is nowhere to hide on stage. Least of all within yourself. It is the hardest thing of all to simply stand on a stage, relaxed but alert, to speak clearly and well, to have your attention focused inwardly, with an objective awareness of what you are doing outwardly.

Many of us at the beginning of our working lives think that the character we are playing is somehow 'out there', a 'something' to be grabbed from out the ether and put on us like a coat. It is the opposite. It is an uncovering and shedding of all the layers in the self that are not relevant to the part, a letting go of all the tricks of the ego – 'look at me, how clever/funny/skilful or just damn talented, I'm being' – until there is an interlocking between the essence of the character and the essence of the actor that is forceful in its simplicity, undeniable and mesmerising in its truth.

Easy to say. Hard to do. Very difficult to be simple. Takes years of practice. Years to learn that the actor is, at best, an uncluttered medium through which the spirit of the play may then freely travel. Get that ego out of the way. Then one may be blessed with that best of experiences as an actor, when you don't play the play, but the play plays you.

One of the blessings of teaching something you actually *do* is that it means you have access to a whole range of practical notions and aids that may have been of use to you when doing that work. You are familiar with the rigours of the job. You know what devastation first night nerves can cause the voice. You know the agony of trying to stuff lines into an overloaded brain when it is simply too tired to take on any more. You may have an idea why a certain line isn't getting a laugh – because someone is moving during it and deflecting the attention. Or the feed line – the line before it – isn't being served up the right way. And best of all you can help with self-consciousness, the actor's bugbear. Consciousness of the self and not of what the character is thinking or feeling. Get your head out of yourself and into the part, very like meditation.

There is a great freedom to be subversive, as an actor who teaches, which the rebel in me relishes. You are not constrained by the rules that normally pervade a classroom (as Tom Stoppard put it, 'We are actors – we're the opposite of people!') so by breaking the rules, or simply not abiding by them, often with humour, you can unite and bond and often be just downright wicked. You have the perfect answer when you don't have the answer: 'I'm not a teacher. I'm an actor. Let's try it both ways and see what works. Let's look it up in the book, or let's ask someone more knowledgeable.'

'I'm an actor, not a policeman' is useful when teaching the under sixteens – something I try not to do for the sake of my reluctance to curfew patrol too often, their future safety and welfare being more important than my concern about the short fuse on my patience. But I've found that 'If anyone is bored they may leave the room as long as they tell their teacher where they are' is a very effective tool for keeping all but the seriously recalcitrant firmly in place.

You don't have to use these ploys or waste valuable energy in bringing drama students to the starting post of attentiveness and willingness to learn, they're there already. But one of the hardest things to do is not to make value judgements about their relative abilities. It's not for you to decide whether they have got what it takes or not. Of course you can't help but have your private opinions, but it's wise to keep them private. Theatre criticism at any level is a fiendishly subjective wicket. For every 200 people who think you are the best thing since Sarah Siddons. there are 200 others who think you should never be allowed to put a foot on a stage ever, anywhere. Teaching drama students is a bit like being a barrister. It's not for you to decide whether the defendant is innocent or guilty. That's in the jurisdiction of the jury – the audience. As a teacher/cultivator, your job as the gardener is to ensure that the conditions are conducive to growth. There's little more exciting than seeing a seed of thought or the conjuring of a picture, take hold of a student, who then takes hold of it, makes it their own and both then flourish.

But whatever the boons of holding the reins of a class, and guiding its direction so that the greatest number benefit from the time, I couldn't do it for long. My estimation and respect for teachers has doubled and trebled since I first started sharing what was taught to me. I don't have the stamina for that sort of dedication. I often end up like a wrung-out rag after a class, similar to a post-performance wreck, as I said, but one important bit of the energy exchange I receive as an actor is missing. The energy that an audience gives back unwittingly to the players in performance. That energy is a teacher, too. The quality of an audience's attention will inform the actor's work as she travels through the part. A slow reaction may mean a mistimed line, restless inattention may mean that the text isn't coming out freshly, but is being generalised, coated with the dulling veneer of habit as each moment and word isn't being really lived in, energised and found anew. The need to want to speak has to be rediscovered every time.

No actor can inhabit every corner of a role each night, every night. It's a complex business being a human being, and doubly complex portraying one. Swayed by this or that emotion, troubled by this or that problem, the actor goes into the theatre with certain facets of her personality uppermost, according to the kind of day she's had. On good days it's easier to access the truth of a joyful emotion, on bad days it's easier to be sad. Though it's never quite as simple as that. The play has an organic life of its own, too.

I wanted to be an actor for the most clichéd of reasons. Not having had a mother or father to love me, I wanted all those people 'out there' to love me. That makes me squirm to write it, so it must be true. It's no longer the reason why I act of course. In fact the supposition that I do is at present undergoing stern review. The physical demands on the actor are often similar to those of an athlete, and the physical reaction after a first night is not too dissimilar to the aches and pains experienced as the result of a mild car crash, if such a thing could ever be mild. The body goes into a state of numbness after all that adrenalin, and often the second performance seems an insurmountable hill to climb. The body is empty, dulled and just refusing to be kick-started. Always a useful knack to have as an actor, the kick-start. The

machine can't be allowed to idle just because it's tired.
There's an audience out there who've paid to see it run. So
run it must, whatever its condition and whatever the attitude
and whereabouts of the driver.

And it's that that I'm beginning to object to. Or rather what
my ageing body is beginning to object to. Now I know that age
is all an attitude of mind. And my attitude is changing.
Changing from finding the prospect of going through the
shredder, both emotionally and physically, a stimulating
challenge, to finding in its place the magnetic lure of the
armchair by the fire. In a manner of speaking. Friends of my
age who do 'normal' jobs are thinking of retiring. I'm thinking
of retiring from the front. Getting behind the line of fire.
Maybe directing a bit more. Or rather holding the reins a bit
more. Acting is such a passive job. Unless you do it all yourself.
All of it – the writing and the acting, and most of the directing,
which this last year I did. Given the ambivalence I've just
expressed about working as an actor this act may seem more
than paradoxical. But being perverse by nature I've just gone
and put myself right back in the front line. I've just done my
first ever one-woman show, which is when you really take all
the flak, as there's no one else for it to hit.

Shakespeare As I Knew Her

The labour we delight in physics pain.

WILLIAM SHAKESPEARE, *MACBETH*, 1606

Intrigued? Barely curious? Or perhaps the mere word Shakespeare puts you off completely? Maybe your reaction is similar to that of a governor of the Bristol Old Vic where I first performed this show: 'Oh Lord, it's not a *feminist* thing is it?' 'It' is actually the title of a one-woman piece I've written for myself. Well, I didn't write it completely alone – I had a little help from my writer friend in Stratford. But believe me, it wasn't easy. For a start, as a member of a theatre audience I've always felt uneasy about watching a solo performance. No, it's not only the boredom of flicking through the programme and finding only one name there – no one else, and not even another costume coming on to relieve the gloom. Ah hah, I think, or perhaps more accurately, Oh no! – here's an ego large enough to think it can entertain an entire auditorium of 200 plus for (please God, not more than) two hours. And that feeling of discomfort has always kept me from ever entertaining the idea of attempting such a thing for a good thirty years of working life.

So what made me change the habit of a lifetime?

'A one-woman show? Oh no I couldn't, it's such an ego trip!'

'That's such an icky Calvinistic attitude,' said dear Patty Schvey, the open-hearted and generous wife of my host when I teach Shakespeare at Washington University in St Louis,

Missouri. Her frankness was couched in that endearing and devastatingly honest manner that Americans have, bless 'em. 'You owe it to those kids to share what you've learned. Do you realise what an opportunity you had working with Laurence Olivier, Paul Schofield, Peter Brook, Tyrone Guthrie, John Gielgud, Irene Worth?' I could go on. Me I mean. But I won't. Coming from her it sounds all right, coming from me it sounds an awful lot like name-dropping.

'Do you realise how many people would just love to hear about all that? Are you crazy?'

Er... no, Patty dear, to both questions.

But it was an impressive list. I was impressed and that was only the half of it.

The other names that could have been added – not quite so cataclysmic in their screen cred, but much beloved or revered within the profession – names like Colin Blakely, Nigel Hawthorne, Nicol Williamson...

So the two weeks after this chastising conversation from big-hearted Patty found me almost permanently attached to Henry's old electric typewriter, secretly bashing out SAIKH in order to present it to him, foil-wrapped and tied in a big red ribbon, magicked from somewhere in the folds of their voluminous house, so that it was waiting for him on his breakfast plate the morning of my annual, and now annually sad, departure from St Louis.

Between the unwrapping of the foil and the only slightly later locking of my suitcases, the manager of the large university theatre, the Edison, was round, schedules discussed, dates chosen, a caricature of Shakespeare requested for the programme, quickly squiggled by me, and the deed done. Two performances of *Shakespeare As I Knew Her* were set in concrete for February 1997. Search me where the jokes about slow movers in the Mid-West come from.

I experienced then just the slightest tremor of fear. What had been just paper in the typewriter for two weeks, one of those days I was going to have to learn. And speak. In public. All sixty pages of it. But those days were distant. The tremor was duly dispatched.

So apart from this Missouri mangling, what else prompted me to string together excerpts from twelve of the main female roles I've played in the canon, compare Juliet's balcony scene with that of Jessica, play the end speech of Kate's from the *Shrew* two ways, throw in a bit of *Hamlet* and intersperse it all with anecdotes and jokes about the productions the excerpts come from? Well, as for the jokes, I've always wanted to do comedy and I'm not above basking in the reflected glory of those greats, or stooping low enough to tell a few gags at their expense. There's hopefully the odd bit of enlightenment about some of the text thrown in for good measure too.

So why have I done it? Well, I guess the glib answer is, now that my fast-held Calvinism has been well and truly pooh-poohed out of me, that I must be addicted to terror. Alone on stage for two hours? Well, forty-three and forty-eight minutes each half respectively. We timed it at our first read through.

I mean *my* first read through.

'Perfect timing. Leave them wanting more,' said my director, a very old friend, Charles Savage, chosen because he knows me well enough to be an outspoken crap-detector. Wanting *more?* I thought, gasping. I was shattered. What more? I wasn't capable of more and I'd just been sitting on a chair reading it, tense as a board, waiting and hoping, subconsciously I suppose, to hear someone else's voice join in. No one did.

Mind you, I had been rehearsing Katherine of Aragon in *Henry VIII* for the RSC from 10 a.m. to 5.30 p.m. That was my little day job. It just happened to coincide with *SAIKH*.

That's the trouble with this business. Feast or famine. One minute you're staring into the middle distance wondering if you'll ever work again, and should you have done that sensible secretarial course 'they' all said you should instead of going to drama school, and the next moment work's coming at you from all directions.

I opened *Shakespeare As I Knew Her* at the beloved Bristol Old Vic, where I trained and first trod the boards, and where I am excessively proud to be the Hon Pres of the Theatre Club. It was

the fiftieth anniversary of the Old Vic, for the Theatre and the Theatre Club, so this show was aptly timed to be my offering as part of their celebrations.

So I was working morning and night on Shakespeare, and Shakespeare and Fletcher, deep in a glut. A glut of iambic pentameters, a sea of caesuras and a mountain of irregular verse and feminine endings. And I loved it. Loved it that is, in the brief intervals that I wasn't stricken with paralysing terror. The initial tremor once neatly dispatched, resurfaced super-sized. It manifested itself at the most unseasonable and unreasonable of times. That was usually around four in the morning, when my overtired brain would wake me, go into overdrive, and decide to do a quick run of all twelve roles simultaneously, with a little bit of Katherine thrown in as an extra challenge. Simultaneously.

I know of a lot of male actors who've done one-man Shakespeare shows, but no women. Women do Virginia Woolf, yes, even a woman Dickens and of course the ubiquitous Jane Austen (there should be a moratorium on the work of that particular woman before we expire from the vistas of heaved-up busts and reel from middle-class obsessions with acreage and the suitability for wedlock thereby conferred) – but few lone female voices in Shakespeare.

'Every actor should do a one-person show. It's good for them,' uttered my mentor, guru and, for many of us who've had the luck to pass through his hands at the RSC, Shakespeare's representative on this planet, belovèd John Barton.

I thought at the time, when terror was momentarily assuaged by his approval, and my insecurity about the excerpts I'd chosen calmed by his eloquent blue pencil, which made radical cuts and changes to some to best know speeches in the canon – 'Don't worry, no one will every know we've moved that bit' – 'But John...'

'Don't fret!'

My fear level, in the face of his ostentatious reassurance dropped to about minus three (the norm most days, as I headed for D-Day, was about plus seven).

He made it sound a bit like taking sennapods; not very nice, but awfully good for you. Very British that. Calvin would have approved.

But back to the lone voice, and that's not just on stage. Who is there to natter to in the interval about the audience? The corridors backstage echo with emptiness. All the other dressing rooms are vacant. No one to joke with, or moan about, or take comfort from or even threaten revenge to: 'You sod, you cut the best line of my speech, you wait till Act Two.' If I'm lucky, I might catch a glimpse of the stage manager for a second or two, especially if I've really made a cock-up of the lines and her lighting plot has consequently gone haywire because all her cues are off. She might need to check, for her own peace of mind, that I haven't succumbed to early Alzheimers. Some kind soul might make me a cuppa, but I won't even have a dresser to chat to. I mean what woman needs help to get into a pair of trousers, a top and a skirt for goodness sake, if she's under eighty?

So I'm obviously not doing it for the company, which is the reason I'm usually lured back into the classical theatre, aka the breadline. It's axiomatic about the quality of scripts – the higher the crap factor the more you get paid. So you look on theatre work as food for the soul and close your ears to the screams from your bank manager and agent.

So why am I putting myself through this? Well, I'm a sucker for a challenge, as I've said before. And it's something new. Something I've never done before. Novel challenges are a bit thin on the ground after thirty years in the same job.

Also, I love those words. I want to get those words back into my mouth again.

I cried, I have to admit, on my last night of playing Rosalind in *As You Like It*, because I thought I would never have a chance to say those witty, exhilarating lines again. I felt the same sadness about saying goodbye to Viola's poignancy and Isabella's passion and Kate's delicious wilfulness... Cleopatra was even worse, because I only got to live with her for four weeks, as we did it on television. Ditto Lady Macbeth.

We live in such an ageist age. Edith Evans played Rosalind when she was forty-seven. Can't see that happening now. Over forty and you're on the leading lady classical past-it heap, with little to look forward to but earnest Emilia in *Othello* or voracious Volumnia in *Coriolanus*. Get the picture? Somebody's maid or somebody's Mum. Well, I don't feel quite ready yet to don either the mob cap or the matron's robe. So I'm stepping right back into Viola and Kate and Isabella etc etc and even Juliet – trying hard to eliminate from aural memory the distant, but nonetheless vividly embarrassing, inflections of my sixteen-year-old performance at Northgate Grammar School for Girls, and replacing it with a hopefully much improved model, in the light of thirty years of playing, and some fifteen years of teaching, Shakespeare.

It was studying Juliet for that performance at school that made the scales drop from my ears; 'The orchard walls are high and hard to climb…' What's difficult to understand about *that,* my sixteen-year-old self thought.

Anyway, this Juliet is unique. It's the first time that Juliet's ever been played by someone on Hormone Replacement Therapy…

We live in an age, too, of street cred, reductionism, estuary English – if it's slightly 'off' it must be right on. Now I'm all for blurring distinctions about who went where to school. We must be the only country in the world where education can be distinguished by accent. I try hard not to be resistant to change, if it's change for the good. But when language itself begins to be devalued, its resonances lost, its poetry belittled, or, worse, ridiculed, as machines isolate us and eliminate the need to actually speak to each other, and entertainment becomes machine-based too, rather than contact with people – then perhaps it's time to check whether we are wasting our inheritance and tarnishing the greatest living language in the world.

Unlike the French with their Académie Française, we have no official group to protect the undermining of our cultural icon – the spoken and written word. 'mericanisms now abound in our language, and I don't necessarily means words that come from

America. I mean flip-talk, sloppy modern-speak, shorthand slang-speak, words that don't really communicate anything other than very basic information, the item they represent. Language without resonance.

The spoken work can convey many levels of meaning, diffuse magic and reverberate myth. It can change us by the sheer exchange of energy in words from one person to another. It can unlock depths understanding within us that remain latent in everyday life. I don't dare to presume or begin to hope that *Shakespeare As I Knew Her* will manage some or any of that; let's just say I hope that it's a small step to reclaiming the feminine within the Bard and a little dollop of anti-word-tarnish polish.

Oh, yes and why have I called the show by this title?

Rosalind says in *As You Like It,* 'Do you not know I am a woman? When I think I must speak!'

As Robert Graves said, 'In spite of what people say about Shakespeare being good, he really is very good!'

That terror-tinged but rose-coloured optimism that marked the initial launching of the show, has now been well and truly weathered. At the beginning, the luxury of being driven back from Bristol (courtesy of the RSC, for this relief much thanks) in the last week of the performances after the show at 11 p.m., arriving in the deep dark of a Warwickshire night at my cottage, the relief was somewhat blurred by having to get up relatively early each morning to go to the rehearsals for *Henry VIII* in Stratford. Rehearsals from which I had been absent for a week. In politics that may well be a lifetime. In theatre it's a new production. There were bits of the play that were unrecognisable to my dazed eyes, from what they'd been when I'd last been part of it in a previous life, in the Clapham rehearsal rooms. More dazed, head spinning from new moves and new bits of songs that I'd had to pick up from the rest of the cast as they sang them – I would get into the car at the end of the day, and be driven back to Bristol, biting my nails and praying for no traffic jams on the M5. On arrival I'd grab something to eat, hurl myself through the well-meaning members of the Bristol Old Vic Theatre Club in the bar, and pray again, as I put on my make-up, that the words of *Shakespeare As I Knew Her* would come out in the right order and that I could keep the snippet of Katherine of Aragon down to the four lines we'd planned and not launch, on automatic pilot, into the entire role.

I did have a major blip one night. Not with Katherine, but with lines that I'd written myself – always the hardest to have conviction in. As I now know.

'Rosalind is the biggest female part in *Hamlet*.' Yes, well. I thought it sounded odd at the time. I said out loud that I was just checking to see if they were on the ball. They knew it was a lie. What's more they knew I knew. So we all had a laugh. I corrected it to 'in Shakespeare', aged fifteen years in three seconds (and this project is supposed to be part of my old-age pension plan) and the show went on, with me running fast behind to catch it up.

Now I spend my time wondering if the show will catch me up. I arrive and wonder whether dear Don the odd-job man, he of the wise saws when my son left home, will have successfully negotiated the tortuous roads from the farm in Compton Scorpion where my new friend Patricia gives house to my set in one of her barns, and that the throne, red backdrop, floor-cloth, stool and tailor's dummy – on which I hang my bits of costume – will ever arrive in the same town, in time for the stage crew, whom I've never seen before and who've never seen me or it, to set it all up before the audience arrive.

The Bristol crew drove it to Stratford, Don drove it to Salisbury. In Antibes I was minus my director and the set, British Airways excess baggage charges being what they are. I had to light the show myself and improvise with furniture generously loaned or acquired from Hilary King and her Red Pear Company. I stayed in the Kings' exquisite villa, ran my lines by the Mediterranean, did two masterclasses on Shakespeare in French at local schools and plunged my scrambled brain at the end of the day in the Kings' azure pool. Don has to face Cornwall and Cumbria in a couple of months, and a month after that I may have to face audiences in New York and Washington DC. I don't think thrones are easy to come by in America. Don says he'll drive his van there too. But I think he's kidding.

The show for some inexplicable reason now runs fifty-two and fifty-four minutes. We've sharpened lots of flabby lines, tightened up some jokes, cut others and I've learned not to go at it like a bull in a china shop, but to pace myself, and give myself moments in which to take stock. 'Réculer pour mieux sauter'. Or at least mieux stagger. I've learned to play the linking bits between the Shakespeare almost like cabaret. Or at least that's how the audiences have taught me to play them. I've learned to wait for the laughs to come, and not to hurry by those lines in case they don't. It's a double dollop of embarrassment if they don't, of course, as I've written those linking bits, and then I learn that *they* don't think they're funny. I've learned a lot. I've learned to be a van loader, a lighting designer, an assistant stage manager, a wardrobe mistress and a sound adviser. That's before I go on stage. I carry my props and costumes everywhere myself. It's been a heavy lesson which has made my very grateful for those people actors so often take for granted. The Stage Management.

Shakespeare as I knew her
Jane LAPOTAIRE
RED PEAR COMPANY

26 / 27 septembre 20h00

Jane LAPOTAIRE présente un one-woman show plein de sensibilité et d'imagination, fruit de sa longue carrière classique à travers le monde. Ce spectacle, tout en légèreté et en anecdotes, comprend des extraits de douze rôles féminins majeurs de SHAKESPEARE.
Réservations : 04 93 61 01 71
Places : 120 F

I think that's what John Barton meant. What he didn't know or didn't say, was how grateful I would be to my fellow actors once I returned full-time to *Henry VIII*. The luxury of standing on a stage when someone else is talking. The luxury of having that time to think. The sheer bliss of leaving the stage in a break between entrances, and going to the Stratford green room for what is described as a coffee. Now there's gratitude indeed.

After *Shakespeare As I Knew Her* had been safely stowed away in Patricia's barn, I was free to have the odd glass of red wine. I'd been off the booze for three months and on a strict energy-promoting regime. Athlete-like, I'd had to keep my strength up. I couldn't afford to fall ill, having been crazy enough to take on such a workload of my own volition in the first place. No encouragement came from anyone to be *that* stupid.

I was free, too, to settle into *Henry VIII* and find that the price of learning and working on two things at once, was that every performance of Katherine held a little bubble of panic

about whether I would remember the lines. Often I didn't. A
new and unnerving experience for me, as I'm usually a quick
study and once learned, never word-shy. I excused my lapses
of memory by thinking that the occasional hiatus gave the rest
of the cast a free, and perhaps, as some of them were
generous enough to assure me, a necessary shot of adrenalin –
often a welcome shock in what can be the tedium of a long
run. I experienced many involuntary kick-starts as the brain
would blank and then miraculously jerk back into the text or
at least an approximation of it. It's hard to ad lib iambic
pentameters, but even an overloaded, tired actor's brain will
surprisingly come up with a similar word of the same syllables.
Most of the time.

I was also free at last to enjoy being in Stratford, at least
during the winter months when tourists are at a minimum.
Free, too, to escape to the rambler-free hills and fields around
my cottage when, from the onset of spring, they are at constant
bobble-hat saturation point.

Stratford doesn't have quite the same feel if you're not a
member of the current company.

'Back again are you?' says Denis Marks, the ever-patient
chemist, over-familiar with actors' throat, chest and confidence
problems.

'No, just visiting my cottage,' I reply rather lamely.

So I tend, then, to shop in Shipston on Stour or Mickleton,
to avoid feeling that my presence in Warwickshire doesn't have
quite the same Good Housekeeping seal of approval as when
I'm bona fide RSC. One year I made it into the Holy of Holies
(The Shakespeare Birthday Marquee) when I wasn't a member
of the company, but I had to sing for my supper. There is no
such thing as a free lunch. I had to give one of the two
speeches that commemorate 23 April – Shakespeare's birthday
– and conveniently too his deathday. I'm convinced there's
been more than meets the eye for some aeons to the official
record-keeping strategies in Stratford.

It's a fallacy that actors make good public speakers. It's quite a different kettle of fear, hiding behind a wig and a costume, speaking someone else's lines in a play, to standing up in front of 500 people, knees visibly knocking and speaking your own words. So I read them. The sheets of quivering paper were held out at arm's length so I could see them through my glasses, and occasionally, when an uncharacteristic moment of bravery assailed me, peer over the top of them at my well-lunched audience. To mark my point, Wole Soyinka, the Nigerian playwright, spoke, before his toast to the Immortal Memory, for about twenty-five minutes without a single note.

A young actor asked me recently about the sense of satisfaction I'd gained from doing my job. I searched long and hard in my memory. I couldn't honestly come up with much. There's always the pervading sense of wanting to have done it better. Wanting to get back on stage to have another go. Satisfaction isn't part of the job description. I'm sure it's the same for painters and musicians. That yellow ochre seems misplaced now, and that end cadence now unnecessary. Your work changes with your perception of life and your perception is constantly undergoing change.

The most fun and freedom is to be had in the rehearsal room, when the play just belongs to us, the actors and director and there's no pressure to present or perform it. Time is spent researching the background of the play, getting to grips with the tricky bits of language, uncovering layer after layer of the person you're playing, and observing all the different strata of the play melding together. Discovering, too, how different the play that you're *now* doing, is from the one you read at the beginning of rehearsal. It may be disappointing to members of an audience to know that as comforting as it is, the applause at the end of the play actually means very little. Conversely, no applause would mean an awful lot. It's a bit like money. It assumes an importance when you haven't got it.

No, I have to confess to a suspicion that the best bit about being an actor is the moment you hear you've got the job.

Stratford upon Haven

All of Stratford in fact suggests powdered history –
add hot water and stir – and you have a delicious,
nourishing Shakespeare.

MARGARET HALSEY, AMERICAN WRITER, 1910–

To play Shakespeare *and* live in the country? Bliss. 'What girl could ask for more?' I said jokingly, as a defence against being thought too eager and enthusiastic about joining the RSC (cynicism was de rigueur in the seventies), but I was seriously overjoyed at the thought. That thought, twenty-three years old now, has been weathered and reshaped since when, in 1974, I first played Viola in *Twelfth Night* for Peter Gill; Lady Macbeth (and other parts too embarrassing to mention) in Trevor Nunn's production of *Macbeth*, and Sonja in *Uncle Vanya*, played and directed by Nicol Williamson. But apart from a few nips and tucks in my attitude to tourist-filled streets when I'm pressed for time shopping for Sunday lunch before a Saturday matinee, not much has changed in the surge of pleasure I feel when I say I'm in the RSC at Stratford for a season. But the reasons for that delight are now manifold. They and I have changed with 'the inaudible and noiseless foot of time'.

There is a bonding that takes place amongst actors, left to their own devices and the sole companionship of their colleagues at the end of the M40, that is particular and special to this place. The company grows very close without the distractions or dispersal of the London effect. Actors fall out of their rented homes on Waterside a few seconds before the half is called, instead of having to trek into The Barbican from the wilds of Kensal Rise, despite the vagaries of the Northern Line, or arriving jaded by the traffic jams in Lewisham. I can make it into the theatre in twelve minutes from my rented cottage, if I put my foot down. A drive largely through country lanes season-ally edged with hoar frost, or the first brave green spears of snowdrops, or heavy-eared waves of wheat. The journey from my home in Putney – the same distance of some eight miles or so, from SW15 to EC2 – takes me the best part of a nerve-frazzling hour. The majority of the company (apart from the young mums with young children learning how to juggle acting, mothering and housekeeping in a new home) are freed from the albeit endearing but intrusive demands of family, and, living alone in Stratford, at least during the week, have the luxury of being able to concentrate solely on The Work.

The play's the thing. Or the voice classes (individual tuition, or company warm-ups before each show) or John Barton's sonnet classes; reacted to prior to the event with some groaning or occasional mutters of 'School', and referred to afterwards with astonishment, gratitude and pleasure. John can untangle the trickiest of texts, the densest of imagery, with such ease and naturalness that even the most terrified of actors coming to the Bard for the first time feels empowered to do their own decoding and demystifying after a class with John. A season at Stratford is now the longest contractual opportunity for actors to work on classical texts. Even at the National Theatre actors are employed play by play. There are eleven months of work on a Stratford season (including early rehearsals which often take place initially in London) and then a further two months in Newcastle and Plymouth before a possible run of another four months or so at the Barbican.

It is vitally important for young actors to have a sense of conti-nuity in their professional development. Vitally important, too, that barriers and defences are removed so that the actor is in touch with her centre, and from this centre is able to grow. There is skill and support available for this at every hand. It is not every actor's choice, of course, this continuation of the learning process begun at drama school. But for those of us who want more than a ten-day shoot on a TV programme, four days on a radio play or a couple of days on a feature film, where there is neither the inclination nor the possibility of lowering defences amongst strangers for so short a period, or the time or facility for learning, it is a heaven-sent opportunity to push professional horizons back and grow. And it's free. Eleven months with some of the greatest texts in the English language, and some of the greatest classical texts in any language. We live on words. The actual bread and butter of living is a different matter. Keeping a home on in London as well as renting in Warwickshire is a luxury and a struggle. Two electricity, gas and telephone bills. The pay isn't up to TV levels, but the work is soul food. We love words.

After all this edification we can then fall out of the theatre into the Dirty Duck pub for legalised drinking after hours. An arrangement solely and specially for the actors. Special. That's what this place makes you feel. Even the Lowliest of Company Members straight out of drama school stands a chance of being recognised, and having their work appreciated by passers-by in the streets, especially if they happen to be outspoken and open hearted American students, and especially if they, the LCMs, happen to look shapely in a doublet and hose. Little groups of autograph hunters huddle round the stage door after a performance in the hope of chatting to the actors. Or if Ken Branagh's in the show, you can expect a healthy gang of Branagh groupies, giggling and jostling in their dozens. Most of us are blessed with one avid fan. I have an inexplicable following of gay guys and a curious collection of middle-aged women, who I suspect either want to mother me or give me a square meal. One woman, respectably dressed and quite shy, said modestly to me one night, 'I laughed and I cried, I can't say more than that.' No indeed, ma'am. That was special. I've never forgotten it.

It's special, too, to be playing Shakespeare in his home town. Audiences are drawn here from all over the world, a sobering honour especially if you're unhappy with your performance or, worse, the production. There's a little you can do about the former but precious little about the latter. Multi-national audiences are not always a blessing for performers either, when line after comedy line is met with a crashing silence resounding from the auditorium.

'What's wrong with me tonight?' said Mary Rutherford to me in the wings after one of her entrances as Olivia, 'not a single laugh.'

'Hang on,' I said, trying to be comforting. 'I'm long-sighted. I'll give them the once over. Maybe we're all off tonight.' We talk like that backstage, when we're not chatting in iambic penta-meters, of course. What the audience is like is always the main consideration in the wings during a performance. After my next entrance I said, 'Wall-to-wall Japanese. All smiling politely and enjoying themselves immensely, but probably understanding nothing and uttering nary a sound.'

Of course there are days when you feel that the performance is on a tourist itinerary – yesterday Canterbury, tomorrow the Lake District, today, the theatre – and that a visit to see a Shakespeare play in Shakespeare's home town is more an oblig-atory notch on a tourist trophy than a real pleasure, but those occasions are rare.

At the opposite end of this scale are the Shakespeare buffs, who religiously attend each summer school or lecture; the Academics at the Shakespeare Centre and the Institute. These places are bowers of intellectual stimulus (especially the Institute, with its exquisite garden) and sometimes places of acute nervous tension, too, for the actor faced with an inquiring audience at a question and answer session about a specific production in which they are appearing. Members of the public from every walk of life, who are drawn to the various Shakespeare courses and summer schools, have often made a lifelong study of the entire canon and their knowledge and percipience can be quite daunting, when an average acting career spanning some thirty years may give the actor only a working knowledge of some fifteen or so of the thirty-seven plays. But it's frequently a fruitful exchange: the actor departs gratefully with a small fee and a more specific understanding of what has been understood and appreciated, or misinterpreted in both directions. And the audience has had a chance to taste what it's like to be up there on the stage doing it and not simply reading it or watching it.

The still small centre in this learning world is for me Holy Trinity Church. Here He is buried. Or at least He is reputed to be. Almost all aspects of Shakespeare's life and work are disputed, and his last resting place is not exempt from the continuing debate. Perhaps the fat burghers of Stratford knew they were on to a good thing, even then in 1616. It certainly seems questionable, even given the small amount of fame he had accrued in his lifetime, that what amounted to a middle-class family should be buried in the chancel of a church. That was a last resting place usually reserved for the nobility of rank, not of literature. And the flagstone with his name on it and its admonitory poem as a warning to body snatchers, seems to indicate a person of exceptionally small proportions unless, as the common rather irreverent parlance goes, he was buried standing up.

However, little of this matters when the failing day's light bathes the waters of the Avon and the branches of the overhanging willows dapple the lapping waves and the backs of the many swans and ducks that flock here. A time when all but the most ardent of tourists have departed with their ashtrays stamped with that famous picture of His head, and their oven gloves replete with pictorial evidence of Anne Hathaway's cottage, it's then easy to turn one's back on the chatter and the clatter of supper in the canteen (that overlooks one of the most beautiful views of the river, as do the leading actors' dressing rooms with their little balconies that give out on to it) and difficult to resist the lure of walking quietly through the gardens in the gathering dusk up to the church, stealing a sprig of rosemary on the way, to pay silent and grateful homage at the altar rail that guards that grave.

It's rare that a walk like this, or any through Stratford, won't bring you face to face with a local shopkeeper with time to chat – a nicety lost in the turmoil that's London – who will smile and say how pleased they are to see you back. Or to recognise the more familiar face of someone who works at the theatre. Usherettes, front of house staff, stage crew – we're all in it together. Bootmakers, swordmakers, dressmakers, all those people that the actor meets in the frantic costume fittings prior to an opening night in the little warren of rooms across the road from the stage door, are mostly local and, as such, take enormous pride in their theatre and their work. Nothing is too much trouble. I've known dressers hoof it up three flights of stairs minutes before an actor's entrance to retrieve a forgotten prop, a handkerchief, a mislaid rosary, and be back down in the wings as fast as the forty-two steps will allow.

The Swan! Whole eulogies have been written, and rightly so, about this beautiful theatre. Suffice it for me to say I don't know an actor in England who has played in it and not loved its brick and wood warmth, and the vibrancy of its relationship of stage to stalls, or an actor who hasn't played it who isn't envious of those of us who have. I remember it originally as the rather sombre and musty conference room where we would rehearse. Not a sad loss, especially as the building of the Swan now gives us actors an exquisite rehearsal space on the top floor, again all golden wood, with a panorama of the rooftops of the town and a spectacular bird's-eye view of the river (safe from the questionable smell that rain often churns up from the river bed) – a room named after one of the most loved and innately gracious of all great actors, Peggy Ashcroft.

That's another thing about playing great classical roles at Stratford. There is a degree of stepping into other people's shoes. That can be quite daunting. Taking on the mantel from names that were heroes in one's theatre-besotted youth. 'Best not read the reviews,' advised Peter Gill, wisely at it turned out, just prior to my first night in *Twelfth Night*. They'll only compare your Viola to Dorothy Tutin's/Vanessa Redgrave's/etc., etc. Best not to know.' It was advice I heeded. I haven't read a review from that day to this until long after the production is over; then it's just so much fish and chip paper or a question of 'Death where is thy sting?' Any actor that says he isn't affected by bad reviews isn't being honest, and the good ones may isolate certain moments in a performance for praise that are then dead to you for ever. As you flip out of the play and remember this is the moment the *Evening Post* thought I played 'elegantly'. In that moment elegance, your concentration and the rôle die.

Shakespeare's birth and death are celebrated on the same day, when the town is closed to traffic and literally hundreds of people walk through the streets, then through the birthplace. All of us laden with posies and garlands of flowers, and bedecked with buttonholes of sprigs of rosemary for 'remembrance' tied with yellow and purple ribbons, and one by one the bouquets are laid in tribute on his grave. It's a great honour to be asked to walk in this procession as a member of the RSC, and hard not to be affected by the excitement and the general air of festivity that commingle after the service to his memory in the church, at which actors and musicians from the RSC take part, and finally come to a halt in the huge marquee in the gardens nearby. This huge and tepid tent bursts with sweltering dignitaries from all over the world, be-chained and be-furred mayors from local boroughs, churchmen and members of Parliament all replete with the importance of their office and a usually large and lavish lunch.

It's a day that makes me proud to be in the theatre. No easy feat, given the bad press and the belittling 'luvviedom' label that the tabloids seem to delight in giving the profession – a term never used by any of us in the business. But this is not a day for carping. It is a day for being proud to be an actor. A day for remembering that the greatest playwright who ever lived also trod the boards.

Many actors, avid walkers like myself and country lovers, once seduced by the beauty of the neighbouring Cotswold hills, and their exquisite villages of thatched roofs and Tudor beams, often make their permanent homes here. It's a dream

I've had for most of the twenty-four years that I've been in and out of the RSC. But there's a disquieting rumour that once you move here, chances are that you never work for the company again. So for the moment it must stay a dream and I'll stay put, and take out that season ticket on the M40, and still feel that surge of pleasure when I see the theatre as I round the Clopton bridge.

Actors talk often about Their Agents – much maligned creatures – because rarely does the actor get over the fact that at the beginning of a career *we* need them more than *they* need us. This attitude sticks later when *you're* really employing *them* with your payment of the ten per cent or more. The old, but untrue adage is, if you didn't get the job it's your agent's fault, if you did, it's a confirmation that you're good.

Many actors talk about the directors they've worked with, and more about those they wouldn't work with again, what's wrong with the production they're in, and how they'd put it to rights, and indeed sometimes try to, if the director is (fortunately) absent for long periods once the play is up and running. But hardly ever do we discuss how we work as individuals, how we put a role together. Everyone's work process is different. And private. Apart from the bit of the iceberg that's visible in the rehearsal room. The ingredients that are contributory to a role are common knowledge. There for all to see is the text, the structure of the play, the function that your character fulfils, the words your character actually has to speak. But the coming together of the actor and the role is a mysterious business. Mysterious to the actor often too.

One day there's just a person fumbling through the words of the text, next there's an irrefutable fleshed-out whole life on view. That moment of arrival at the incontrovertible, of the meshing of character and actor I can't describe. That flight from the known into unknown. There are no words for that. But I can describe the scaffolding.

Part pageant, part history play, part the personal downfall of Buckingham, Wolsey and Katherine, but in keeping with the last great plays of the canon, *The Tempest* and *The Winter's Tale*, *Henry VIII* is also a play about spiritual rebirth, not just in the symbol of the baby who is to become Elizabeth I, but through that most difficult of human experiences – the humbling of the worldly state that leads to the spiritual one of forgiveness.

The Role Is Greater than the Sum of the Part

Nobody expects the Spanish Inquisition!
Our chief weapon is surprise – surprise and fear,
fear and surprise –
our two weapons are fear and surprise – and ruthless efficiency –
our three weapons are fear and surprise and ruthless efficiency
and an almost fanatical devotion to the Pope...
our four... no... AMONGST our weapons –
amongst our weaponry – are such elements as fear, surprise...
I'll come in again.

GRAHAM CHAPMAN, *MONTY PYTHON'S FLYING CIRCUS*, 1970

My first reaction when Greg Doran rang to ask if I'd like to play Katherine of Aragon was, 'Do I have to play it in a flak jacket?' As frivolous as this question might sound, and as inaccurately corroborative it is of the assumption that all female actors care about is what they look like, it contained a fundamental seriousness. We as an audience lately have been subjected to much directional updating: *Hamlet* in Edwardian tails (so much for Ophelia's 'With his doublet all unbraced, his stockings foul'd, Ungarter'd, and down gyvèd to his ankle'), *Two Gentlemen of Verona* set to Charleston time and *The Merchant of Venice* replete with mini-skirts and mobile phones.

In spite of how these comments might be interpreted, I'm not a dyed-in-the-wool purist, especially if updating makes the play more accessible to a younger audience unfamiliar with Shakespeare's work, but I felt that we had recently run the gamut of directional modernising, and that the wave of making Shakespeare fashionable and fashion-full had mercifully run its course, and that it would be a relief to us all as audiences to have that unique experience of seeing a Shakespeare play in the costumes of the time.

Henry VIII is so essentially Tudor in its mores, its history, its hierarchy, in its treatment of women as male property and heir-bearing machines, that to shift it out of its time zone I felt would be inappropriate and perverse.

'No,' said Greg firmly and with great meaning. I breathed out.

My second query (although the play is rarely performed, the last production being at Stratford in 1983 – as academics still dispute how much of it is Fletcher and how much Shakespeare) was to myself: 'Who had played her before?'

This is a daunting question that all classical actors have to face when confronted with a role that the late and the great have put their unique mark on and, as a consequence has to a certain extent become identified with them.

The list was awesome.

Mrs Siddons, Ellen Terry, Flora Robson, Diana Wynyard, Gwen Frangcon-Davies, Edith Evans and latterly the much-loved Peggy Ashcroft. Admiration, fear and flattery mingled. I put the list out of my mind and held my breath. I'm still holding it now, some fourteen months into the playing of her.

We started with three weeks of simply sitting round a vast table reading each speech in turn as it became one's turn – much like the dreaded drama classes at school in my teenage years, nothing dramatic about them at all, no sense of character, no sense of development, but eventually a thorough under-standing of every single syllable of the text, seen more clearly as we were freed from the dreadful obligation every actor feels when confronted with a new role – how am I going to say/inflect/interpret this line? Or this? Or this?

Then we progressed to the heady level of being able to read the same character – but not one's own – for a whole scene. So, for example, the actress cast as Patience would be reading the Lord Chamberlain, and the actor cast as Wolsey would be reading Katherine. And again in turn, each actor having read a speech, would then have to paraphrase that speech in their own words. This meant that every single member of the company knew exactly what was happening at any given moment of the play, whether they were in that scene or not. This volte-face of roles was hugely useful too, as it often gave one a chance to read one's opponent. I gained great insight into Wolsey, Katherine's arch-enemy, by, as luck would have it, having to read him for the whole scene and therefore empathising with his predicament and feelings in a direct way that might otherwise never have been opened up to me.

As always with a Shakespeare history play we did our research faithfully. The walls of the rehearsal room were plastered with family trees; who had married who and why, what for and when. Then, as always with a Shakespeare history play we had to put all that out of our minds and play his own particular version and timing of the events, not minding the exclusions – notably Sir Thomas More – and stomaching what seemed initially the fulsome premonition at the end of the play of Elizabeth's glorious reign, written with hindsight and not a small degree of flattery and propaganda for James I's court, populace and benefit.

So, separating the real history from the history in the play, but using what was of consequence to both, became for me a way of substantiating Katherine's lines and enriching her character. What were the facts that were true to both regarding this woman?

I've always felt a double obligation when playing a character that actually lived. Every avenue of their life and experience must be opened up: what food they ate, what music they listened to, who they liked and disliked, what they themselves looked like, etc., etc., so that no false value judgements are made about them, and by a process of osmosis, all about them is absorbed by the actor, all the pores opened to let the wind of that essence blow right through you. Then you put all that out of your mind too, and simply play the play, hoping that all this knowledge will somehow filter through and inform your every move and gesture.

So who was Katherine of Aragon that is relevant to this rarely seen but frequently maligned piece of theatre by Fletcher/Shakespeare?

A Spanish princess.

The decision to play her with an accent came relatively late in rehearsals (week four or five) and came as a shock when Greg suggested it to me. I had been so caught up in the history of the period of both England and Spain, in all our projects on Tudor London: sewage, streets, crowds, conditions; instruments of torture of the time; our differing personal reactions to Hampton Court; besides the difficulties that we all had in dealing with such an irregular text, mostly twelve (dreaded Alexandrines) or eleven-beat lines – even some thirteen-beat (heaven help us!) and then great wodges of so very regular ten-beat lines, that the words themselves demanded consciously careful handling and skilful playing in order to avoid a straitjacket monotone of rhythm and delivery. So suddenly to be faced with an accent that is famously difficult on top of all this (by comparison Russian is a doddle) – all those 'th's for 'd's, 'j's in place of 'y's and all those guttural 'h's (how was I not to sound like the waiter in *Fawlty Towers?*) was, to put it mildly, fairly alarming.

In the end, with Charmian Hall, the RSC's dialect coach's invaluable help, we dropped the guttural 'h's' and played it safe with the rest. The thing with an accent is not to play it once you've learned it, of course, you simply try to do what you normally do in any acting, which is to play *the intention of the line*. In the same way you don't play drunk, you play sober.

Of course Greg was right. The accent was essential. It was vital for Katherine to be seen as the outsider, the stranger that she is described as ('Alas poor lady, she's a stranger now again') and

Backstage with RSC dresser Jill Osman

the foreigner that she was. In the same way that Wolsey's Suffolk accent marks him, in spite of his learning, his ecclesiastical power and wealth, as a man from rural England – Ipswich Suffolk.

She was the youngest of five children born to Isabella of Castile and Ferdinand of Aragon. Four daughters, and a son who died relatively young, she must therefore have been familiar from an early age (and was to be reminded constantly throughout her marriage to Henry) with the terrors that a male childless heir held for a dynasty of kings, especially the one so recently established by her parents, the first Reyes Católicos, who by their marriage combined the centre and south of Spain, thus uniting the country after 880 years of Moorish rule.

Not long after, the ships of the Conquistadors crossed the Atlantic loaded with crosses, missionaries, missals and Christian convictions, and Spain in her heyday saw herself as the champion of Christian Orthodoxy whose task was to unite the world in Catholicism.

Only in Spain do you hear not only 'Adios' but 'Vaya con Dios' – Go with God.

Catalina – her Spanish name – was born in Granada, but took as her emblem (a more peaceful symbol than the seven arrows in a yoke that formed the crest of Isabella and Ferdinand, which she can be seen holding in the Holbein-like painting of her in more mature years) the pomegranate (*la granita*), which can be seen to this day on the colours displayed above her very modest grave in the north transept of Peterborough Cathedral. It was to prove, as much in Katherine's life, deeply ironic, as the pomegranate is also the symbol of fecundity.

So her Catholicism – although a political statement that was born and strengthened by the early years, in which she grew up from the age of six in the Palace of the Alhambra, where every vestige and emblem of Islam must have been firmly replaced by her parents with a crucifix – was also, as I was to find, a richly vibrant living faith to her personally, and one that was to sustain her through more hardship than most queens have to undergo.

On arriving in England aged sixteen, after a tortuous journey that had taken five months, to be married off to Arthur, Henry VII's heir, and speaking only Spanish, her first action on English soil – the land that was to be her home through two marriages, a widowing, a divorce and five stillbirths or miscarriages – was to give thanks to God in the nearest church. This seemed ample evidence already, and was borne out later by much in the text, to warrant my wearing a rosary and a missal on all my costumes at all times.

It's been a personal foible of mine, developed over the years, to find one line that refers to the character that I'm playing, that seems to hold all the quintessential elements of that character. For example, when I played Viola I found Sebastian's line 'She bore a mind that envy could not but call fair' replete with everything that Viola is. For Gertrude, Claudius's description 'The Queen his [Hamlet's] mother lives almost by his looks' helped me make the decision that faces every Gertrude – whose side to come down on, her husband's or her son's.

I was spoilt for choice with references to Katherine. They abound throughout the play and are spoken by every echelon of society:

The good Queen... (Second Gentleman)

Her that loves him with that excellence
That angels love good men with... (Duke of Norfolk)

    ...and she
So good a lady that no tongue could ever
Pronounce dishonour of her –
She never knew harm doing. (Anne Boleyn)

That man i' the world who shall report he has
A better wife, let him in naught be trusted
For speaking false in that. Thou are alone
In thy rare qualities, sweet gentleness,

Thy meekness, saint-like, wife-like government,
Obeying in commanding, and thy parts
Sovereign and pious else could speak thee out
The Queen of earthly Queens. She's noble born,
And like her true nobility she has
Carried herself towards me.
(Ironically Henry again, after Katherine has refused to acknow-
ledge the divorce court and has turned her back on the
proceedings.)

That honour every good tongue blesses...
... good lady. (Wolsey)

...good lady (Wolsey)

... she was divorced
And the late marriage made of none effect
Since which she was removed to Kimbolton
Where she remains now sick.
Alas, good lady. (First and Second Gentlemen)

So 'good' seems to be the operative word. But you can't play
'good'. Good is a value judgement, and all value judgements are
made from a standpoint outside the character, which for me is a
very unwise and unhealthy place to be. If you stand too long
outside the character, you risk putting it 'out there', i.e. not
letting it 'travel through' you. Also 'good' often equals boring.
And Katherine is anything but boring. Besides, I had already
begun to love her (as she must have loved the greatest icon of
goodness, Jesus Christ). But He also had moments of despair
and flashes of anger; later, as the work progressed, I was to find
these, too, in Katherine. So, I turned to Katherine's own words;
her motto was 'Humble et loyale' and this was to be borne out
again and again in the text of the play.

In her first scene in the play, (Act 1, Scene 2) her initial gesture,
although a queen (and she uses the royal 'we' in her very first

line) is to kneel to Henry. Thereby acknowledging his sovereignty, and also his embodiment of the Divine Right of Kings – he is God's representative. Her humility and devotion to him both as king and as husband, and her ability to flatter him and yet remind him gently of his duty to his position, always keeping within the confines of what is no more than appropriate, is finely contained and superbly phrased in her first complete speech:

That you should love yourself, and in that love
Not unconsidered leave your honour nor
The dignity of your office, is the point
Of my petition.

In this relatively short scene for her (she has only nine speeches), she calls Henry 'your Majesty,' 'the King our master', 'my sovereign' and 'your highness.'

Humble and loyal indeed.

She wins the first round as Henry publicly rebukes Wolsey for instigating a tax that had no precedent, and offers a free pardon to every man that refused to abide by it. But she doesn't fare so well in her second mission for mercy and clemency, for the Duke of Buckingham. Buckingham receives the death sentence, aided and abetted by the put-up evidence of the surveyor, who has been schooled by Wolsey to incite the King's anger and insecurity about Buckingham's threat to Henry's life and crown.

She has lost the battle for Buckingham's life, but the war with Wolsey has only just begun.

This first scene held for me all the elements that are essential pointers to the character of Katherine. It also contains what I suppose students of Stanislavski would call super-objectives and objectives, and these have become markers that I remind myself of before each performance.

In order of importance, Katherine's devotion, loyalty and duty are 1) to her God, 2) to her King, 3) to her husband and 4) to her people. This is more than just a neat little formula. These four obligations hold water in all of the four scenes that she has in the play. Four scenes that Greg and I developed a shorthand for by calling them, albeit loosely, because the analogy doesn't totally hold, Spring, Summer, Autumn and Winter.

Henry 'riseth from his state, takes her up and kisses her' in the first scene. That's evidence of a happy marriage. Spring in deed.

'Summer' is blown, possibly fly blown and tainted before we see Katherine next (Act 2, Scene 4), on trial in defence of the continuation of her marriage through no fault of her own, but through Henry's dual voracious needs – for a male heir and for Anne Boleyn.

The four reminders I give myself before this scene begins, which are vital if I'm not to become lost and bogged down in one of the longest pieces of rhetoric in the canon – her speech in her own defence – are:

'I refuse to acknowledge this court – it's unfair and unjust and English.'

'I have been a true and humble wife, you can't fault me on that score.'

'Wolsey is my enemy and therefore I refuse to be judged by him.'

'I want time – and help from Spain.'

But most of all I remind myself that she thinks she is going to win.

As a child she had been made to study rhetoric along with the accepted subjects for women of rank: music, poetry, grammar, embroidery, painting, illumination, history, Latin and philosophy. She was, according to many historians, a woman of great intellectual ability. Erasmus found her scholarship more impressive than Henry's. She was a shrewd diplomatist and a formidable debater. All this Henry finds to his cost in the trial scene.

Henry cannot fault her on her behaviour, her humility as a wife and her devotion, which she took to such a level that she would suit her every mood to his, she never contradicted him, she tried to love his friends even though she knew they were her enemies (this is an indirect reference to Wolsey which she picks up in more direct manner later), she gave up her own friends if they angered him, and sums it all up by reminding him and the court, that this devotion, and this marriage have lasted some astonishing twenty years. The only time I decided that she would falter in this rhetoric would be at the mention of the dead children that she had borne him. The emotional pain at her failure to produce an heir for her beloved husband, and the grief that she must feel for those dead children, plus the unpalatable thought that childbearing is now an unlikely possibility, threatens to overwhelm her. But she's her father's daughter, and drawing on her innate Spanish sense of honour and dignity she regains her composure and challenges Henry that is she is at fault in any way, that he take her life.

Henry says nothing. She then reminds Henry and the court that both Ferdinand of Spain, *her* father, renowned for his wisdom, and his own father, Henry VII, a prudent and intelligent man, had agreed, along with the assembled clerics of that time, that this second marriage of hers was indeed lawful. She is sure of her ground and the justice of this point on which the whole intended divorce rests, and sums up by asking for more time to be advised by her friends in Spain.

That for me became over the weeks of rehearsal quite clearly the end of the speech. She knows she is right. She knows the law is on her side. She knows that Henry cannot fault her. And in the true sense of theatre, drama can only come from the juxtaposition of opposites. She assumes that Henry will be won over. She assumes that Henry will agree. Again, but cataclysmically for her this time, Henry again says nothing, and in those few seconds between

Wherefore I humbly
Beseech you sir, to spare me till I may
Be by my friends in Spain advised, whose counsel
I will implore

and

> If not, i' the name of God
> Your pleasure be fulfilled

her whole world comes crashing down about her ears. She realises that Henry doesn't want her any more.

The emotional backwash that this devastating pain causes her is mostly fired thereafter in Wolsey's direction. She turns her tears into anger and turns on him as the reason for her husband having turned on her. She now publicly accuses Wolsey of being her enemy and a liar, although her Christianity tempers it into 'not at all a friend to truth'.

The extent of her distress at the whole proceedings, which she is no longer able to hide, is perhaps nowhere more evident than when she snaps at her faithful and beloved manservant Griffith, who reminds her quietly as she attempts to sweep out of the court, having appealed to be tried by the Pope:

> (Madam, you are called back.)
> What need you note it? Pray you keep your way.
> When you are called return. Now the Lord help.
> They vex me past my patience. Pray you pass on.

She finally leaves with:

> I will not tarry, no nor ever more upon this *business* – (I pronounce it *baseness* as I did in reference to Wolsey's unfair taxations in the first scene, experiencing another of many moments of gratitude for the initially unwelcome Spanish accent)
> My appearance make in any of their courts.

The money lenders have been scourged in the temple.

The placing of the interval after this scene is of huge benefit to Katherine as it adds to the sense of time passing as she waits for news and help from Spain.

It seemed perverse for a Spanish princess, faced with the possibility that grows more likely every day, of losing her husband, her status, her homes and her daughter, when asking for a song to cheer her up, that she should be happy with an English madrigal. (Odd too, that it should be a song about that most faithful of lovers Orpheus!) So the *Spanish* rendering of Orpheus with his lute was born. I compounded the felony of suggesting that Katherine and her Spanish maid (who we named Inez) should sing several lines of it translated into Spanish – her homesickness is much evident later in the scene and this confirmed the justification for this element. So Katherine's blue mood is nicely lifting with memories of home, as she is drawn into the Spanish dance, that she surely must have taught them in her younger days, when Griffith interrupts it with the alarming news that the Cardinals Wolsey and his man from Rome, Campeius, have sprung a surprise visit. Obviously the next unwelcome round in the divorce talks are about to begin.

Katherine three times in this scene makes references to the frailty of her womanhood (as she did to Wolsey in the trial too) – all this from a woman whom Thomas Cromwell later described in these terms: 'Nature wronged the Queen in not making her a man. But for her sex she would have surpassed all the heroes of history.'

They are here to castigate her for her behaviour in the trial. The other cardinal, Campeius, puts his oar in – Wolsey has forgot 'like a good man her late censure both of his truth and him' and offers her a sign of peace and counsel which she reads, in part correctly, as betrayal. But the devastating extent of that ruin and betrayal she has yet to find out. She gets dangerously near to betraying Christian respect for the representatives of God by belittling 'such men of gravity and learning' here on 'such business', which I again pronounce as 'baseness'.

A stern look of reprimand at such levity from the devout Griffith puts her back on course, and she addresses the heart of her problem. She knows her position is in jeopardy – 'I feel the last fit of my greatness' – and begs once more for time and counsel, as she did in the trial scene. The echo in the words 'friend less, hope less' adds to our understanding of her forlorn state.

Again Wolsey wrong-foots her by reminding her of 'the King's love' – inappropriate to say the least – and of her infinite number of friends ('in England'?) – inaccurate at the most. She now gives reign to a fury that until now she has held in check. A spurned wife and a lonely homesick woman is a potent mixture, and by the time Campeius reminds her of her 'loving King' and warns that the divorce may go ahead in spite of her wishes, she has all the ammunition available for a full attack on them both as vacuous representatives of the God they serve, and in Wolsey's case, a man who has been corrupted by a king – the nearest she ever gets to a criticism of her sovereign and her husband.

Having skirted self-pity with 'a woman lost among ye, laughed at, scorned', she now gives full vent to that most human of anguishes, a woman rejected because she is old; a self denigration made all the more potent by the presence of the beautiful and young Anne Boleyn.

Alas, he's banished me his bed already,
His love too, long ago. I am *old* my lords,
And all the fellowship I now hold with him is only my *obedience*.

A Christian duty that hardly describes a matrimonial passion.
It is autumn indeed.
This for me is the crux of the scene and the heartbreaking core of Katherine. It makes her the emotional heart of the play. She says as she goes to leave, a broken woman, a forsaken wife and a ruined Queen: 'Pray do my service to his Majesty.' In that formal phrase is all that she has lost since she first put her foot on English soil, and all that she has had to agree to lose, in order to keep her dignity.

When we next see her – her last and 'Winter' scene – she has precious little, other than her dignity, apart from the faithful Griffith and her maid Patience. I asked for my last costume to be changed from the original drawing, although there was a clear progression in what Rob (Jones) had designed, a progression downwards from the splendour of the Cloth of Gold Dress, to the almost nun-like garb for the trial scene (Katherine, in keeping with her Christian modesty, had in the first four and a half years in England only two new dresses). But I still felt that a structured Tudor dress with its corseting and boning was too definite somehow in its silhouette for the frail and ill wraith that she has become. So with amazing speed and generosity Rob jettisoned it and produced a grey shroud-like smock that hung and clung in ageing folds about my body and accentuated bones and skeleton.

Bereft of everything except her two faithful servants, almost unable to walk, we wonder what has kept her going. We are surprised to find that it is hatred. Hatred of Wolsey has fed her fires and fuelled her since we saw her last. And like all creatures who have fed on poison she has been eaten up by it mentally and physically. She becomes alert, is intrigued by the manner of Wolsey's death and makes a joke of him managing it well, as an example for her to follow. But the laugh is wiped off Katherine's face when she learns that he did die in a state of grace. But she can't resist another defamatory outburst against the man who she has blamed all these years for the destruction of her marriage.

How often must the poor Patience have been needful of the quality of her name, and the ever-loyal Griffith had to hold on to his 'religious truth and modesty' in the face of frequent outbursts of this nature against Wolsey?

Griffith makes a stand to speak of the transience of Good in general and of Wolsey's good in particular, and he does it in such a way that the years of Katherine's hatred melt away. Her mere admission of the fact that she hated Wolsey is a giant revelation to her and a huge step towards the Truth. She hears that Wolsey, for all his materialism and ambition, at the end of his life 'felt himself/And found the blessedness of being *little*'.

This must hit hard, as she has never found that blessedness. She has spent her years in exile surely inwardly bemoaning the wrongful removal of her divine right as Queen, a right that she had learned at Isabella's knee.

But this huge step of forgiveness, the humbling of her pride and the ultimate blessing of Wolsey's departed soul, takes its toll on her strength and she then wants to rest, listening to the music that she wishes to hear at her death.

She sleeps and as she sleeps sees a vision.

The vision that she sees caused us much debate. Finally to my great relief, the idea of the younger members of the cast tripping round me in white dresses and cherub wings, was scrapped for the simpler (and to my mind more effective for an audience familiar with the cinematic skills of Spielberg) pillar of golden light. In this she surely, as a reward for her forgiveness of Wolsey, sees 'a blessed troop', 'spirits of peace,' who invite her to 'a heavenly banquet, whose bright faces cast a thousand beams' upon her 'like the sun'. (What a potent reminder of Spain, even at this late stage in her life and the play!)

Their departure leaves her saddened to recall the wretchedness of her earthly state. But the spirits have promised her eternal happiness – the greatest accolade (if that's the right word for humbling through suffering and Christian endurance), but as ever, with her truthful mind, she knows that she is not ready for this greatest of tributes yet.

Greg asked a very potent question at one point during the rehearsal of this scene, when it seemed to be stuck, not growing or going anywhere. 'What would we lose if the scene ended after the vision?'

Quick as a flash we saw what the end of Katherine's role was about.

We have to see that she has no grudges against Henry, that she is still concerned for his welfare, that she must remind Henry of his duties towards the child of their 'chaste loves', Mary Tudor (especially as another child from Anne Boleyn is on the way), and she must make provision for her faithful servants, albeit that her proud estimation of how many she has is slightly awry. To the last she is the champion of the poor, albeit that her manservants have grown poor because of cleaving to her despite her change in fortune.

The energy with which she finally puts her earthly house in order so that she may depart in peace costs her dear. She knows that she is near death. With her recently learned humility she tells the messenger to inform the King that 'his long trouble is now passing out of this world'.

What a heartbreaking but nevertheless accurate description of herself.

'Tell him in death I blessed him, for so I will.'

What utter Christian forgiveness and love. This is all the more poignant now, of course, since we have seen her, frail as she is, claw herself back from the jaws of bitterness and hatred.

Again the word 'chaste' appears. How strongly she must have held on to this through all her years of exile and rejection: 'I was a chaste wife to my grave.' And she leaves us having detailed her burial instructions, with a last reminder of who she really is – 'a queen and a daughter to a king'. Spanish, noble, and dignified to the end, till she 'can no more'.

Her actual last words, after she had heard mass at daybreak said by her Spanish chaplain, were in a moving letter to Henry, in which she declared:

For my part I pardon you everything... I commend unto you our daughter Mary, beseeching you to be a good father unto her... lastly I make this vow, that mine eyes desire you above all things.

'Humble et loyale' to the very end.

The Imperial ambassador Chapuys wrote of her 'that she was the most virtuous woman I have ever known, and the highest hearted'.

Me too.

It is a privilege and a joy to play her.

May she rest in peace.

End Time

What a case am I in then, that am neither a good epilogue,
nor cannot insinuate with you on behalf of a good play...

WILLIAM SHAKESPEARE, *AS YOU LIKE IT*, 1599

Vladimir:	That passed the time.
Estragon:	It would have passed anyway.
Vladimir:	Yes, but not so rapidly.

SAMUEL BECKETT, *WAITING FOR GODOT*, 1955

I have lived with Katherine now for over a year in Stratford,
Newcastle and latterly Plymouth – the place where significantly
she first put foot upon the earth of England. Katherine and I are
now about to take up residence in London, New York and
Washington DC. Such worldly places, bereft of the peace and
harmony of spirit that she so valued and sought, that would
surely have sent her scurrying to her prie-dieu and clutching her
rosary even more often. In the break between airing my Spanish
accent in the capital and on Capitol Hill, I have been once more
to St Louis armed with John Barton's Shakespeare teaching
tools. I had a new group of American students, and as ever their
infectious energy, from which I gain much, became infected

with a passion for the Bard, which left me as ever overawed, moved and grateful. This April visit I saw leaves on the Missouri trees, waxy magnolia flowers the size of dinner plates and an abundance of eye-catching, vividly coloured blossom well in keeping with all things big and bright and American.

I also saw – thanks to the generosity of American audiences who came to a benefit performance I did of *Shakespeare As I Knew Her* to raise funds for Wash U students to visit Stratford and the Globe for a summer Shakespeare course – my first standing ovation since *Piaf* on Broadway seventeen years ago.

Some ten days after my return from the 'Show Me State', when I was still suffering the affection- and attention-withdrawal that always hits me the minute I sit in the departure lounge at Lambert Airport watching the Schveys depart in the opposite direction, the echo of the American cheers were somewhat dimmed in my memory by a rather silently appreciative audience for *Shakespeare As I Knew Her* in Cumbria. My by now usual apprehension about whether Don the van man with the set will ever get to the same theatre as the one I'm about to perform in, was tinged with a rather crisper edge of panic than usual. Fifteen minutes before curtain up, my dresser had not showed up, so the only available female, the catering manager, was ushered into my dressing room, to be told about the three quick changes in the show. She did not know stage left from stage right and had to be put right pretty sharpish. She managed well and fortunately I did not come on dressed as Isabella the nun when I should have been disguised as Jessica the boy. I must have been the most quivering jelly she had every put a jacket and a hat on.

A year does much for change.

The Globe has now officially opened. There were many of us who have been with it since the beginning, when for many years it was just a slab of concrete with a puddle in the middle, who had a tear-blurred vision of the fireworks that ended the gala night. The night 'they' said we'd never see. 'They' said we couldn't do it but we did. Some fifteen years and £11 million later, money that we raised ourselves before the lottery bid

matched our cash, the Globe flag fluttered in earnest atop the tower, while the first company of actors trod the stage and worked out how best to dodge the much-disputed, much-moved pillars. The spirits of Sam and Charlotte Wanamaker and Theo Crosby the architect must have smiled, or something very like it, up amongst the clouds that held on to the threatened rain that by some miracle thankfully never fell. I had trouble seeing straight but that was also due to the weight of the Elizabeth I bald cap, wig and hat, which topped a costume it took two people an hour to get me into, and then three people to heave me up to sit side-saddle on a suspiciously benign and rather dozy horse. Elizabeth II said to me she 'thought the horse was good'. I said I thought it was on valium.

For the few days that we rehearsed the Globe gala show, my Katherine of Aragon wires were well scrambled. Somewhat due to Paul Jesson (Henry VIII) telephoning me on my way to a rehearsal to wish, with his wicked sense of humour, his *daughter* good luck. I had been playing his wife for over seven months. I tried hard not to think of Katherine as I got to know, albeit slightly, the offspring of her greatest rival.

I am now the proud possessor of a new Hearing Aid, which cost double the price of the old one Many radio recordings contributed to the HA Fund, so I pretend that it's superior to the ten-year-old model I had previously and wear it quite a lot. But not professionally of course. That would be too much like admitting defeat.

I have two new friends, Sal and Patricia, who do much to guide, chivvy and amuse, whose common sense and wisdom I am grateful for, and whose presence in the villages on either side of my cottage does much to eliminate unwelcome solitude. N and I have been in touch again, much to my surprise. I am pleased but wary.

My cat is still resident, although his trajectory of daily existence is now somewhat reduced to the limited area between the food bowls and the best chair in the sitting room which he has lately

designated for his sole occupancy. When I stroke him, which he only allows me to do after several days of playing hard to get, after I return from my many trips away from home, I notice that his backbone has become ridged and knobbly with age. But then the MRI scan that I had when I began to lose the use of my left arm through the weight of my Katherine of Aragon costumes, showed the same disfiguration. He also no longer comes when I call him. At first I thought it was part of the cold-shoulder treatment for my long absences, till one day I walked right up to him to stroke him as he slept and he jumped. My cat is deaf. His once luscious black fur is lifting to a manky dull brown spiked with white. And there the comparisons must end.

My waistline seems to be expanding in direct proportion to the length of time that I have been on HRT. So I am seriously debating the reduction of the latter in order to safeguard the expansion of the former. Apologies to Teresa Gorman, but she doesn't have to undergo the strictures of Tudor corseting. I think.

My general well-being was boosted no end by being made an Honorary Doctor of Bristol University. A Doctor of Letters. Paul Jesson, ever the wit, said, 'Are you sure they don't mean a Doctor of Postcards?' The glorious July day was shared by the Rev Nev Boundy, Ray Price, Chairman of my beloved Bristol Old Vic Theatre Club, Erika Neumann, who *is* the Bristol Old Vic Theatre School, has been for many years, and is also an equally passionate friend of the late, much-loved Nat Brenner, my son and about two thousand other people. Dressed in my red, burgundy and pink robe and clutching my black velvet *Tudor* hat, I couldn't quite believe that I would have to stand on a stage for about half an hour in front of such a large audience and not be required to say a single word. My son, with his double first from Oxford, muttered, 'I'm so proud of you, Ma.' With my six O-levels and two A-levels that was praise indeed. I still can't quite believe it when a letter addressed to Dr Jane Lapotaire plops on to my doormat.

I didn't live alone in London for a while. Claire moved into my son's old room upstairs, which did a little to diminish London loneliness and much for my kudos in the street, as she was as shapely as she was beautiful. I enjoyed for a while her presence in the house and the company of her young friends. I indulged myself in the fantasy that some of their collective youth would brush off on me. She said she enjoyed my tidiness, and was surprised by the fact that all the machines in the house, unlike the previous places she'd lived in, worked. I was surprised too. My mothering muscles were re-activated with great joy as I fell on her laundry at every opportunity and folded it neatly into piles. But she has moved on, and I welcome the silence of my sanctuary with a new appreciation. I have more time and space to pray and meditate and think. So I pray and meditate and think more. Living alone has a different colour now.

A lot of sequences have come or are coming to an end. I shall have left the RSC by the time the American tour is over, and I shall release Katherine's spirit into the ether above the Potomac, with gratitude for all the dignity that she shared with me, and all the devotion that she allowed me to see, and I shall then be a free spirit once again, aka freelance, or in my less positive moments, unemployed.

But nothing, not even the perennial fear of a week with no money coming in, or no teaching or writing prospects on the horizon, would ever induce me to consider that getting up at the same time every day, catching the same bus or tube into work, to toil in the same office or factory, was a preferable or tolerable alternative. Although, as I've said, I have more than a sneaking feeling that my work pattern is about to change. And I am doing the changing. I lost the use of my right arm for almost a year after the Broadway run of *Piaf*, at the time I just considered to be the natural outcome of doing a drug withdrawal fit flat on my back on the stage seven times a week. This shaking and trembling for over a minute, not surprisingly split the nerves in my shoulder blade, and my arm hung painful, withered and useless by my side. No one in the audience fortunately ever remarked on my one-armed performance.

Getting ill playing Joy Davidman in *Shadowlands* had a similar cause and outcome. Falling on my left hip (she eventually died from the cancer that provoked the fall), eight times a week, twice on Thursday and Saturdays, kept my osteopath busy for months and my intake of painkillers constant even though I wore stuntman's knickers with their thick foam padding to soften the falls. Gertrude, leading me into the valley of the shadow and eventually hospital, I reasoned at the time was the conglomeration of everything in my own life being a contributory factor, plus the fact that she is a very unsatisfying, negative, small and depressing role.

But the MRI scan for the Katherine injury, coinciding with my reading about neuro-linguistic programming, gave me a chance to put what I had pondered rather vaguely over the years of playing tragic roles into more precise terms. Sticking one's fingers into past personal pain, in order to motor the appropriate negative emotions demanded by the role, which in the case of tragedy is nearly always an abundance of despair, rejection, isolation, fear and anxiety – a jolly crew – causes the same reactions physically in the body as if those emotions were real. The body doesn't know the difference between an actual and an imagined scenario. When I, astonished by this shattering revelation, shared it with my son, his response was rather scathing:

'But, Ma, you've always known that.'

I suppose I did know it – in my head – but I chose not to connect it to my body. Dr Brian Bates, a psychologist at Sussex University, had, some eight or so years ago, given me a copy of his book *The Way of the Actor*, in which he explores the role that the actor takes on as shaman, embodying the ills and pains of the society for whom he performs. I thought at the time it was an interesting, if perhaps rather over-generous, assessment of the actor's importance, function and powers. Now I think otherwise. So my osteopath, and the painkiller manufacturers are about to, as far as my expenditure is concerned, experience a sharp decline in income. I shall give in to that magnetic lure of the armchair by the fire, after a day of simply standing teaching, or sitting writing, and my friends in the future perhaps won't be quite as hesitant as they were in the past about asking me how I am. My response will hopefully be short and to the point: 'Well, thank you.'

A friend of mine who lives in the country is dying. He doesn't see it that way and that is perhaps best for him. He is a simple man and like lots of innocent people who live close to the vagaries of nature, very wise. He has an intuitive understanding of others and can detect bullshit a mile off. It's hard to watch him driving his thinning frame, trying to go about his life as he always has, and not over-fuss him with offers of food and pleas for him to sit down and rest. I've learned from my journey with two other friends towards their deaths, that the dying must be allowed to make their own agenda. It's hard to separate the pain of one's own need, because of the impending loss of that person's company, wisdom and friendship, and the distress we feel at seeing someone we love in great pain. I wish he had my faith, little and imperfect as it is. And I wish my faith were strong enough to embrace wholeheartedly and with joy this next step of his soul's journey. I shall miss him.

My son has really gone. I thought we had relinquished our bond in stages – childhood visits to Los Angeles, the teenage departure for far-flung places in the gap year, culminating in leaving for university, then ultimately the final move into his own flat. I little thought there was another layer of relinquishing which had to be discharged. But it seems for him there was. I now wait for him to contact me. Being respectful of his need for total independence, and trying hard to put my needs after his. That's the official line. In my head, I have many heated arguments with myself and him, in which graciousness hardly figures at all.

Older friends with older sons say give it time.

Time. For years time was my enemy. There was never enough of it for all the jobs I had given myself to do. It was a daily battle to complete the list. A battle I never won. From the moment I entered my day at full tilt, I would not stop running until the day and I were spent. The more I had to do, the quicker the time seemed to speed sneakily by. Now I've developed my own retaliatory sneakiness and time has become elastic. I only do what I feel comfortable doing, and when that's done I have time for myself. A day that I have deemed chore-free, seems to stretch luxuriously around me and ahead of me. Time slows down as I've slowed down. It's a delightful realisation that never ceases to surprise me. The less I have to do, the more time I have to do it in.

Time is malleable. 'It travels in divers paces with divers persons.' Indeed. I couldn't have put it better myself. What a case am I in, then, just to have realised that this journey through one year has in fact taken me more than two.